ADHD

A Wiley Brand

ADHD

2nd Edition

by Jeff Strong and Carol MacHendrie, LCSW

ADHD For Dummies®, 2nd Edition

Published by: **John Wiley & Sons, Inc.**, 111 River Street, Hoboken, NJ 07030-5774, www.wiley.com

Copyright © 2024 by John Wiley & Sons, Inc., Hoboken, New Jersey

Published simultaneously in Canada

For general information on our other products and services, please contact our Customer Care Department within the U.S. at 877-762-2974, outside the U.S. at 317-572-3993, or fax 317-572-4002. For technical support, please visit https://hub.wiley.com/community/support/dummies.

Wiley publishes in a variety of print and electronic formats and by print-on-demand. Some material included with standard print versions of this book may not be included in e-books or in print-on-demand. If this book refers to media such as a CD or DVD that is not included in the version you purchased, you may download this material at http://booksupport.wiley.com. For more information about Wiley products, visit www.wiley.com.

Library of Congress Control Number: 2024930171

ISBN: 978-1-394-21908-7 (pbk); ISBN 978-1-394-21910-0 (ebk); ISBN 978-1-394-21909-4 (ebk)

Contents at a Glance

Contents at a Glance

Table of Contents

Introduction

A lot of people have attention deficit/hyperactivity disorder (ADHD). Researchers estimate that in the United States, people with ADHD constitute anywhere from 3 to 6 percent of the population (or more, depending on which study you read). On the low side, this totals about 9 million people. Almost everyone knows at least one person with ADHD (whether they're aware of it or not). So rest assured that if you have ADHD, or are related to someone who does, you're not alone.

Even though so many people have ADHD, the condition is widely misunderstood. Some people — including many healthcare professionals — believe that ADHD isn't real. These people believe ADHD is a made-up excuse for bad behavior and bad parenting.

We want to assure you right from the start that ADHD is a real condition that affects millions of people. For many, it makes life very difficult. ADHD has a biological cause and can't be willed away through discipline or hard work. And the symptoms of ADHD can't be ignored in the hopes that the person will simply grow out of them.

To reduce (and sometimes eliminate) the symptoms of ADHD, you need to understand this condition and receive knowledgeable intervention. The purpose of *ADHD For Dummies*, 2nd Edition, is to help you gain a better understanding of ADHD and discover where to look for help. Our goal is to give you the tools to effectively address ADHD in your life, whether you, your child, your spouse, or your friend is the one with ADHD.

About This Book

ADHD For Dummies, 2nd Edition, is unique among books on this condition in that we've written it with the ADHD person in mind. We don't go into long explanations with obscure points; we go right to the heart of the matter and give you the information you need to know with as little fuss as possible.

When we set out to write this book, obviously we wanted to offer basic information about what ADHD is and where it comes from. But we also wanted to provide information on cutting-edge treatment approaches and simple, effective strategies to help you start getting the symptoms under control and begin living the life you want to live. As a result, this book is short on background details and jargon and long on real-world advice. Both of us have many years' experience working with people with ADHD, and we draw heavily from these experiences in the pages that follow.

In this book, we don't assume that you're the person with ADHD. Instead, we try to offer a view of this condition as if you, your spouse, your child, your grandchild, your friend, or your student has ADHD. (Whew, that's a lot of perspectives in one book!) Given the enormity of perspective that we try to cover, we can't very well list each of the possible relationships you may have with ADHD in each paragraph. To keep things simple, we generally refer to *you* throughout the book as if you're the person who has ADHD. However, in some instances we do mention a specific perspective as it relates to a particular relationship, and in those cases we write about *your child, your spouse,* and so on.

Another convention we want to clarify up front is how we reference the condition we're writing about. In the mental health field, this condition is called *attention deficit/hyperactivity disorder,* or ADHD. Most likely, you've also heard it called simply *attention deficit disorder,* or ADD. We're talking about the same condition; we've simply chosen to use its formal name in this book. (As you find out in Chapter 2, this condition has had many names over the years).

Foolish Assumptions

In this book, we make only one assumption about you: We assume that you want to read a book about ADHD that doesn't dilly-dally around with poetic descriptions and lengthy anecdotes, because you have very little time and want to get the bottom line quickly. We don't waste your time with lengthy explanations, but we do want to make this book engaging to read, so we include some references to people we've worked with to give you insights into life with ADHD.

Icons Used in This Book

As with all *For Dummies* books, we use a few icons to help you along your way.

REMEMBER

Certain ideas and techniques are very important and worth remembering. This icon gives you those gentle nudges to keep you on track.

TECHNICAL STUFF

This icon sits next to paragraphs that are interesting but ultimately aren't critical to understanding the discussion at hand. You can skip them if you need to.

TIP

The Tip highlights expert advice and ideas that can help you to better deal with ADHD in your life.

WARNING

This icon alerts you to instances when you need to take special care not to hurt yourself or someone else.

Beyond the Book

In addition to the abundance of information and guidance related to ADHD that we provide in this book, you get access to even more help and information online at Dummies.com. Check out this book's online Cheat Sheet. Just go to www.dummies.com and search for "ADHD For Dummies Cheat Sheet."

Where to Go from Here

This book is set up so that you can read it cover to cover or jump around and read only those parts that interest you at the time. For instance, if you don't know anything about ADHD and want to get up to speed on the basics, start with Chapter 1. On the other hand, if your child is having trouble in school and you want to find some ways to deal with their challenges, you can head straight for Chapter 16. If you want to find out about the latest alternative treatment methods for ADHD, check out Chapter 11, 12, or 13 first.

Regardless of where you start in this book, if you run across a term or idea that's covered in more detail somewhere else, we offer a cross reference so you can locate the background information you need.

1

The ABCs of ADHD

Chapter **1**

ADHD Basics

I n 1980, a new term entered the common vocabulary: *attention deficit disorder*. It described a condition that has been recognized since the latter part of the 19th century but called a variety of other names. This term — which later morphed into *attention deficit/hyperactivity disorder (ADHD)* — often rears itself whenever someone has difficulty in school or work, can't sit still, or is unable to control their behaviors. The symptoms of ADHD can affect anyone — people of all ages, genders, and socioeconomic backgrounds. Because of this fact, and because the symptoms of ADHD are simply extremes of everyday behavior, this condition is often misunderstood and misdiagnosed.

In this chapter, we introduce you to ADHD. We give you a brief overview of the common symptoms, biological causes, diagnosis, treatment approaches, and life strategies for coping with ADHD. This chapter gets you up to speed on the basics, and we deal with each of these topics in much more detail in the rest of the book.

REMEMBER

As we point out in the Introduction, ADHD is a complex condition that's estimated to affect between 3 and 6 percent of the people in the United States. Rest assured that many happy, successful people live with ADHD, including both of us.

Having so many people around you with ADHD means that quality information, support, treatments, and life strategies are available that can help minimize the negative effects and maximize the positive. (And yes, ADHD does have positive attributes. You can read about these in Chapter 14.)

Identifying Symptoms of ADHD

If you have ADHD, you may have trouble regulating yourself. This difficulty can exist in the areas of attention, behavior, and motor movements. ADHD looks different in almost everyone. For example, one person may have no problem sitting still but gaze off into space unable to focus at all. Another person may constantly fidget but be able spend seemingly endless amounts of time focusing on one thing, often to the exclusion of everything else in their life. Yet another person may not be able to stop themself from impulsive and often dangerous behaviors but may be able to sit calmly in school. The following sections break down both primary and secondary ADHD symptoms.

Peering into primary symptoms

Despite all the different ways that ADHD manifests, the condition has three basic symptoms:

» **Inattention/distractibility:** People with ADHD have problems focusing. You may be able to focus sometimes but not others. This variable nature of being able to pay attention is one of the main features of ADHD. Because attention is inconsistent, people can easily rationalize or dismiss this symptom.

» **Impulsivity:** Many people with ADHD have trouble regulating their behavior. In this case, you often act without thinking, perhaps talking out of turn or taking unnecessary risks.

» **Hyperactivity:** Someone who is *hyperactive* is frequently moving in some way. You may be able to sit but may need to move some part of your body when doing so; leg rocking or shaking is one common example. This hyperactivity is more of a problem with children than adults because most ADHD adults have less physical restlessness as they get older and often find activities to channel it.

The term *attention deficit/hyperactivity disorder* (ADHD) comes from the American Psychiatric Association's *Diagnostic and Statistical Manual of Mental Disorders* (DSM-V). The DSM-V outlines three types of ADHD:

» **Inattentive type:** Having this type of ADHD means that you have difficulty focusing but are able to sit still.

» **Hyperactive/impulsive type:** If you have this type of ADHD, you struggle to sit still and have difficulty considering consequences before doing or saying something, but focusing isn't an issue.

» **Combined type:** If you have a hard time focusing as well as difficulty sitting still or doing things without thinking, you have the combined type.

The DSM-V also rates the current severity of ADHD from mild to moderate to severe. These ratings are helpful to understand where you fit within the overall spectrum of the condition.

Seeing a few secondary symptoms

Aside from the basic three symptoms of inattention, impulsivity, and hyperactivity (which we discuss in the preceding section), ADHD has a ton of other symptoms. These symptoms can include, but aren't limited to, the following:

» Worry

» Boredom

» Loss of motivation

» Frustration

» Low self-esteem

» Sleep disturbances

» Hopelessness

In Chapter 3, we discuss these and other symptoms in detail.

TECHNICAL
STUFF

These secondary symptoms are also connected to other common disorders. The overlap of symptoms among a variety of disorders is called *comorbidity* and is one of the reasons that diagnosing ADHD is so difficult. (See the "Getting a Diagnosis of ADHD" section later in this chapter, or check out Chapter 5.)

Clueing in on ADHD's Origins

Many people used to believe that ADHD (before it even had this name) was merely a behavioral disorder and had no biological basis. However, research since then has shown that people with ADHD have something different happening biologically than people without the disorder. What exactly that biological basis is no one knows for sure. Some of the discoveries that researchers have made include the following:

» **Genetic links:** Having the disorder frequently is a genetic predisposition. ADHD runs in families; you're more likely to see a child with ADHD born into a family where at least one parent has it.

>> **Neurological activity:** Some studies show that people with ADHD have brain function differences. For example, some studies have shown a lower level of activity in the front of the brain — the area that controls attention. Others have discovered activity abnormalities in other regions deep within the brain.

>> **Chemical differences:** Certain chemical activity, such as dopamine and norepinephrine, seems to be different in people who have ADHD. Several studies suggest that there are differences in the responses when neurochemicals are created and released by people with ADHD compared to people who don't have the condition. This is an important component when it comes to choosing medication (Chapter 8 explores ADHD medications in more detail).

REMEMBER

Even after decades of research, the actual cause(s) of ADHD aren't known. But despite this lack of completely detailed understanding of the causes, they do know a lot about how to treat the disorder. We give you an introduction later in this chapter in the section "Viewing Various Treatment Approaches," and we write about treatment options in detail in Part 3 of this book.

Getting a Diagnosis of ADHD

Diagnosing ADHD can be frustrating for some people because there's no definitive way to check for it. You can't see it in a brain scan. You can't test for it with a blood sample. The only way to diagnose ADHD is to do a detailed evaluation of your (or your loved one's) past and present behaviors. This job involves finding a professional who understands the subtleties and variations of ADHD and can make a *differential diagnosis* (a list of conditions that have the same symptoms). The following sections give you an overview of this important process.

Choosing your professional

The first step to finding out whether you have ADHD involves finding the right healthcare professional. You may start with your family doctor or pediatrician, but in order to get an accurate diagnosis (as accurate as possible, anyway), you need to see a professional who understands all the different ways ADHD looks and can review your history properly. Your options can include, but aren't limited to, the following:

>> **Psychiatrist:** A *psychiatrist* is a medical doctor who specializes in mental illness and behavioral disorders. A psychiatrist can prescribe medication and often is up-to-date on the neurological factors of ADHD.

>> **Neurologist:** A *neurologist* is a medical doctor whose specialty is the brain. This person often views ADHD from a biological basis and can prescribe medication. They may not be up-to-date on the best ADHD life strategies or alternative treatments.

>> **Psychologist:** A *psychologist* is trained in matters of the mind. Most psychologists understand the criteria for diagnosing ADHD and can offer many treatment options; some can prescribe medication depending on their license.

>> **ADHD specialist:** An *ADHD specialist* can be anyone from a teacher to a therapist who has experience and expertise in working with people with ADHD. Specialists likely have knowledge of many treatment and coping strategies, but they aren't able to prescribe medication.

>> **ADHD coach:** An *ADHD coach* helps you improve your functioning in the world. Coaches can come from many backgrounds — education, business, psychology — and their focus tends to be on practical, day-to-day matters, such as skills training. Like an ADHD specialist, a coach has expertise in working with people with ADHD but usually can't prescribe medication.

Each professional will immediately recommend the approaches that they're most familiar with and that fit with their treatment philosophy, so choosing the best professional for you depends partly on your values regarding medication and partly on how open you are to unconventional ways of approaching treatment.

TIP

In Chapter 4, we help you explore your values and how they fit with each type of ADHD professional. You also find out how to question a professional to see whether their philosophy fits with yours. Knowing this information prevents you from feeling pressured to attempt treatments you don't agree with and helps you find treatments that fit your style.

Preparing for the evaluation process

After you've chosen a professional to work with (as we explain in the preceding section), you can dig into the actual process of evaluation. This process involves answering a lot of questions and looking at your past. Chapter 5 gives you a heads up on the types of questions you have to answer, as well as the official criteria for being diagnosed with ADHD.

REMEMBER

Diagnosing ADHD isn't easy, and a diagnosis either way isn't the final word. ADHD is one of many similar conditions, and even the best professional can place you or your loved one in the wrong category. We recommend that you seek a second opinion, especially if you have any doubts about the diagnosis. Chapter 6 introduces you to many conditions and symptoms that can appear to be ADHD or that can accompany it.

Viewing Various Treatment Approaches

Treating ADHD has so many approaches that one of the main struggles most people have when they're diagnosed with the disorder is to weed through all the treatment options and choose the best ones to try.

Treatment options break down into several broad categories, which include the following. The most conventional treatment methods for ADHD are medication and behavior modification. Both are useful and effective approaches, but many other types of treatment can work wonders with the right person:

» Medication

» Counseling and therapy

» Coaching

» Training

» Behavior management

» Nutrition and supplements

» Herbs and homeopathies

» Neuromodulation therapies

» Rebalancing therapies

» Social skills training

We discuss each option in detail in Chapters 8 through 13. Each treatment approach has a place, and many of them work well together. Knowing how to choose and what to combine can be difficult. Our goal is to make this challenge more manageable, which is why we wrote Chapter 7, where we help you develop and implement a plan for treatment success.

Recognizing ADHD's Role in Your Life

One of the best ways to deal with the symptoms of ADHD is to have a toolbox of strategies you can reach into when you run into difficulties. The more tools you have in this box, the easier life becomes. As we explain in the following sections, we dedicate an entire section of this book (Part 4) to helping you fill your box with the best tools possible.

Accentuating the positive

ADHD doesn't just create challenges. In some areas, people with ADHD have multiple strengths. When you understand these positive attributes — such as heightened creativity, high energy, hyperfocus, and a willingness to take risks — you can discover ways to maximize and amplify them to help you succeed in the world. For example, you can identify your style of working to keep you on task and motivated to get a job done. We created Chapter 14 to inspire and encourage you to find your strengths and make the most of them.

Dealing with daily life

Whether you're at school, at home, or at work, you can develop ways to minimize the negative impacts of your ADHD symptoms by using some strategies that have worked well for other people, including us. In Chapters 15 through 17, we offer you insights, tools, and ideas for making daily life as successful and stress-free as possible.

For example, we suggest ways to help you develop healthy family relationships, motivate your child with ADHD to do their homework, know your legal rights at school and in the workplace, keep organized on the job, develop a solid career path, and much more. We hope the information in these chapters also spurs you on to create your own unique ways of dealing with ADHD in your life.

Chapter **2**

Exploring the Causes of ADHD

N o one completely understands the causes of ADHD. However, significant advances in brain science mean researchers understand more about the chemistry, structures, and workings of this complex organ than ever before.

In this chapter, we review several theories about the causes of ADHD — both those that have broken new ground and others that have severely missed the mark. We also explain some studies that indicate that ADHD has a biological basis and/or neurodevelopmental basis and others that address the role of genes and gene behavior. We explore where the worldwide research on ADHD is heading and what it means for the future of diagnosis and treatment.

Gaining Perspective from Past Theories

The earliest reference to the symptoms of ADHD comes from the ancient Greek Hippocrates, who thought it was an elemental imbalance (too much fire over water). Sir Alexander Crichton, a Scottish physician, made the first medical reference to these symptoms in 1798. In 1902, British physician George Frederic Still lectured about patients he'd seen with symptoms of ADHD, and since then numerous theories about the causes of ADHD have been considered.

In the following list, we offer a brief overview of the more common past theories of ADHD for a historical perspective. Some of these theories have been based on behavioral problems (bad parenting, willful children), but many have viewed ADHD as having some biological basis:

>> **Bad parenting:** Blaming parents for the behaviors a child with ADHD exhibits is, on the surface, logical. After all, plenty of kids act inappropriately when adults don't supervise them properly. The difference is that children with ADHD can't be disciplined into not having the symptoms. They can be taught ways to cope and strategies to lessen their symptoms, but these strategies don't remove the ADHD.

WARNING

The blame-the-parents theory is, without a doubt, the number-one misconception about ADHD. Unfortunately, a lot of people still believe it. Don't buy into this theory — it's just not true.

>> **Defiance/willfulness:** Like the bad parenting theory, the theory of defiance is based in logic, because when kids without ADHD act out, they can be taught not to behave that way. The problem is that people with ADHD can't concentrate better by trying harder, and they can't stop hyperactivity or restlessness by willing it away. This theory is still perpetuated among people who don't understand ADHD.

>> **Poor diet:** After researchers realized that ADHD wasn't caused by bad parenting or willful defiance, they started looking at other causes. Diet was one theory that garnered a lot of attention. A poor diet can, in fact, cause some ADHD-type symptoms in people without the condition, and it can worsen the symptoms of ADHD (see Chapter 11), but it doesn't cause ADHD.

>> **Allergies and sensitivities:** Much like a poor diet, allergies and sensitivities can create symptoms similar to ADHD, such as inattention and forgetfulness. And these sensitivities can worsen symptoms for some people with ADHD. People who have these symptoms (but not ADHD) see them disappear when they get their allergies or sensitivities under control. Red dye No. 3, which has been banned in California, is a good example of this type of substance sensitivity.

>> **Brain damage:** One of the early nonbehavioral theories involved the idea that people with ADHD have some sort of brain damage. This view was partly a result of the 1918 influenza epidemic, when some children who had influenza encephalitis developed hyperactivity, inattentiveness, and impulsivity.

>> **Toxic exposure:** Exposure to lead and the accumulation of lead in the brain were once considered the cause of ADHD. Studies have suggested that some people with lead exposure may display symptoms similar to ADHD. However, lead exposure isn't the cause of ADHD for most people who have it. And lead isn't the only offender; exposure to other environmental toxins during pregnancy or after birth can also cause ADHD-like symptoms.

>> **Traumatic brain injury:** Like the brain damage theory, some people have believed that ADHD stems from lack of oxygen during birth or a head injury early in childhood. Although brain injuries can induce the same symptoms as ADHD (depending, of course, on where the injury is), they aren't the cause of ADHD.

REMEMBER

Several theories on the origins of ADHD actually led to the identification of disorders that are distinct from ADHD. This connection illustrates how the primary symptoms of ADHD can be found in more conditions than just ADHD. We discuss various disorders that share the same basic symptoms as ADHD in Chapter 6.

WHAT'S IN A NAME?

ADHD has been called many things since it was first observed. Two early names were *Minimal Brain Damage* and later — because at the time no one actually saw any damage in the brain — *Minimal Brain Dysfunction*. Since its inclusion in the American Psychiatric Association (APA) listing of mental disorders, ADHD has been officially called the following names:

- Minimal Brain Dysfunction

- Hyperkinetic Reaction of Childhood

- Attention Deficit Disorder With or Without Hyperactivity (ADD, a name that's still widely used outside the professional community)

- Attention Deficit/Hyperactivity Disorder (ADHD)

Coming at ADHD Research from All Sides

Since the first edition of this book, scientists have a much greater understanding of genetics and *epigenetics* (how your environment and behavior cause changes that affect how your genes work without actually changing your DNA). This explosion of knowledge is due in large part to the mapping of the human genome, which led to new theories about and treatments of many diseases, particularly cancer.

So how do neuroscientists come up with a working hypothesis that can be turned into a theory? They start by trying to understand how the brain and the mind (your thoughts and memories, for example) interact to produce particular types of learning, emotions, and behaviors. Then they try to understand how the study group (in this case, people with ADHD) functions differently from the general population, and they try to find evidence of some biological difference to explain the differences they've observed.

Studies for looking at causes of mental health conditions, including ADHD, are global and widescale. In practice, scientists from different disciplines are trying to understand ADHD from different angles:

>> Geneticists are looking for unique characteristics of the genes that people with ADHD inherit. Epigeneticists are looking at how different genes are expressed and what environments influence that (because environmental factors seem to heavily determine whether a gene gets turned on and expressed or turned off).

>> Neuroscientists and physiologists are trying to find differences in brain function between people with ADHD and people without it.

REMEMBER

No single factor — genetic or environmental — causes ADHD. Rather, developing ADHD involves a complex (and not yet fully understood) interplay between them. Both the genetic/biological and the environmental determinants sides have their theorists. More research is necessary to understand the roles of risk factors before birth, of epigenetics, and even of intergenerational trauma.

Examining Self-Regulation's Role in ADHD

The ADHD research taking place today is rooted in the recognition that people with ADHD have one core problem: the inability to consistently regulate their attention and behaviors. The following sections explore the nature of this problem and the various brain functions that contribute to it.

Recognizing self-regulation as a core issue

ADHD may be primarily a problem with self-regulation. *Self-regulation* refers to your ability to attain and maintain particular states of functioning in a consistent and predictable way. Although anyone can struggle with self-regulation, especially when they're tired or uninterested, people with ADHD are more likely to have problems controlling their attention, managing their impulses, modulating their moods, and managing their activity levels.

You must be able to self-regulate to be able to plan, organize, and perform complex thoughts and behaviors like you want, when you want. Otherwise you aren't confident that you can call on the skills you already have when you need them, and you have no guarantee of being able to learn something new.

On the surface, self-regulation seems to depend on your desire to control your behavior. That's true, but much more than simple willpower is involved. All higher brain functions are partly hard-wired from birth and partly learned. (Learning is just modifying the wiring through experience.) In other words, your ability to self-regulate is a characteristic of the brain you were born with as it developed through the experiences that helped you learn how to use it. Neuroscientists use the saying "What fires together wires together."

The areas you try to regulate — such as sustaining your attention on a specific task or sitting still when you're asked — are things you can learn to do more effectively as you grow older if you get the right kinds of experiences. The ability to use your experiences to learn is partly dependent on your ability to attain and maintain consistent brain states — which comes full circle back to self-regulation.

Linking executive brain functions and self-regulation

Executive functions are the brain functions necessary for you to be able to regulate your behaviors. Executive functions primarily cover these areas:

>> **Response inhibition:** *Response inhibition* includes impulse control, resistance to distraction, and delay of gratification. According to researcher Dr. Russell A. Barkley, response inhibition is the core problem in ADHD; the rest of the executive functions draw off it.

>> **Working memory:** *Working memory* is divided into two categories:

- **Nonverbal:** *Nonverbal working memory* allows you to refer to past events to gauge your behavior. For example, if you don't remember that interrupting someone while they're talking results in a negative social interaction, you may interrupt them.

- **Verbal:** *Verbal working memory* allows you to internalize speech, which results in the ability to understand other people as well as to express yourself clearly.

>> **Motor control:** This function not only allows you to keep from moving impulsively but also helps you plan your movements.

>> **Regulation of your emotions:** Without this function, you may find yourself getting frustrated easily or reacting extremely to a given situation.

>> **Motivation:** This function helps you get started and persist toward a goal.

>> **Planning:** This function works on many levels, but the most significant involves being able to get organized and to develop and implement a plan of action.

Executive functions are controlled in several areas of the brain, including the following (see Figure 2-1):

>> Frontal lobe

>> Basal ganglia, including the caudate nucleus (which is located deep inside the brain and therefore not indicated in Figure 2-1)

>> Cerebellum (the small area by the back and base of the brain)

As we discuss in the later section "Anatomical," current research is finding that at least one of these brain areas seems to work differently in people with ADHD from the way it does in people without ADHD.

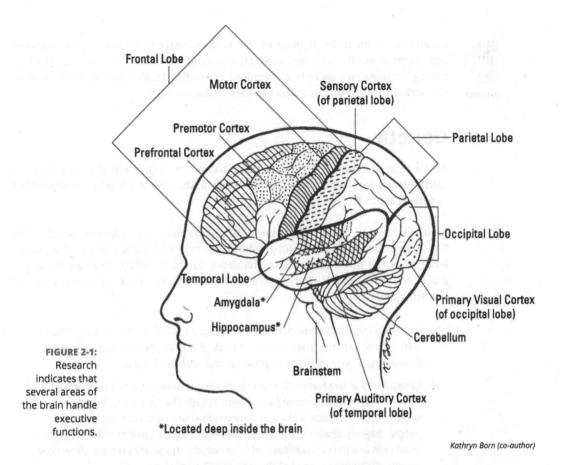

Frontal Lobe

Motor Cortex

Sensory Cortex
(of parietal lobe)

Premotor Cortex

Parietal Lobe

Prefrontal Cortex

Occipital Lobe

Temporal Lobe

Amygdala*

Primary Visual Cortex
(of occipital lobe)

Hippocampus*

Cerebellum

FIGURE 2-1:
Research
indicates that
several areas of
the brain handle
executive
functions.

Brainstem

Primary Auditory Cortex
(of temporal lobe)

*Located deep inside the brain

Kathryn Born (co-author)

Exploring Current ADHD Research

Although the exact cause of ADHD is still unknown, you can find no shortage of research into the biology of ADHD. This research fits into four broad categories: genetic, anatomical, functional, and chemical.

If you know someone with ADHD, the focus on biological causes shouldn't surprise you. When you watch someone struggle with ADHD symptoms, you know that this person wants to pay attention, sit still, or control their impulses. But try as they may, they aren't able to (as we discuss in Chapter 3).

Because we want to focus most of this book on ways to treat and cope with the symptoms of ADHD, we have to limit the amount of research we cover. In the following sections, we include a sampling of studies to give you an idea of what researchers are looking at and what they're discovering.

Genetic

ADHD runs in families — so much so that when diagnosing the condition, an ADHD professional's first step may be to look at the person's family to see whether anyone else has it.

Along those lines, many studies have examined ADHD from a genetic perspective. These include studies that look at adoptive versus biological parents, the prevalence of ADHD in families, twins' tendency to share ADHD, and specific genes associated with ADHD. Here's a short sampling of some of these areas of investigation:

» In 2023, a large international study identified 27 places in the human genome with genetic variants that increase the risk of ADHD. This number of locations is more than twice as many as previous studies have found.

» Researchers at the National Institutes of Health have identified differences in gene activity in the brains of people with ADHD. The NIH study, led by scientists at the National Human Genome Research Institute, found that people diagnosed with ADHD had differences in genes tied to chemicals that brain cells use to communicate. In other words, this study's results show how genetic differences may contribute to ADHD symptoms.

This research is one of the only studies to use brain tissue post mortem.

» Several studies by Dr. Joseph Biederman and his colleagues at Massachusetts General Hospital have shown that ADHD runs in families. In one study, Dr. Biederman and his colleagues found that first-degree relatives (parents or siblings) of someone with ADHD have a five times greater chance of also having ADHD than someone who has no close relatives with the condition.

» A 2016 published in *The Journal of Child Psychology and Psychiatry* showed that identical twins were almost 60 percent more likely than fraternal twins to share an ADHD diagnosis and that fraternal twins were still significantly more likely to share a diagnosis than nontwin siblings.

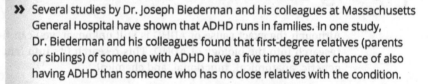

Anatomical

Researchers have conducted a few studies into the size and shape of the brains of people with ADHD compared to those of people without it. A lot of conflicting data exists in this area, but a few basic ideas have been suggested:

» One study suggested that the size of the *corpus collosum* (a bundle of nerves that ties the hemispheres of the brain together) is different in some people with ADHD than in some people without it. Other researchers have suggested that this part of the brain operates differently in people with ADHD than in others.

» A 2017 imaging study found that overall brain volume and specific brain regions were slightly smaller in participants with ADHD than in those without ADHD.

Although anatomical research continues, most of the ADHD research being done right now focuses on differences in brain activity between the ADHD and non-ADHD populations.

Functional

The brains of people with ADHD seem to function differently from the brains of people without it. This area of study is important not only because it helps explain the cause of ADHD but also because these studies use relatively new technologies for imaging — specifically, functional MRI (fMRI).

Here are some highlights from this field:

» Much attention is being paid to the task positive network (TPN) and the default mode network (DMN). Functional MRIs show that when you do a task, the cluster of neurons in the *task positive network* light up. When you daydream or use your imagination, you use your *default mode network*. fMRI shows that in people with ADHD, the TPN and the DMN are turned on simultaneously, whereas in a neurotypical brain the DMN is turned off when the TPN is turned on. (You can read more about this "glitchy switch" in *ADHD 2.0* by Drs. Edward M. Hallowell and John J. Ratey [Random House Publishing Group].) This inconsistency is one theory on why some people with ADHD show such a difference in both distractibility and negativity compared with people who don't have ADHD.

>> A study by Dr. Alan Zemetkin using PET scans on adults with ADHD discovered that when the subjects concentrated, the level of activity in the front part of the brain (the frontal lobe) decreased from its level at rest. People without ADHD have an opposite response — an increase in activity in the frontal lobe when they concentrate.

Chemical

For information to pass from one part of the brain to another requires the action of *neurotransmitters* — chemical messengers within the brain.

A neurotransmitter allows one *neuron* (nerve) to communicate with another. When the upstream neuron gets excited and wants to pass on information to the downstream neuron, it releases the neurotransmitter molecules into a closed connection (like an airlock in a submarine or a spaceship) called a *synapse*. The neurotransmitter then crosses the space to the downstream neuron's membrane and binds to specific receptors that cause an effect inside the receiving nerve.

As we explain in Chapter 8, certain medications are generally effective for treating ADHD symptoms, and most of these medications affect one or both of two neurotransmitters: norepinephrine (also called noradrenalin) and dopamine. This effectiveness indicates that these two neurotransmitters are involved in causing the condition. These neurotransmitter systems are distributed throughout the brain in specific locations, and they have different effects based on the types of receptors that the downstream neurons have on their membranes. The receptors determine what effect a neurotransmitter has, and different types of receptors exist in different regions of the brain.

A lot of research has been done in this area showing a link between certain brain chemicals and the symptoms of ADHD. Some of the more elegant theories about ADHD consider the balance between norepinephrine and dopamine in the various areas they affect, including the idea that one neurotransmitter has more effect in one hemisphere of the brain than the other (see Figure 2-2). Most of the neurons that have norepinephrine as their transmitter are contained in one area of the brainstem, the *locus coeruleus*. It's part of the *reticular activating system*, which is the area of the brain that controls the general level of activation of your nervous system (how aroused you are — whether you're awake or asleep). Dopamine is found in several different areas of the brain, but the area that seems most important for ADHD is the part that projects to the prefrontal cortex and is probably responsible for significance, meaning, and motivation.

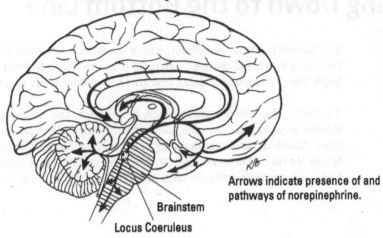

Median section through the left side of the brain

Arrows indicate presence of and pathways of norepinephrine.

Brainstem

Locus Coeruleus

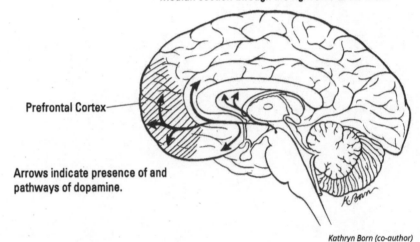

Median section through the right side of the brain

Prefrontal Cortex

Arrows indicate presence of and pathways of dopamine.

Kathryn Born (co-author)

FIGURE 2-2:
The dopamine-norepinephrine connections in the brain may have a lot to do with ADHD.

One way to think about ADHD is that it's a problem of deficiency in the activities of norepinephrine and dopamine. When you have too little norepinephrine working, you aren't paying attention to your environment. When you have too little dopamine activity, then you lack motivation, determination of salience, sustained attention, and engagement.

Getting Down to the Bottom Line

The human brain is *neuroplastic,* which means the networks in the brain change through growth and reorganization. So if you're trying to rewire your brain, have hope. You can teach an old dog new tricks, metaphorically speaking.

The fields of genetics, neuroscience, epigenetics, and neuroimaging continue to expand at rapid rates. We imagine that knowledge of the causes of ADHD and the brain functions and chemicals involved will increase dramatically in the near future. As this all becomes clearer, you can expect that clinicians will have much better ways to help someone with ADHD cope with the condition.

Chapter **3**

The Many Facets of ADHD

E veryone has a unique nervous system. In fact, the infinite variability in how humans' brains work has given rise to the popular term *neurodivergence*. ADHD fits into this concept.

ADHD can look different in everyone. One person may be able to sit still but not focus, another may have very little trouble sitting still but constantly speak without thinking, and yet another may not be able to sit still for any length of time while also having problems keeping focused on a task. Such is the nature of ADHD and one of the reasons many people have a difficult time believing this condition exists.

In this chapter, we list the primary symptoms of ADHD and discuss how these symptoms often give rise to others. We also examine how gender, age, race, and sexual orientation create special issues for people with ADHD.

Picturing the Primary Symptoms of ADHD

ADHD has three primary symptoms: inattention/distractibility, impulsivity, and hyperactivity. These symptoms don't all have to be present for you to have ADHD, and if you do have one or more of them, they may not be present all the time. (Chapter 5 explains how this inconsistency works.) The following sections explore these symptoms and many of the ways in which they manifest in people with ADHD.

Inattention/distractibility

REMEMBER

Inattention means you have a hard time focusing on something. *Distractibility* means your attention is easily pulled from one thing to another.

Inattention is at the core of ADHD, and it isn't as simple as never being able to focus. Nothing about this condition is as clear-cut as that. Inattention is more accurately a problem in being able to control or regulate how and when you focus on something. (*Regulation* is a key word for people with ADHD; check out Chapter 2 for more about regulation.)

We much prefer thinking about attention as variable or inconsistent. This point is where distractibility comes in. External and internal stimuli pull on people with ADHD much harder than on people without it. As a result, people with ADHD have a hard time staying focused on one thing.

A key thing to know about this symptom is that it can look different in almost everyone, and it can change from day to day in each person. But even with such variability, a few basic characteristics of inattention and distractibility occur in people with ADHD:

>> **Not being able to concentrate:** Try as you may, keeping focused on something is difficult and, at times, impossible. The worst part is that the harder you try, the harder concentrating is. Your mind may go blank, or you may have other thoughts come into your mind.

>> **Being able to focus well on some things but not on others:** This symptom is one of the most confusing aspects of inattention in ADHD. Many people think that just because a person can concentrate on something means they must be able to concentrate on everything if they just try hard enough. That's not the case for people with ADHD.

For example, your coauthor Jeff worked with a 9-year-old boy who couldn't stay on task at school. He often stared out the window, spaced out, and sometimes almost dozed off. At home, whenever he had to do homework, he had the same difficulties. However, if you gave him a model rocket to build or a book about rockets, he was in his element and could often focus for hours. In fact, he'd get so engrossed that he often forgot to eat or go to the bathroom.

Some people with ADHD claim that they don't have the condition because they can focus "as long as it's something I'm interested in." The criterion for ADHD isn't about being unable to focus ever; instead, it's about not having control over when and how this focusing happens. This discrepancy leads to another aspect of ADHD, which we describe in the next bullet.

>> **Being able to focus sometimes but not other times:** For many people, this feature of ADHD is one of the most frustrating. As an example, the same 9-year-old boy we mention in the previous bullet experienced many times when he couldn't even focus on the model building that he loved so much. Some days he'd start putting a section together and lose track of what came next or end up gluing that section to the wrong part of the main model. This scattered thinking made tackling complex projects very difficult for him because he'd often lose track of what he was doing.

>> **Being easily distracted by things happening around you:** Many people with ADHD are unable to filter out all the things going on around them and are easily pulled away from what they want to focus on.

For example, Jeff worked with a man in his 40s whose relationship was in trouble because he was unable to effectively listen to his wife when she talked, which led her to believe that he didn't care about her. This man explained that as he tried to listen, he found himself distracted by the sound of the refrigerator turning off or on, a passing car, or some other sound that his wife didn't even notice. For him, these sounds were irresistible. As much as he tried to ignore them, they seemed to draw him in. The result was that even though he genuinely wanted to listen to his wife, he caught only parts of the conversation and often ended up misunderstanding what she said.

>> **Being easily distracted by your own thoughts:** For many people with ADHD, having a series of unrelated thoughts flowing through their minds is common. Many people think of this issue as "daydreaming."

>> **Losing track of your thoughts (spacing out):** An extension of being easily distracted is spacing out. This symptom is common for people with ADHD — they seem like they have gaps in their awareness.

>> **Being forgetful:** A lot of people with ADHD tend to lose their keys, forget to turn in assignments, space appointments, can't remember simple instructions, and get lost.

>> **Being late:** Because many people with ADHD have trouble organizing their time, they're often late to appointments. Sometimes they're purposely early everywhere they go because they know they tend to be late.

>> **Being unable to finish things:** People with ADHD are notorious for starting a project and then moving on to something else before finishing it. Jean, a woman in her late 30s whom Jeff worked with, was extremely bright and ambitious, with tons of great ideas and the talent to back them up. The only problem was that every time she'd work on one of her projects, she'd leave it half finished. She always had an excuse for abandoning a project, such as another, more important project coming up. She also had a long history of quitting jobs after just a few months even though she performed them very well.

>> **Procrastinating:** Because people with ADHD are often poor at organizing their thoughts and time, they often fail to even start something. Also, after repeated failures, many people avoid starting projects because of the fear that they'll fail again. Many people with ADHD wait until the last minute to do things because the pressure helps them focus.

>> **Not attending to details:** People with ADHD are often "big-picture" people. They can think up new and exciting ideas, but they just can't seem to follow through with the details needed to make those ideas happen. They often miss important details when given instructions on how to do something.

>> **Making careless mistakes:** Not attending to details leads to careless mistakes. This problem is common with people who are easily distractible, because they drift from one thought to another and lose track of what they've done and what they need to do next.

This list can't even come close to detailing all the ways that inattention and distractibility manifest in people with ADHD. The main aspect of inattention and distractibility for people with ADHD is a reduced level of activity in the frontal lobe of the brain. The frontal lobe, as we describe in Chapter 2, is responsible for motor planning, organization, problem-solving, attention, and impulse control, to name a few.

Impulsivity

Impulsivity is the inability to consider the consequences of your actions beforehand — in other words, doing before thinking. When you have this symptom of ADHD, it's almost as though you have an involuntary response to a stimulus. The response can take the form of actions or words.

Like the other symptoms of ADHD, impulsivity looks different depending on the person. Some people have difficulty considering what they say before saying it, whereas others may act at times without thinking. Here are a few ways that impulsivity can manifest in people with ADHD:

>> **Blurting out answers before a question is finished:** Many teachers of children with ADHD complain that the children shout out answers before questions have been asked. Many ADHD adults have a habit of finishing other people's sentences.

>> **Saying inappropriate things:** Having successful interpersonal relationships often involves being diplomatic — knowing when *not* to say something because it wouldn't accomplish anything useful. People with the hyperactive/impulsive type of ADHD have a difficult time censoring themselves, and they respond to other people without considering the consequences of what they say. Most often, the person saying these things feels awful afterward and wonders in amazement why they said what they said.

>> **Butting into conversations:** Because of the inability to keep from saying the first thing that comes to mind, people with impulse problems often butt into conversations. This tendency is due partly to the lack of impulse control but also to the difficulty that many people with ADHD have in being able to "read" conversations. In other words, they can't pick up on and interpret subtle signals (body language) and the rhythm of a conversation. When this person butts into the conversation, they may do so with a comment or story that doesn't fit with the current conversation. Interrupting is another variant of this symptom. Coauthor Carol has worked with countless couples for whom interrupting is a significant issue in their relationship.

>> **Intruding on others:** Another characteristic of ADHD sufferers is that they often don't know where their bodies are in space, so they tend to be some-what clumsy. Couple this characteristic with the lack of impulse control, and you often find people with ADHD intruding on others — bumping into them, grabbing at a toy, and so on.

>> **Acting without considering the consequences:** Lack of impulse control often leads to doing something before thinking about whether it's a smart thing to do. Many people with ADHD act from impulse to impulse. For example, Carol has worked with many adults who surf the Internet and make impulsive buys — everything from cleaning cloths to watches to cars — only to regret their purchases later. The hunt, whether for a bargain or an item, is what's so alluring.

>> **Engaging in risky behaviors:** Because people with ADHD often crave stimulus, they may get into situations where they do dangerous things. This tendency is related to another aspect of ADHD: thrill-seeking. Pushing life to the limits can really help some people focus and feel more in control.

>> **Being impatient, especially in line:** Impatience comes in many forms, some of which we cover in previous bullets, such as butting into conversations and blurting out answers before a question has been fully asked.

One thing that's particularly difficult, even excruciating, for people with ADHD is waiting in line, which requires someone to stand relatively still. People with the hyperactive/impulsive type of ADHD have symptoms that cover both impulsivity and hyperactivity or restlessness. As a result, they're more likely to fidget and squirm while waiting. Jeff had a client who would do his grocery shopping after midnight to avoid standing in line. Having a smartphone has helped many of Carol's clients deal with the impatience and restlessness of waiting to check out at the store.

Some people with ADHD can't stand to drive the speed limit or stop at stoplights. This kind of impatience obviously can cause myriad problems, including increased traffic violations and accidents.

>> **Wanting things immediately:** This symptom can take many forms, such as wanting to have your needs met immediately, as in the case of buying on credit or of a child who has a tantrum when you don't come running to their aid. Shopping on the Internet can satisfy this need but also create financial and relationship distress.

Impulse control is regulated in the frontal lobes of the brain — the same part of the brain that controls attention. Because people with ADHD often have less activity in this part of the brain, they have less control over their impulses. Often, their bodies react to a stimulus before the reasoning part of the brain can stop, choose the best response, and then act.

Restlessness/hyperactivity

Restlessness and *hyperactivity* are essentially the same thing — the inability to regulate your physical movements. For the person with this symptom of ADHD, sitting still is difficult (especially at school or work, where sitting for extended periods of time is expected), as is doing activities that require minimal physical movement, such as study hall or staff meetings. Restlessness is subtler than hyperactivity because it's often internal rather than external.

Hyperactive children are probably the poster children for this disorder, even though only about half the people with ADHD have the symptom of hyperactivity.

REMEMBER

Most young children exhibit what would be called hyperactivity — frequent movement and activity. That isn't necessarily a sign that your child has ADHD. Most children outgrow this level of activity by the time they're 4 or 5. And even before then, most kids have periods of time where they're able to sit quietly, such as when reading a book with a parent or older sibling.

Hyperactivity is easily seen in children running around, but in adults, it can be much subtler — so subtle, in fact, that many professionals have suggested that adults outgrow their hyperactivity. This suggestion is proving to be inaccurate. Adults don't outgrow their hyperactivity; they grow into their restlessness. And they often learn how to deal with the symptoms by disguising them.

Restlessness and hyperactivity are so variable in people that in one instance this symptom may be obvious, and in another it may be almost completely disguised. Following are a few of the ways this symptom can present itself:

>> **Being unable to sit still for any length of time:** This characteristic is especially obvious in younger children. As children grow older, they often develop the ability to sit, although they may squirm in their seats or, as they grow older still, just fidget.

>> **Being always on the go:** The classic descriptor is that people with this symptom of ADHD seem to be "driven by a motor." As much as they want to stop moving sometimes, they can't seem to do so.

>> **Feeling edgy:** Adults with ADHD often have this form of restlessness. They're generally able to control their movements to the point of not drawing attention to themselves, but they still feel the need to move and release the energy that builds up inside them. For people with the combined type of ADHD (inattention and hyperactivity/restlessness), these feelings of restlessness often make the inattention worse because the restlessness commands their attention. Restlessness can also manifest in the medium- and long-term parts of a person's life. People with ADHD quite commonly move or change jobs frequently just because they're restless. These feelings of restlessness aren't confined to adults, however; children can have them, too.

>> **Fidgeting constantly:** When hyperactivity and the need to frequently move are internalized, this symptom often manifests as fidgeting. Fidgeting can take on several forms, from seemingly repetitive tapping to random movements. Fidgeting doesn't necessarily relate to restlessness in some older people with ADHD. Some people fidget to try to focus on a task.

>> **Talking nonstop:** Rather than move their bodies, some people with ADHD run their mouths. Constant talking is simply another way to release the energy that seems to build up from ADHD. Often this nonstop talking moves from subject to subject, following the somewhat random thought patterns that go through the person's mind.

Obviously, hyperactivity and restlessness can manifest in people with ADHD in many other ways. The main thing to be aware of is that these actions aren't voluntary. They aren't the result of defiance or bad behavior.

Considering Some Secondary Symptoms

Additional symptoms, such as boredom, frustration, and low self-esteem, often accompany the core symptoms of ADHD (which we discuss in the preceding section). For many older people — adolescents and adults — with ADHD, these symptoms can be more of a problem than the primary ones. The sections that follow give you a glimpse into these secondary symptoms and how they can impact your life.

Anticipation of failure

Much of the anxiety that people with ADHD feel is the result of repeated failures, such as losing track of thoughts, forgetting, being late, getting lost, saying the wrong thing, and so on. With a history of making these types of mistakes, many people get worried because they're afraid that they're going to make another one. The sense of failure this history evokes is painful. Working with a therapist or a coach can significantly reduce the feelings of anxiety and shame that accompany this aspect of ADHD. Flip to Chapter 4 for more on finding a coach or therapist.

Worry

People with ADHD often worry excessively. This worry is actually another expression of the pent-up feelings of restlessness. That makes worry both a symptom and a method for people with ADHD to try to control how their minds work. If they can focus on a thought — in this case, anxiety over some trivial thing — they can avoid spacing out.

REMEMBER

Anxiety disorders have similar symptoms to ADHD — restlessness, inability to concentrate, and hyperactivity — so someone who appears to have ADHD may actually have an anxiety disorder. Approximately 25 percent of people have both. To rule out these possibilities, you need to have a professional explore a *differential diagnosis*. A differential diagnosis is made by a professional to distinguish one condition or illness from another that presents with similar symptoms. We cover this subject in detail in Chapter 6.

Boredom

For people with the hyperactive type of ADHD, almost any stimulus can become boring — especially something that happens repeatedly or is part of someone's everyday life. These types of people seek new and exciting stimulation to keep them interested, and they often partake in high-risk behaviors in order to quell the boredom that can so easily overtake them.

WARNING

People whose ADHD manifests as boredom sometimes create conflict in their lives — whether at school, at work, or at home — in order to "spice things up." This behavior can look as benign as waiting to do a project until the very last minute, or it can take the form of instigating an argument. This need for stimulation can also be as risky as driving recklessly, seeking out high-risk sports, gambling, or compulsively overspending.

Loss of motivation/feelings of hopelessness

Many people with ADHD feel as if they're failing in the world, which erodes their self-esteem and can lead to loss of motivation or feelings of hopelessness. Unfortunately, for many people these feelings exacerbate some of the other symptoms of ADHD (such as forgetfulness, inattention, and spacing out), thus further reducing self-esteem and creating more social isolation. They can also lead to depression (see Chapter 6 for details). Depression in people with ADHD is a serious factor and needs to be dealt with by a professional.

REMEMBER

Depression can be a coexisting condition and has many similar symptoms to ADHD — inattention, poor memory, and negativity — so it can be confused with ADHD. In fact, according to the American Psychiatric Association diagnostic manual (DSM-V), depression must be considered when diagnosing ADHD. Chapter 6 details this process.

Frustration

Imagine not being able to control your ability to focus, to keep from moving, or even to keep from saying something inappropriate. This situation is very frustrating. People with ADHD have to deal not only with their inability to do these things but also — and probably more importantly — with their inability at one time and their ability at other times. The symptoms of ADHD, as we explain earlier in this chapter, can come and go. Sometimes you can concentrate, and sometimes you can't. Sometimes you can sit still, and sometimes you can't.

Not having control over attention, motor activities, or impulses leads to feelings of frustration, and people with ADHD have a lower threshold for this frustration than others. Couple this feeling with lower self-esteem, which most people with ADHD experience (as we explain in the following section), and eventually the person with ADHD may stop trying to do things altogether.

Low self-esteem

Years of not measuring up to others' or your own expectations, experiencing failures at home and school, and struggling in social situations often lead to low self-esteem. Negative messages, whether internal or external, such as "if only you'd apply yourself" or "you aren't living up to your potential" have an erosive effect on how people perceive themselves. People with ADHD generally struggle with low self-esteem, and this second skin of shame colors the way they view and act in the world.

People with low self-esteem have a hard time accepting compliments. They often interpret what others say as criticism even though it may, in fact, be a compliment. Low self-esteem also leads to an overall negative outlook and can be accompanied by moodiness and eventually followed up by depression.

Sleep disturbances

Many people with ADHD have trouble sleeping. Some have a hard time getting to sleep, others wake up often at night, and still others have a hard time waking up in the morning.

TIP

For some people, changes in sleep can be one of the side effects of taking medication. In this instance, you need to adjust the dose and the time of day that you take your medication. Be sure to consult with your doctor before making any changes to your medication dosage or schedule.

Sleep problems can have many causes. Some people actually get hyperfocused on something and forget to go to bed. After a few times doing so, they may develop a sleep debt and need time to sleep longer than usual. This cycle happens to many people with ADHD: During the week they don't get enough sleep, and on the weekends they sleep most of the day away.

For other people — mostly ones with the hyperactive type of ADHD in particular — getting to sleep may be difficult. Winding down is next to impossible, so falling asleep may take hours. For many people with ADHD (regardless of the type), getting up and moving in the morning can be especially challenging. The person may need an hour or so to fully wake up.

REMEMBER

The concurrence of sleep disorders and ADHD is common, so a person with one condition may also have the other. To make matters more complicated, many sleep disorders share the same basic symptoms as the inattentive type of ADHD — such as forgetfulness and inability to concentrate — so what looks like ADHD may actually be a sleep disorder. Chapter 6 digs into this subject more deeply.

Substance abuse

Although substance abuse is technically a *co-occurring condition* with ADHD (meaning simply that the two coexist; see Chapter 6), it's common enough among people with ADHD that we include it in the list of secondary symptoms. Boredom leading to impulsive behavior increases the risk of substance abuse, especially in adolescents with ADHD. Abusing drugs and alcohol may result from trying to numb feelings of failure and from trying to self-medicate.

Certain drugs, such as cocaine, don't offer a high for people with ADHD. Instead, these drugs work much like the prescription stimulants (such as Ritalin) people with ADHD use to reduce some of their symptoms. The problem with this approach — aside from the fact that it's illegal — is that getting any consistency by using street drugs to try to deal with ADHD is impossible because you never know what's in them, and you don't know how strong they are.

Half of all adults with untreated ADHD develop a substance use disorder at some point in their lives. The good news is that people who are properly treated for ADHD have less of a tendency to abuse alcohol and drugs than people who don't have ADHD.

Facing ADHD in Different Populations

Although ADHD manifests differently in everyone, it can show some common characteristics within a given population. In some cases, knowing how other people of their same demographic behave similarly may benefit a person with ADHD.

Children

REMEMBER

Almost all young children exhibit ADHD characteristics, such as darting from one thing to another or climbing on everything in sight. That's why the DSM-V (the manual for mental disorders) stipulates that in order for a child to be classified as having ADHD, they must be acting in a way that isn't appropriate for their age.

Regardless of age, kids without ADHD can often sit still for periods of time — such as when reading a book — whereas kids with the hyperactive type of ADHD can't.

Hyperactive children can be *really* active, which is why hyperactivity is most problematic when kids are young. As kids age, they mellow out a bit, and their hyperactivity turns more inward. By the time they're in their teens, they don't run around as much, although they often squirm or have feelings of restlessness.

Difficulties with attention and organization can have a lasting impact on children with ADHD because ADHD can interfere with learning the basic skills necessary for development into the next stages of education and life. Many children with ADHD have difficulties learning to read, spell, or do arithmetic. These problems can come from not being able to sustain attention and focus, or they can stem from specific learning disabilities that sometimes accompany ADHD (see Chapter 6).

Some, but definitely not all, ADHD children have difficulties getting along with others. A lot of ADHD kids have problems taking instruction, being disciplined, or respecting rules. These problems can follow them into adolescence and adulthood.

Adolescents

For adolescents, the primary symptoms of ADHD are often overshadowed by the secondary symptoms of low self-esteem, frustration, and boredom, to name a few. After years of not being able to get things "right" in school or at home, many teens with ADHD are demoralized.

REMEMBER

Dealing with boredom, low self-esteem, and frustration in adolescents becomes a priority because they have the potential of causing many more problems down the road.

Adolescents with the impulsive/hyperactive type of ADHD are often able to sit and don't exhibit the same level of activity as younger people. Generally, their hyperactivity manifests more internally as a general sense of restlessness and as fidgeting. This internalization doesn't indicate that the symptom of hyperactivity has lessened; instead, it indicates that the person is finding a way to release the kinetic energy in a way that is more socially appropriate. In other words, the hyperactivity is still there; it's just been transformed to be less obvious.

In school, adolescents with ADHD may have a harder time than younger children with ADHD. This shift is partly due to the way schools operate: After children leave elementary school, they often have classes in different rooms with different teachers and have access to fewer support services for kids who are behind in their study skills. Children with ADHD also tend to be somewhat behind their peers in emotional development, and this delay continues into adolescence.

WARNING

Because of the expanding world that adolescents inhabit, especially social media and substance use, the effects of impulsivity can be far-reaching. Impulsive behavior that may have been relatively benign at a younger age can become downright dangerous as adolescents reach their teens. Another problem adolescents experience is that the hormonal changes occurring during puberty often coincide with an increase in the severity of the symptoms of ADHD. (Some adolescents actually have a decrease in ADHD symptoms during puberty, but they're in the significant minority.) Plus, monitoring the dose and drug used becomes increasingly important because as adolescent bodies change, their need for medication changes, too. Unfortunately, many teens don't want to take medications and often sabotage a treatment regimen that would otherwise work for them. All these factors can create a very difficult period for families.

Adults

ADHD used to be known as a childhood disorder. People assumed that after a child with ADHD grew up, they also grew out of their ADHD symptoms. This premise has proved to be false — so much so that a plethora of books are now on the market addressing adult ADHD.

ADHD in adults does exist, but it often manifests differently than in children. Hyperactivity gives way to restlessness; most adults are able to find a way to sit reasonably still even though they desperately want to get up and move around. Adults often develop ways to avoid the signs of hyperactivity obvious in children. For example, they may stay very busy or exercise.

Many of the inattention symptoms of ADHD don't improve with age. Adults have often developed strategies to deal with the symptoms, but they still have them. Unfortunately, most adults with ADHD still suffer from the effects of inattention/distractibility to the point where it impacts their lives. Money problems, frequent job changes, and family and interpersonal problems can wreak havoc and cause the secondary symptom of low self-esteem or the co-occurring condition of depression to develop.

REMEMBER

One of the most important and difficult things for adults with ADHD to do is find the right occupation, and the right job within that sector. Many small business owners are adults with ADHD because many of the positive attributes of ADHD, such as creativity, innovation, and risk-taking (which we discuss in Chapter 14), are essential attributes of entrepreneurs. In addition, many people with ADHD are self-employed because they find working for someone else and meeting the strict requirements of the corporate world very hard.

Unfortunately, running their own businesses can be especially difficult for people with ADHD because of the tendency to procrastinate, be unorganized and impulsive, and so on. For these people, life strategies, good assistants, and technological aids are invaluable tools. Chapter 17 has details about making the most of your work environment.

Women

REMEMBER

One of the biggest challenges women with ADHD encounter is a lack of awareness about the condition, because the perception has been that ADHD typically affects males. Research indicates that males are 69 percent more likely to be diagnosed with ADHD than females. Does this discrepancy mean that fewer women have ADHD? Or is it possible that many women with ADHD aren't being identified because the symptoms associated with ADHD are primarily the ones of hyperactivity most often found in males, and females' symptoms are more likely to be inattention?

Note: When we discuss the research and references to males and females, we are referencing the sex assigned at birth and not gender identity. To date there have not been enough studies that look at trans women with ADHD or the prevalence of ADHD in that population.

Traditionally, more males are hyperactive than females. That doesn't mean you don't see hyperactive or restless girls, but this symptom is less common among females and often doesn't manifest itself as extreme levels of activity. It tends to be internalized more. In young girls, hyperactivity may take the form of excessive talking; for example, Carol was consistently reprimanded in elementary school for excessive talking and blurting out answers. On the other hand, boys tend to get up and move around.

Traditional gender roles that dictate being the organizational hub of the family also worsen inattention in women and girls. This situation can prove to be challenging for women with ADHD, who often try to mask their symptoms while experiencing a sense of shame and inadequacy that can lead to reactive depression. Women with ADHD are diagnosed with depression and low self-esteem at a higher rate than men.

REMEMBER

Different phases of the life cycle, particularly menopause and *perimenopause* (when the body transitions to menopause), affect women with ADHD. Drops in vital hormones and neurotransmitters make this life stage particularly challenging for women with ADHD. Many of this stage's symptoms mimic ADHD and can exacerbate ADHD symptoms of forgetfulness and inattention.

We discuss lifestyle strategies for women in Part 4.

Black, Indigenous, People of Color (BIPOC)

Black, Indigenous, and People of Color (BIPOC) communities have experienced a significant disparity and underrepresentation in both diagnosis and treatment of

ADHD. In numerous studies Black, Latino and Asian children were less likely to be diagnosed and treated for ADHD than white children.

REMEMBER

In addition, stigma, stereotypes, and biases affect how BIPOC families experience living with ADHD. For example, institutional racism and bias about behavior and parenting have interfered with Black families' ability to trust they're receiving the care they need. There is understandable distrust based on healthcare biases that make it challenging for Black families to feel understood and receive an accurate diagnosis.

Visibility — for instance, through culturally sensitive practitioners from BIPOC communities as models and advocates — is one thing that can help.

It's important to dig further into this topic through online resources and reading works by practitioners and advocates from the Black and Hispanic communities. CHADD.org and ADDA.org have numerous webinars, podcasts, and online articles on this topic. There are also a few children's books aimed at this population. One example is *Black Boy, Brown Boy: ADHD & Me* by Marquesha Gulley, Jeremiah Bolden, and Joshua Bolden (Independent Press, 2021). The resources are quite scant, however, compared to the research, books, and articles about white children and adults.

LGBTQIA+

In certain studies, more adults with ADHD identified themselves as bisexual compared with individuals without ADHD. People living with ADHD may experience *gender dysphoria* (conflict between your gender identity and the sex you're assigned at birth) or question their gender identity more frequently than those without ADHD do. Yet no evidence supports a direct cause-and-effect relationship between gender nonconformity and ADHD. Neuroqueer individuals, who are both neurodivergent and queer, experience challenges and discrimination that often compounds marginalization and stigma as well as the misdiagnosis of ADHD. This population is understudied, and the intersectionality of people with ADHD and gender nonconforming people needs much more research.

2

Diagnosing ADHD

Meet the many types of professionals who can diagnose and/or treat ADHD.

Walk through what to expect from the evaluation process.

Explore conditions that often share some symptoms with ADHD (which can make diagnosing ADHD tricky).

IN THIS CHAPTER

» **Exploring the different types of ADHD professionals**

» **Considering your own beliefs about diagnosis and treatment**

» **Knowing what to ask your potential treatment partners**

» **Making sure your diagnosis is as accurate as possible**

» **Tracking your treatment**

» **Determining what services your diagnosis provides**

Chapter **4**

Moving Forward with a Diagnosis

The first step in getting diagnosed with ADHD is finding a professional who understands the condition and can most accurately assess your situation. Not all professionals are the same when it comes to diagnosing and treating ADHD. This chapter helps you understand the roles different professionals play in ADHD care and walks you through the process of choosing the best person(s) for you. You also discover how to ensure that your insurance covers the cost of diagnosis and some treatment.

Help Wanted: Searching for the Right Person or People

You need to consider two primary aspects of ADHD care when looking for an ADHD professional: diagnosis and treatment. The right professional for one aspect may not be the best person for the other.

One of the most common questions we get asked is "Which healthcare provider is the best for treating ADHD?" As we show you in this section, we can't really give just one answer to this question. Essentially, your goal is to find a professional who has experience in diagnosing ADHD and who's aligned with your personal beliefs. (We help you determine your personal beliefs in the section "Examining Your Values" later in this chapter.)

REMEMBER

In this chapter, we refer to an *official diagnosis* as one that's legally recognized. This designation doesn't mean it's a more accurate diagnosis, only that it's made by a professional who's legally entitled to offer one, such as a medical doctor or mental health professional. An unofficial diagnosis can be just as accurate, but it doesn't afford you the same protections as its legally recognized counterpart.

Many different health professionals can look for the basic symptoms of ADHD and let you know whether you fit the profile for the disorder. However, only certain professionals can look at the nuances of your condition to see whether ADHD is the best diagnosis. Likewise, some professionals are good at diagnosing, while others are better suited to offer treatments or life strategies that can help you cope with the symptoms — regardless of what label is placed on them.

TIP

Bottom line: The best professional for you is one who has experience in your condition and who has the resources to effectively deal with the symptoms present. For some people, this person may be the family physician; others may determine that a psychologist or psychiatrist is best. In the later section "Evaluating Your ADHD Professional," we offer tools for locating an individual whose experience, beliefs, and treatment approaches meet your specific needs.

Table 4-1 gives you an at-a-glance overview of the types of diagnostic and treatment services various health professionals provide. The sections that follow provide more detail and make generalizations about who may work best for you.

TABLE 4-1 **Diagnosis and Treatment Capabilities**

Provider	Diagnose (Officially)	Prescribe Medication	Counseling	Nonconventional Treatments	Life Strategies
ADHD specialist	Yes (Sometimes)	Depends	Sometimes	Yes	Generally
Family physician	Yes (Yes)	Yes	Sometimes	Sometimes	Sometimes
Pediatrician	Yes (Yes)	Yes	Sometimes	Sometimes	Sometimes
Psychologist	Yes (Yes)	Sometimes	Not usually	Sometimes	Yes
Clinical social worker	Yes (Yes)	No	Yes	Sometimes	Yes
ADHD coach	Yes (Sometimes)	No	Sometimes	Sometimes	Sometimes
Psychiatrist	Yes (Yes)	Yes	Yes	Sometimes	Yes
Neurologist	Yes (Yes)	Yes	No	No	No
Neuropsychiatrist/ behavioral neurologist	Yes (Yes)	Yes	Sometimes	Sometimes	Sometimes
Educational diagnostician	Yes (Yes, according to school district)	No	No	No	Yes, but only for school situations
Speech–language pathologist	Yes (No)	No	No	Yes	Sometimes
Occupational therapist	Yes (No)	No	No	Yes	Generally

ADHD specialist

An *ADHD specialist* is a professional who specializes in working with patients with ADHD and is a trained expert. A specialist can be an excellent choice for diagnosing and/or treating ADHD. For example, one situation in which the ADHD specialist may be your best choice is when you're dealing with a multidisciplinary clinic that specializes in evaluating and treating ADHD and related conditions.

WARNING

The only problem is that anyone can call themselves an ADHD specialist; using this term doesn't require any licensing or certification. As a result, the term itself means virtually nothing and is hardly an indication that a person is qualified to treat or diagnose ADHD.

TIP

The main thing to look for when considering an ADHD specialist is the background of the person using this label. You may find educators, psychologists, psychiatrists, or any of the other professionals listed in this chapter also calling themselves ADHD specialists. Dig deeper than the label and find out what this person's educational background is to determine whether they're someone you want to work with.

Family physician

Your family doctor is often a good place to start to look for ADHD in you or your child. They can often spot the basic symptoms and may be able to perform some simple evaluations to quickly rule out ADHD in most people. But a family physician may not be the best solution for doing detailed evaluations and exploring the subtleties of ADHD — and keep in mind that ADHD is all about subtleties.

REMEMBER

Family physicians have to focus on the big picture with their patients and often aren't as knowledgeable about current trends and research as specialists. Also, most family physicians don't have the time to perform the detailed evaluations necessary to rule out all the other possible conditions that look like ADHD (which we discuss in Chapter 6). Some family doctors don't even believe that ADHD is a legitimate disorder and may blame the problem on bad behavior or bad parenting. (This viewpoint is becoming rarer, but it does still exist, especially when patients are from historically marginalized races).

On the other hand, because your family doctor knows you or your child best, they can often get you started and then refer you to the appropriate professional if you need to dig deeper (assuming they believes ADHD is real). They may also be able to rule out any physical conditions, such as thyroid problems (see Chapter 6), that can have the same symptoms as ADHD.

TIP

To find out whether your family doctor can help you with ADHD, simply ask about their view of ADHD as a disorder and what experience they have with the condition. Some family physicians have had enough experience dealing with patients with ADHD that they're aware of the possible treatment strategies and current medications and their efficacy.

Pediatrician

Pediatricians often diagnose and treat ADHD in children and adolescents. In many cases, they have a great deal of experience dealing with ADHD. However, like the family physician (see the preceding section), a pediatrician has little time available to do extensive evaluations and follow-up. Pediatricians do their best to treat patients with ADHD; however, their medical training is often inconsistent in providing them with the skills to evaluate and treat children with ADHD. Ask your pediatrician if they have had training and their experience in managing children with ADHD.

One subspecialty to consider when identifying the right person to evaluate your child is the *developmental pediatrician.* This person involves themselves in all sorts of problems with development, including behavioral problems.

Psychologist

A *clinical psychologist* is a mental health professional who is well versed in mental disorders and is often an excellent choice for someone to root out a diagnosis of ADHD. You can also find educational psychologists and neuropsychologists who may have even more capacity to analyze your situation and make a thorough assessment ending in diagnosis. These specialists sometimes participate in the diagnosis but leave the treatment to the clinical psychologist and the physician.

Most independently practicing psychologists have PhDs. Some psychologists are licensed in states that allow them to prescribe medication like a psychiatrist. If you think you want to try medication for your symptoms, ask the psychologist about their experience with treating ADHD.

REMEMBER

Where psychologists shine is in being able to help you deal with many of the secondary symptoms and *co-occurring* (coexisting) conditions of ADHD, such as depression, anxiety, trauma, and low self-esteem. (Check out Chapter 3 for more on secondary symptoms and Chapter 6 for a discussion of co-occurring conditions.) These secondary symptoms and co-occurring conditions are often more of a problem for adults and adolescents with ADHD than the primary symptoms of inattention, impulsivity, and hyperactivity are, and they can make life very difficult unless they're dealt with effectively.

Some psychologists are also up-to-date on alternative treatments, such as neurofeedback (see Chapter 12) and can help you with other life strategies that can greatly ease your symptoms and make ADHD less of an issue in your life.

Clinical social worker

Licensed clinical social workers (LCSW) have a master's degree and specific, advanced training in psychotherapy techniques. Because they're trained in social work first, they may have unique capabilities in terms of dealing with your interactions with other people, "the system," and society. In many respects, they work in the same ways that clinical psychologists do (see the preceding section), especially treating coexisting conditions. You have to find out whether your particular social worker is familiar or experienced with ADHD.

TIP

Because LCSWs are licensed mental health professionals, they can make an official diagnosis of ADHD.

ADHD coach

An *ADHD coach* is someone who specializes in helping you improve your functioning in the world. ADHD coaches can come from a variety of backgrounds, including counseling, psychology, business, and mediation. No official, regulated criteria for becoming an ADHD coach currently exists. However, the ADHD Coaches Organization does provide specific criteria for someone to be recognized as a legitimate ADHD coach.

ADHD coaches often see themselves as being action-oriented. That is, they focus on practical skills and offer support for your everyday struggles. Most ADHD coaches don't offer any kinds of treatment other than skills training and some minor counseling, but some may have a referral network in place to help you find other types of treatments to use. Generally, ADHD coaches aren't able to provide you with an official diagnosis and can't prescribe medication.

Psychiatrist

A psychiatrist is a medical doctor who specializes in the mind. *Psychiatrists* are mental health professionals specifically trained to diagnose and treat psychiatric conditions, including ADHD. The *Diagnostic and Statistical Manual of Mental Disorders* is published by the American Psychiatric Association, so you can be sure that a psychiatrist is qualified to explore whether you have ADHD. Because psychiatrists are medical doctors, they're able to prescribe medications and are often very experienced in finding the best drug for each patient.

Some psychiatrists (especially child and adolescent psychiatrists) know a lot about ADHD, and some even know a lot about adult ADHD. A psychiatric diagnosis is most often made based on information the psychiatrist gathers from interviews with the patient and their family members. Sometimes psychiatrists obtain test results from psychologists or physiological data from laboratory tests to help make a diagnosis.

The biggest advantages of seeing a psychiatrist for ADHD are that psychiatrists are very familiar with the medications used to treat it, and they're very familiar with — and used to treating — other mental conditions that can accompany or mimic ADHD. As with any healthcare professional, look for a psychiatrist who has experience working with people with ADHD.

Neurologist

A *neurologist* is a medical doctor who specializes in diseases of the nervous system. However, people don't usually use them for diagnosing ADHD.

One situation in which the neurologist may be the best choice for you is if you or any of your family members have known or suspected neurologic disorders other than ADHD (such as seizures or tics). As in the case of the psychiatrist and the psychologist, whom we discuss earlier in the chapter, you can benefit from the specialist's knowledge of similar-appearing conditions that can have other causes.

Neuropsychiatrist/behavioral neurologist

Two subspecialties cross the boundaries of neurology and psychiatry: the neuro-psychiatrist and the behavioral neurologist. These subspecialties are similar in that they emphasize problems of behavior that result from abnormal nervous system function — problems like ADHD. If you have one of these specialists in your area, they may be a good choice for an evaluation. Both are MDs, so they can prescribe medication.

The only drawbacks to these professionals are that they're usually in major metropolitan areas only and are often in great demand because of their expertise. They may not have time to manage the case after making the diagnosis. However, they should be well connected to a treatment team that can do the case management.

Educational diagnostician

An *educational diagnostician* is trained to assess learning problems in students. These professionals are required to have master's degrees and, generally, several years of teaching experience. They also need state certification. Educational diagnosticians are employed by the school district and go by different titles depending on the state you're in: educational consultants, learning consultants, or learning disabilities teachers (not to be confused with *special education teachers*, whose job is to actually teach special education classes).

Educational diagnosticians usually work in concert with school psychologists and can do a good job of identifying learning difficulties (including ADHD) in students. You don't get much from these professionals in the way of treatment approaches, except for maybe educational strategies and recommendations for your child's Individual Education Plan, or IEP (which we discuss in Chapter 16). However, an educational diagnostician can be helpful in first identifying that your child may have a problem in school and can offer insight into what that problem may be.

Speech–language pathologist

A *speech–language pathologist* (SLP) deals with issues related to speech, language, and hearing. Because many people with ADHD have some problem understanding verbal instructions, an SLP can be helpful in rooting out the problem and offering some treatments and life skills that can minimize this issue. SLPs are in the best position to diagnose and treat a condition known as *central auditory processing disorder*, which often mimics parts of ADHD and sometimes accompanies it (see Chapter 6). These professionals can also be very helpful if you're dealing with language delays or dyslexia as part of the problem.

REMEMBER

Although many SLPs claim to be able to diagnose ADHD, they aren't specifically trained to do so, and many don't look nearly as deeply into the other possible diagnoses as other mental health professionals (such as psychologists and psychiatrists) do. That doesn't mean, however, that SLPs can't offer insight into your or your child's symptoms.

Speech–language pathologists often have quite a few nonconventional treatment plans that can help people with ADHD (or at least the symptoms of ADHD). These treatments include vision therapies and sound therapies.

Occupational therapist

An *occupational therapist* (OT) is trained to help people with everyday tasks (occupations) and can often help people with ADHD deal with the sensory issues involved with the condition. OTs can have either master's or doctorate degrees in occupational therapy, and many have a lot of experience with ADHD. OTs aren't able to prescribe medication, and most prefer to use techniques they've learned to deal with the symptoms of ADHD, most notably sensory integration, vision therapies, and sound therapies (see Chapters 12 and 13).

Other professionals you may encounter

You may work with a host of other professionals when trying to get a handle on your or your child's symptoms. These include homeopaths, acupuncturists, nutritionists, and others. Each of these professionals can offer some help for some people. In Part 3, we detail many of the treatment approaches that these professionals offer, and we give you a heads up on what each can do. You can often find these professionals online listed under the name of the discipline they practice.

Examining Your Values

When you seek professional help for diagnosis or treatment of your or your child's ADHD-like symptoms, thinking about what you want from your relationship with a professional can be helpful. In the following sections, we help you investigate your values as they relate to diagnosis and treatment of ADHD.

Digging into your ideas about diagnosis

Because a diagnosis of ADHD can be difficult to pinpoint, and because many conditions share the same symptoms (as we explain in Chapter 6), you really must trust yourself and your professional to be able to identify the problem. Here are some things to consider:

>> **How important is an official diagnosis to you?** Some people want the label to make them feel as though they've done everything possible to get the "right" diagnosis or to receive services that may be available to them. Other people are happy just having some sense of what the problem is so they can get down to the work of minimizing their symptoms and maximizing their ability to function in the world. We cover the concept of an official diagnosis in the earlier section "Help Wanted: Searching for the Right Person or People."

>> **How much are you willing to do to get this diagnosis?** Depending on which professional you go to, you may encounter a simple questionnaire or a whole slew of evaluations to root out the cause of your or your child's symptoms. You can be assured that an official diagnosis requires much more documentation and evaluation than an unofficial diagnosis. (Chapter 5 covers the evaluation process in detail.)

REMEMBER

A diagnosis is a double-edged sword. On the one hand, it can offer you peace of mind, the best place to start looking for treatment, and possibly some much-needed services for you or your child. On the other hand, some people don't want to have a label placed upon them and don't have the desire to lobby for special services. Some people also may be tempted to use a diagnosis as an excuse for their behavior rather than as a road map to making changes.

Tackling your thoughts on treatment

Successful treatment of ADHD depends largely on identifying the right treatment for a specific person. This process involves finding not only the potentially most effective treatment but also a treatment that the patient can stand behind and give their full attention. For example, even though a particular medication may have the potential to work for someone, that potential is wasted if they don't take the med according to the schedule the doctor prescribes.

Many parents of children with ADHD are adamantly opposed to using medication because they're unsure of the long-term effects on the delicate nervous systems of their children and don't want to take even the remotest chance of contributing to problems later in life. As a result, some children who could respond well to the right medication don't have the opportunity to try it.

Likewise, many people (even some professionals) don't believe that nonconventional therapies can have a positive impact on the symptoms and underlying causes of ADHD. As a result, they reject these therapies outright without exploring them first.

REMEMBER

We strongly encourage you not to dismiss any possible treatment approach without having at least explored the issue with a professional who's personally experienced with that approach. And before you agree to a specific treatment plan, take the following steps:

>> **Find out what's expected of you as a patient (or the parent of a patient) in order for the treatment to work its best.** Honestly ask yourself whether you have the time, energy, and desire to follow the necessary protocol.

>> **Make sure you understand the side effects of any treatment plan before starting it.**

>> **Make sure your expectations for the outcome of the treatment plan are realistic.**

Evaluating Your ADHD Professional

When you choose a healthcare professional to work with, you invest a lot of time and effort in the relationship. Therefore, finding a professional whose experience, approaches, and beliefs fit with your needs and expectations is very important. One way to determine the fit of a healthcare provider is to interview that person first. The following sections suggest some considerations, as well as questions you can ask a prospective professional.

Selecting a diagnostician

When you look for a professional to help you weed through the diagnostic process, here are some recommendations for finding the right person:

>> **Take an active role in the diagnostic process.** Educate yourself (as you're doing by reading this book) about ADHD and similar conditions, and come to your first meeting with a potential diagnostician armed with any questions you have.

>> **Ask the professional you're considering how involved they want to get in the diagnostic process.** To be relatively sure about the diagnosis, the evaluation needs to be fairly in-depth. The problem is that performing in-depth evaluations takes time and can cost a lot of money. Most evaluations require at least two to three hours and assessment tools. Even if your insurance covers the cost of your evaluations, you don't want to have a longer assessment procedure than necessary. On the other hand, some cases are a lot more complicated than others, and you don't want to quit the evaluation before the diagnostician knows what's going on.

TIP

An ethical diagnostician uses a "take it one step at a time" approach and performs only those evaluations they deem necessary to root out the problem. This stage is where the information in Chapter 5 can come in handy; it lays out the process of evaluation so that you can go to a professional with a clear understanding of what to expect.

After you select a diagnostician, ask them to keep you informed about any diagnosis they make and who they're sharing this information with (such as your insurance company).

Partnering up for treatment

You may want to use the same professional to treat you as you did to diagnose your ADHD, or you may decide to work with someone new. Either way, you can get a glimpse into a professional's treatment philosophy by asking a few simple questions:

>> **What's your professional experience and training?** Knowing a provider's educational and professional background can help you determine whether this person can offer you the service you need. Their experience and background can likely inform you about the types of treatment approaches they can offer.

>> **How do you generally treat people with ADHD?** Expect a long answer here — one that essentially says, "It depends on the patient." Most healthcare providers have a few treatment approaches that are first on their list to try. Some prescribe medications, some look toward diet, and some use treatments such as sound therapies or neurofeedback (see Chapter 12). And some offer all these treatment options. Choose a professional who has an open mind and is willing to think outside the box.

>> **Can you recommend other professionals for different treatments?** Most providers have a referral network of professionals who specialize in different treatments than the ones they typically use. The best professionals have the most complete lists and freely share this information while offering guidance along the way.

>> **What if a treatment fails?** One reality of trying to treat ADHD is that not everything works for every person, so you're going to have to adjust along the way in order to find the right combination of approaches for your situation. Knowing up front how to deal with these minor setbacks can keep your relationship with your provider on the right track.

Here are some other things to consider when choosing a healthcare provider:

REMEMBER

>> **Does your provider show up on time?** If you arrive on time for your appointments but have to wait a long time to be seen, that doesn't reflect very well on how the provider views you as a patient. A single instance is one thing — it may just be one of those days — but a pattern of running late speaks volumes about how the doctor values your time.

Some doctors, like other people, have trouble managing their time. They may be in the habit of spending extra time with all their patients, so don't be offended until you have some idea of what's going on. And be sure to extend the same courtesy to your provider as you'd have them extend to you — show up on time and prepared for your appointments.

>> **Are they respectful to you by listening to your questions and concerns and giving them the weight that you feel they deserve?** Good healthcare providers take the time to answer your questions and alleviate your concerns instead of brushing right past them.

>> **How does your provider's staff treat you?** If staff members are impolite, or if all they're concerned about is how you're going to pay, that's a red flag. You should be treated with respect and politeness.

>> **Do you feel comfortable with your provider?** Your provider may be the most qualified professional in the world, but if you're not comfortable in their presence, you probably won't get the most out of the relationship. You can either discuss your discomfort with them or trust that your comfort level and intellect aren't in sync and decline to continue with that provider.

Getting a Second Opinion

The ADHD diagnosis is similar to that of other mental health conditions, such as anxiety and depression: It has its limitations. As we say many times in this book, there's no way to absolutely, positively determine whether someone has ADHD; there's only a best deduction based upon the information gathered. As things stand now (as we write this), the quality of your diagnosis relies on the skills of your evaluator and the depths into which you and your caregiver dig while looking for an answer.

For most people, the first diagnosis they receive is usually sufficient to steer them in the best direction for treatment; even with a cursory evaluation, you may gain enough knowledge to get the help you need. Other people may find that their first diagnosis was inaccurate enough that they weren't able to find a treatment plan that worked. Or they may decide, after receiving an unofficial diagnosis, that they want a more detailed evaluation to make a diagnosis official in the eyes of their insurance company or child's school. In these cases, a second opinion and further evaluation are good ideas.

Managing Your Care

When you begin treating the symptoms of your or your child's ADHD, you most likely work with more than one professional. In fact, we're willing to bet you end up working with several people, each of whom deals with different aspects of your care. For example, you may use your family doctor to handle your medications, a nutritionist to help you develop the best diet to minimize your symptoms, and a psychologist to help you deal with the secondary symptoms (such as low self-esteem). You may also have additional therapists for specific treatments, such as neurofeedback or sound therapies.

Keeping track of all these professionals and varying treatment plans is your responsibility — even if you hire a professional to help with this task — and it can require significant time and energy. The easiest way to manage your care is to document everything about each treatment you try. (Check out this book's appendix for a form for tracking your treatments.) Keep track of the following types of information:

>> **The date the treatment started and ended:** This way, when you reflect on what changes you saw and how you felt at a certain time, you can see at a glance what you were doing.

>> **The details of the treatment approach:** This information is especially important for medications. You want to know how much you used and when.

>> **The professional you saw:** Keeping all the professional contacts you've made handy is important because chances are you'll encounter a lot of people while you seek out treatments that work. You can easily forget specifics about each person. Having an accurate record (including how you felt about this professional) can keep you from covering the same ground more than once.

>> **The results you observed while trying each treatment program:** This info includes both the good and the bad and is probably the most important thing to keep track of. Having a detailed record of the effects of the various treatment plans you've tried offers invaluable information, not only to keep you from repeating an unsuccessful treatment but also to offer insights as to how new treatments may work.

>> **What other treatments were going on at the same time:** Most of the time, you have more than one treatment happening at once. Perhaps you're trying nutrition and medication, sound therapies and homeopathy, or some other combination. Keeping track of overlapping treatments can help you avoid treatment combinations that don't work well together.

REMEMBER

Be sure to share this information with the different professionals you work with; that way, they can design a treatment program around the other things you're doing or can advise you against trying one treatment while doing another. This information is especially important to share when you're taking medications. When you start making changes to your treatments, adjust one variable at a time instead of changing everything at once. Doing so makes keeping track of what works and what doesn't easier for you.

>> **Why you stopped:** Sometimes you stop a treatment because the schedule for it has ended; certain treatments, such as the various neuromodulation therapies we describe in Chapter 12, are time-limited. Other times you may stop because the treatment isn't working for you, such as if you try a medication that has too many side effects.

Being Eligible for Services

The main reason to receive an official diagnosis of ADHD is to be eligible for legal protections, and services from your insurance company or your child's school. The following sections delve more into those concerns.

Getting a diagnosis for legal purposes

ADHD is currently classified as a medical condition. As such, any medical doctor, including family physicians, pediatricians, psychiatrists, and neurologists, can diagnose it. ADHD is also a psychiatric diagnosis, so any licensed mental health professional can make the diagnosis official. The main reasons to have an official diagnosis relate to legal and financial matters. If you want to request accommodations at school or in the workplace, you need an official diagnosis. The same goes for getting disability status with the government. Most health insurance covers ADHD treatments with a doctor, psychologist, or allied health professional if you have an official diagnosis.

Examining your insurance coverage

Some insurance providers cover ADHD diagnosis and certain types of treatment — usually medication and counseling to some extent. To find out whether your insurance company covers diagnosis or treatment, you must contact your provider. Following are some things to consider when dealing with insurance and ADHD (or any other mental disorder, for that matter):

REMEMBER

>> **How much coverage do I have for mental illnesses?** Know which diagnostic and treatment services your insurance company covers and what to expect from it. Depending on your level of coverage, you may not receive many benefits.

The Mental Health Parity and Addiction Equity Act of 2008 (MHPAEA) is a federal law that generally prevents group health plans and health insurance issuers from imposing more restrictive limits on mental health and substance abuse benefits than they do on medical/surgical benefits. Equal treatment of mental health hopefully will become more robust to reflect both the law and need.

>> **What types of treatments does my insurance plan cover?** Many insurance plans cover only certain types of treatments, such as medication and a limited number of counseling sessions. You may find that you're not covered for the types of treatments you want to try, meaning you need to be prepared to pay out of pocket.

>> **What if my insurance company declines to cover ADHD?** ADHD is a mental disorder and should be covered under your policy's mental health benefits. If you're denied coverage, you can appeal it through the insurance company's appeals process. Statistically, you have a good chance of winning with proper documentation.

>> **How comfortable am I with having a label that will be permanently attached to my medical file?** After you file a claim with your insurance and have a diagnosis of ADHD, this diagnosis becomes part of your permanent medical record. Having this label changed or removed is very hard (almost impossible, in fact.) It moves from insurance company to insurance company if you change insurers.

Seeking out school services

Although we discuss school services for children diagnosed with ADHD in detail in Chapter 16, we want to briefly mention how these services relate to the diagnosis you receive from your chosen healthcare professional. School services usually take the form of a *Section 504 plan* (accommodations under the Americans with Disabilities Act) or an *Individual Education Plan* (for children in need of special education because of a specific learning disability or behavioral disorder).

REMEMBER

Before a school will even consider offering services for your child, you need to have an evaluation conducted by the school — usually from the school's educational diagnostician — or a complete diagnosis from either a psychologist or psychiatrist. (What constitutes "complete" in the eyes of a school varies from district to district.) Even with a psychologist's or psychiatrist's diagnosis, you probably still need to go through the school's evaluation process before it recognizes ADHD in your child. You can read more about all these professionals earlier in the chapter.

After the school acknowledges ADHD in your child, you still need to petition for services for your child; these services aren't guaranteed. Some schools bend over backward to help their ADHD students; others don't. To be eligible for services, you must have a "proven" need for the services beyond the diagnosis. And guess who decides whether you need these services or not? Yep, you guessed it: your child's school.

This situation presents a potential conflict of interest because putting a child in the Individual Education Plan process costs the school money. On the other hand, public schools get federal money to keep children in special education, and most schools nowadays are constantly short of money for these services. Your backup in dealing with resistant schools is the state board of education and the federal disability law (see Chapter 16). You also can check on the Internet for organizations and attorneys that assist with advocacy.

If you want school services for your child, you may have a long and difficult battle to get them. Chapter 16 can help you with the process.

Chapter 5

Navigating the Evaluation Process

As we discuss in Chapter 4, ADHD evaluations can be as simple as a single questionnaire and an interview that takes only a few minutes, or they can involve an elaborate series of tests that takes many hours to complete. The intricacy of your evaluation process depends largely on the professional you choose, the degree and makeup of your symptoms, and the depths to which you and your healthcare provider decide to go in assessing your condition. Your insurance coverage and the services provided in your area also play a big role.

This chapter lays out the full-blown (and then some) evaluation process for rooting out the cause of your or your child's symptoms. We explore the many types of assessments that an ADHD professional may use to determine whether you have the condition, including psychiatric/psychological evaluations, educational assessments, performance tests, and physiological tests. You probably won't have to endure all the different tests and diagnostic procedures we cover in this chapter, but most likely you'll experience at least one in your quest to understand the reason for your symptoms.

An adequate evaluation includes several different sources of information — for instance, home and school behavior and performance reports. Also, the more professionals who assess your condition, the greater the likelihood of receiving an accurate diagnosis.

TIP

Preparing for the Evaluation Process

When you hire a healthcare provider to conduct an evaluation of you or your child, they should skillfully guide you through the process. But remember that you're still half the partnership. To have a successful experience that causes as little stress as possible, you can do some things to prepare for your appointment:

» **Write down any questions or concerns you have about the evaluation process and its eventual outcome.** Take this list with you because you'll likely forget these questions when you walk into the diagnostician's office.

» **Bring the results of any questionnaires you may have previously taken.** Doing so may shorten the evaluation process if the questionnaire is something your provider is familiar with.

» **Make a list of any allergies you have, all your current and past medical conditions, and medications that you're taking or have taken in the past.** If you go to your family physician for an evaluation, you may not need to take this step if your doctor already has this information in your file.

» **Make a list of foods you commonly eat and any connections you've seen between these foods and your symptoms.**

» **Write down when you first noticed symptoms and how these symptoms have changed over time.**

» **Think about any strategies or coping mechanisms you've developed to help you deal with your symptoms.**

» **Make a note of any times or environments where your symptoms seem to get better or worse.**

Be sure to arrive on time for your appointment. When you're at your appointment, you can do a few things to help move the process along:

» **Be attentive when your provider is talking.** Depending on the level of your ADHD symptoms, this task may be difficult. If you know you struggle in this type of situation, ask your provider whether you can take notes or record what they say for later review.

>> **Don't be afraid to assert yourself during the appointment.** Giving your power to a professional and having them control the direction of the conversation often feels easy. If you have something to add during the conversation, speak up (politely). This participation helps keep the appointment going in the best direction and helps your provider better understand you and your symptoms.

>> **Reassure yourself that the appointment is necessary.** Cold feet are common at the first few appointments. Thoughts like "I'm fine, I'm just imagining my symptoms" are sure to pop into your mind as you're sitting in your first appointment. Trust that you made the appointment after careful consideration and that the appointment is important. You can assess the need for additional appointments after you've finished with the first one.

>> **Be open and honest with your provider.** Without honesty about your experiences, behavior, and feelings, your provider can't get a clear picture of who you are or the challenges you live with.

REMEMBER

ADHD evaluations don't include a bulletproof physiological test. However, with the interpretation of a skilled professional, the assessments we list in this chapter can offer a pretty clear picture of what's going on and provide direction to help minimize the difficulties that you deal with in your life.

Mental Health Evaluations

Your first step in determining whether you or someone you love has ADHD is to do a mental health evaluation. This step usually involves completing a fairly simple questionnaire where you score your symptoms, rating them from being nonexistent to severe.

You can find about as many ADHD questionnaires available as you can people giving them, but they all use the basic criteria for ADHD as outlined in the American Psychiatric Association's *Diagnostic and Statistical Manual for Mental Disorders* (DSM-V). Research arenas seem to use a few standardized questionnaires over and over again. The advantage of these questionnaires is that they're more scientifically developed than some simple ones.

The most commonly used psychiatric/psychological rating scales include the following:

>> **Conners rating scales:** Several Conners rating scales exist for both adults and children. The most widely used are these:

- **Conners Rating Scales — Revised (CRS-R):** These rating scales are for children 3 to 17 years old. Children ages 12 to 17 complete the form themselves using the Adolescent Self-Report Scales (CASS). Younger kids are scaled by a parent using the Parent Rating Scales — Revised (CPRS-R) or by a teacher using the Teacher Rating Scales — Revised (CTRS-R). Completing these forms takes only a few minutes.

- **Conners Adult ADHD Rating Scales (CAARS):** These scales for adults come in three varieties: long, short, and screening. The long version has 66 items, the short form has 26, and the screening scale has 12. The person who may have ADHD, or someone close to them, completes these scales. They take only a few minutes to do.

>> **Wender Utah Rating Scale (WURS):** This 61-question scale is for adults and is commonly used in research.

>> **ADD-H Comprehensive Teacher/Parent Rating Scales (ACTeRS):** This rating scale for adolescents and adults consists of 35 items that the person thought to have ADHD or an observer can complete. This form takes 5 to 10 minutes to complete.

>> **Adult ADHD Clinical Diagnostic Scale (ACDS):** With this scale, a doctor or other healthcare worker asks you 18 questions about your symptoms during an interview.

REMEMBER

Aside from evaluating your answers to these questionnaires, your healthcare provider must look at your past as well as your present behaviors to make a diagnosis. That means walking into a psychiatrist's office, having someone give you the once-over, and walking out with a diagnosis is difficult. Expect to spend a good deal of time talking with your healthcare provider about your (or your child's) past behaviors, academic performance, and social relationships.

For adults, the past can be a bit fuzzy; having a close family member or friend offer their views is often helpful because adults with ADHD sometimes don't recognize their symptoms. The situation may be easier for evaluating a child; parents often remember details of their child's behavior during the recent few years that can offer insights into the background of the symptoms.

REMEMBER

Keep in mind that a questionnaire can't rule out other conditions that share the basic symptoms of ADHD. For details about these conditions, see Chapter 6.

Medical Testing

As we discuss in Chapter 6, some medical conditions share many symptoms with ADHD. To determine whether one of these conditions is the cause of your symptoms or whether you, in fact, have ADHD, you may have to go through some medical tests, including tests for the following conditions:

>> Lead poisoning

>> Thyroid dysfunction

>> Allergies or sensitivities

>> Brain tumor

>> Traumatic brain injury (including birth trauma)

>> Connective tissue diseases

>> Tourette's syndrome

REMEMBER

Your healthcare professional won't need to order all these tests for you. Many of these conditions are very rare (such as a brain tumor), but your healthcare provider does need to at least consider them before making a final determination that you have ADHD. One indication for further medical testing is a late or abrupt onset of ADHD symptoms.

Educational Testing

Educational testing involves some sort of intelligence test and, for children, evaluations to check for age-appropriate functioning. These tests have less to do with trying to root out the symptoms of ADHD than with helping assess the likelihood of other causes of the symptoms, such as learning disabilities or medical conditions like brain damage.

Providers use literally dozens of different intelligence tests, but the most common seem to be the following:

>> **Kaufman intelligence tests:** Evaluators use two types of Kaufman intelligence tests, depending on the age of the person being tested:

- **Kaufman Brief Intelligence Test (KBIT-2):** For ages 4 and up, this test quickly assesses verbal and nonverbal skills by using two subtests. Like its name implies, the KBIT-2 takes very little time — only 15 to 30 minutes — and offers a pretty good assessment of your intelligence.

- **Kaufman Adolescent and Adult Intelligence Test (KAIT):** This test is more involved than the K-BIT and consists of two levels: the core battery and the expanded battery. The core battery takes about 60 minutes to complete, while the expanded battery takes 90 minutes. This test is designed for people 11 years old and up.

>> **Wechsler intelligence tests:** Wechsler tests come in three types, each for a different age group:

- **Wechsler Preschool and Primary Scale of Intelligence — Revised (WPPSI-R):** This test is used for children ages 2 ½ to 7 ½ and is designed to measure cognitive abilities. The WPPSI-R consists of 11 subtests that evaluate both performance and verbal abilities. It takes between 50 and 75 minutes to complete.

- **Wechsler Intelligence Scale for Children (WISC):** This test is for children ages 6 to 16 and consists of six verbal and five performance subtests. It scores for verbal and performance IQs as well as a full-scale IQ based on these two results and takes 60 to 90 minutes to complete.

- **Wechsler Adult Intelligence Scale (WAIS):** This test is designed for people 16 and older. It evaluates performance and verbal abilities by using 11 subtests to determine verbal IQ, performance IQ, and *full-scale* (combined) IQ. The test takes about 60 to 90 minutes to complete.

>> **Woodcock–Johnson III (WJ III):** This test is for people ages 2 and up. It consists of two sections — achievement and cognitive — that cover academic achievement, general intellectual ability, oral language, scholastic aptitude, and specific cognitive abilities. The cognitive section contains 7 subtests (totaling about 35 minutes), while the achievement section consists of 11 subtests (totaling about 55 minutes). If you don't want to do that math, just know that each subtest takes about 5 minutes to complete.

Psychologists and educational diagnosticians commonly conduct all these tests. If you work with an educational diagnostician (see Chapter 4), keep in mind that you'll likely have to wait a while to get the school to schedule this type of test.

REMEMBER

Making sense out of the results of educational tests takes some skill. These aren't tests you can do at home and score yourself; you need a trained professional to score them for you. Fortunately, anyone who offers these tests has also been trained to interpret them properly and can offer guidance for what to do after you receive your score.

Motor, Cognitive, and Social Skills Testing

Skills testing involves both motor and cognitive skills, including social skills. Physical or occupational therapists usually carry out motor skills evaluations. Speech–language pathologists or educational diagnosticians can assess cognitive skills. You can read more about many of these professionals in Chapter 4.

Psychologists or counselors who have expertise in social skills training can evaluate social skills. This type of evaluation uses some standard rating scales, including

» **Novotni Social Skills Checklist:** This scale is available in two forms: the self-report version and the observer report version. These scales are used for adolescents and adults.

» **Reynolds Adolescent Adjustment Screening Inventory (RAASI):** This scale contains 32 items in 4 categories for 12- to 19-year-olds.

Behavioral Assessment

Behavioral assessments involve observation by a trained behavioral specialist. Different protocols and methods exist for this evaluation, some of them more formalized than others. Often, the academic/educational testing evaluation a school does includes a behavioral assessment. Professionals use many standardized tests, the most common being these:

» **Child Behavior Checklist for Ages 6–18 (CBCL/6–18):** This test is for children ages 6 to 18 and consists of 118 items. A parent or close relative completes it.

» **Adult Behavior Checklist for Ages 18–59 (ABCL):** A loved one of the person thought to have behavior problems completes this checklist, which takes about 15 minutes.

» **Child Behavior Checklist/1½–5 (CBCL/1½–5):** This evaluation is for children ages 1½ to 5 years old; a caregiver completes it.

Performance Testing and Your Ability to Maintain Attention

Performance testing involves assessing your ability to maintain attention. You usually take this assessment by using a *continuous performance test* (CPT). You're instructed to respond to a repetitive and boring stimulus by either pressing or not pressing a key on a computer's keyboard in response to an image on the screen. Because this task is boring and repetitive, it requires sustained attention and control over impulsivity — both areas in which people with ADHD have difficulties. Common CPTs include the following:

>> **Conners CPTs:** The Conners CPTs are available in two varieties covering different age groups. Each test assesses attention by using letters (CPT-II) or images (K-CPT):

- **CPT-II:** This test takes 14 minutes to complete and is used for people 6 years old and up.

- **K-CPT 2:** This test is for 4- and 7-year-olds and takes only 7 minutes to complete.

>> **Integrated Visual and Auditory (IVA) CPT:** This test measures and evaluates both auditory and visual inattention and impulsivity. This test takes 20 minutes to complete and is designed for people ages 6 and up.

>> **Test of Variables of Attention (T.O.V.A.):** This test for people ages 4 and up consists of two subtests — one focusing on visual processing and the other on auditory processing. This test takes between 11 minutes (for 4- and 5-year-olds) and 22 minutes (for ages 6 and up) to complete.

PHYSIOLOGICAL TESTING: MEASURING BRAIN ACTIVITY WITH EEG

Electroencephalogram (EEG) technology has been around for decades and consists of measurements of electrical activity in the brain, known as *brain waves.* These brain waves change when brain activity changes. The more activity in the brain, the faster the brain waves are; the lower the activity, the slower the brain waves are. EEG tracks only surface activity and can't see deep into the brain.

These brain waves are measured by placing electrodes on a person's scalp and sending the signal picked up by these electrodes to a device that amplifies the signal. The data can then be fed into a computer for viewing and analysis.

So far, research done with people with ADHD suggests an increase in slower, larger waves in certain parts of the brain when these people try to concentrate. (Chapter 2 covers some of the research done in this regard.) People without ADHD tend to produce a different spectrum of activity in the same part of the brain when they concentrate. As a diagnostic tool, EEG can offer some guidance, but not enough different organizations have done enough studies to determine with certainty whether this lower level of activity observed is consistent with all people with ADHD or just a certain percentage of them.

EEG is used quite a bit for treating ADHD through a technique called *neurofeedback*. We cover this treatment approach in detail in Chapter 12.

Knowing What to Do after Diagnosis

Most people are somewhat relieved after they receive a diagnosis of ADHD, if for no other reason than they feel like they finally have some sense of why things are the way they are. Even though you may be excited and relieved to finally have a diagnosis, being slapped with a label can be somewhat disconcerting. This conflict is common and is something worth talking about with your therapist.

Ideally, after you finish your evaluations, you and your diagnostician should discuss what the results mean and examine some strategies to deal with your symptoms. Along with diagnosis often comes the first in what may be a long line of treatment plans. Most effective treatments for ADHD involve several different types of approaches — some biological, some psychological, some social (see Chapter 7). The best treatments also are tailored to your needs and goals and modified as those needs and goals change. Part 3 of this book deals with a variety of ADHD treatment options.

REMEMBER

You'll almost certainly run into some dead ends when you start trying to tackle the symptoms that caused you to seek professional help. Here are some things to keep in mind after you've received your diagnosis:

>> **Don't feel rushed into any particular treatment plan.** You've lived a long time with your symptoms and can get by for a little while longer. Take whatever time you need to explore and understand everything involved in each treatment being offered, as well as what results you can expect, before you commit to doing it.

>> **Trust your instincts about a treatment approach.** If it doesn't feel right, don't do it — or at least request further explanations until you're satisfied that the treatment is something worth trying. On the other hand, if a particular

approach seems to fit for you, don't be afraid to give something a try. No single treatment works for everyone; what works for someone else may not work for you, and what didn't work for someone else may make a big difference for you.

>> **Be careful not to take on too many treatments at once.** You may feel like trying everything in the hopes that at least one treatment will work for you. This reaction is okay, but don't do them all at the same time. Make a plan, and methodically work through the different treatments until you find the right balance. This approach allows you to keep better track of what works and what doesn't.

>> **Disclose all treatments you're doing to each of your providers.** They need to be aware of any potential conflicts between therapies. This point is especially true when you start mixing medications, diet, and other therapies that change your chemical makeup.

>> **Allow yourself time to acclimate to the new you — the one with an official-sounding label.** Chances are you'll experience quite a few conflicting emotions about your new status. These can include (but aren't limited to) the following:

- **Relief:** Many people are glad to finally have a way to understand their symptoms and feel validation for the difficulties they go through.

- **Regret:** For older people, regret is a common feeling because of all the time they lost not knowing what was wrong.

- **Anger:** Some people feel anger because of what they've lost out on as a result of their symptoms.

- **Grief:** Grief is common when confronting the losses many people feel over the effects of their symptoms on their lives.

- **Hope:** After people get past the other emotions, they often come to a place of hope in being able to minimize their symptoms (through treatment) and maximize their strengths.

You need time to process all these emotions. Talk with people you trust who can offer perspective and help you move through these feelings, such as close friends, family members, or a qualified therapist.

Chapter **6**

Investigating Conditions with ADHD-like Symptoms

pproximately 75 to 80 percent of people with ADHD also have one or more psychiatric conditions diagnosed in their lifetime. In this chapter, we out-line disorders or conditions that can mimic ADHD or that can accompany ADHD symptoms. When you, your child, or your loved one goes to a professional for an ADHD evaluation, the provider should consider these conditions as well. (We discuss the ADHD evaluation process in Chapter 5.)

We start this chapter by explaining how a professional properly diagnoses ADHD and similar conditions. The bulk of the chapter details conditions that can imitate ADHD and explains why one of these conditions may be a more appropriate diagnosis for you.

The basic symptoms of ADHD — inattention, distraction, impulsivity, and hyperactivity — show up in other conditions. Not all of these other conditions are mental disorders; some are medical conditions, some are sensory processing dis-orders, and one is referred to as pseudo-ADHD. In the sections that follow, we explore these other conditions in detail.

Understanding Differential Diagnosis: Sorting Out Your Symptoms

One of the most difficult aspects of diagnosing ADHD is weeding through what's called the *differential diagnosis*. This phrase is industry-speak for "conditions that may be more appropriate than the one you're currently considering for this person." (The process of sorting through all the possible causes a group of symptoms can come from is also called differential diagnosis.)

REMEMBER

When you see a mental health professional for your ADHD-type symptoms, your professional also considers other causes for the symptoms you're experiencing. This procedure ensures that the person making the diagnosis doesn't just assume that you have ADHD when a better explanation is available. They must look at many other possibilities, including quite a few mental disorders, a handful of medical conditions, and a few conditions that have the same basic symptoms as ADHD but aren't necessarily recognized by the medical community.

Your mental health professional follows specific steps in making a diagnosis and ruling out conditions similar to ADHD:

1. **Discover the symptoms comprising the main complaint.**

2. **Discover *secondary* (additional) symptoms.**

3. **Explore these symptoms in sufficient depth to evaluate their significance: when they started, how severe they are, and so on.**

4. **Make a mental list of all the conditions they know about that are characterized by these main symptoms.**

   This list can get long, but most experienced professionals can narrow it down pretty quickly.

5. **Ask about other information — symptoms or past events — that may suggest support for one or more possible diagnoses.**

6. **Narrow the list down and prioritize the related conditions according to the hierarchy of the symptoms and how they show up in different conditions.**

   Your professional most likely will have more than one possible condition in this list.

7. **Look at the timeline of symptom development.**

   Since ADHD symptoms are often present in childhood, they frequently occur prior to, or along with, co-occurring disorders. If one of the following disorders appeared before the ADHD symptoms, then treating the earlier condition may alleviate the ADHD.

REMEMBER

You'll very likely end up with a multifaceted diagnosis at the end of the diagnosis process because your symptoms aren't easy to categorize and because the many similar conditions overlap considerably. You may be told that you have elements of various conditions without receiving a clear diagnosis of any one condition.

TIP

Don't get hung up trying to tell the difference between the many ADHD-adjacent conditions we list in this chapter. You may not be able to; the differences are subtle, and all the symptoms are simply deviations on what's considered "normal." A good professional, however, often has enough experience to understand the subtleties and commonalities of the many conditions and will likely be able to recognize the core issues well enough to develop a treatment plan that works.

Mental Disorders Sharing Features with ADHD

According to the *Diagnostic and Statistical Manual for Mental Disorders* (DSM-V), several mental disorders have features similar to ADHD. We discuss each in the following sections.

Anxiety disorders

If you have an anxiety disorder, you have a significant, persistent fear or worry that occupies your mind and is difficult to control. Several types of anxiety disorders exist, but here are the three most common with symptoms similar to ADHD:

>> **Generalized anxiety disorder:** In a *generalized anxiety disorder,* the anxiety is persistent, excessive, and unrealistic. It encompasses everyday events and issues, such as your job, your finances, the health and safety of your family members, and minor things like appointments and household tasks.

>> **Specific phobia:** A *specific phobia* is anxiety centered on a particular thing, such as heights, flying, or animals.

>> **Social phobia:** A *social phobia* is fear of social interactions and the fear that you'll be embarrassed or humiliated around others.

Many people with these forms of anxiety disorders experience the ADHD-like symptoms of restlessness, hyperactivity, impulsivity, excessive talking, scattered thinking, and forgetfulness. In addition, if you have an anxiety disorder, you may also experience fatigue, muscle tension, irritability, palpitations, sleep disturbance, dry mouth, abnormal sweating, and stomach upset.

REMEMBER

What distinguishes these symptoms from the same symptoms in people with ADHD is that the symptoms in anxiety disorders come and go with the anxiety (unless you have generalized anxiety disorder that's present all the time). When the anxiety itself isn't present, these symptoms generally disappear, whereas in ADHD these symptoms remain relatively constant.

Many people with ADHD also have some sort of anxiety, some to the degree that constitutes an anxiety disorder. If you fall in this category, you'll likely get a dual diagnosis — one of both ADHD and an anxiety disorder.

Obsessive-compulsive disorder

Although *obsessive-compulsive disorder* (OCD) is technically a form of anxiety disorder (see the preceding section), it occurs frequently enough that we think it deserves its own separate discussion. OCD is characterized by the following symptoms:

>> **Recurrent anxiety-producing thoughts (obsessions):** These thoughts are often repetitive, meaning that you feel driven to reiterate them over and over or are unable to get them out of your mind. As a result, these thoughts interfere with your daily life.

>> **Persistent repetitive actions (compulsions):** These behaviors are also ritualistic and get in the way of your everyday life. They often involve things such as frequent hand-washing, excessively checking that locks are secure and appliances are turned off, or uncontrolled cleaning behavior.

Many people with OCD also have symptoms similar to ADHD, such as problems with concentration, forgetfulness, and difficulty planning. These symptoms are due to the intrusion of obsessions and compulsions They're caused by disturbances in brain function that are different from ADHD, but that can present similarly.

TIP

When getting an ADHD assessment, ask your provider whether they also screen for OCD when they make an ADHD diagnosis. The presence of OCD has implications for the most effective medication treatments.

Post-traumatic stress disorder

Post-traumatic stress disorder (PTSD) happens to some people after experiencing a dangerous, scary, shocking or terrifying event. People with PTSD often have anxiety, disturbing thoughts, nightmares, and flashbacks, among others. PTSD also shares some the following symptoms with ADHD:

- >> Distractibility
- >> Impulsive behavior
- >> Irritability
- >> Memory problems
- >> Restlessness
- >> Sleep issues
- >> Trouble concentrating

Because PTSD and ADHD have a *bidirectional relationship* (each condition can impact the other's symptoms), it can often be difficult to know which is the primary condition. Generally, if your ADHD symptoms appeared after a traumatic event, PTSD is considered to be the cause of these symptoms.

Bipolar disorder

Bipolar disorder, formerly called *manic–depressive disorder*, is similar to depression (which we discuss in the next section) except that instead of just feeling down, you also have periods when you feel excessively up. Following are the two sides of bipolar disorder and their symptoms:

- >> **Depressive state:** The basic symptoms for people in this state are lack of interest in everyday things, profound sadness, fatigue, insomnia, or an excessive need for sleep. When you're in the depressive state, you also show symptoms similar to ADHD, such as inattention, loss of concentration, distractibility, forgetfulness, and restlessness.

- >> **Manic state:** The manic state has the basic symptoms of inflated self-esteem, lack of sleep, excessive irritability, excessive talking, delusions, obsessive behavior directed toward a particular goal, and behaviors that can have harmful consequences. Sometimes irritability is the most pronounced symptom. The symptoms of mania that are similar to ADHD include hyperactivity, impulsiveness, and distractibility. This manic state generally lasts at least a week, but usually longer. *Hypomania* (which is characterized by less severe symptoms) can last from four days up to months at a time.

REMEMBER

Bipolar disorder has been increasingly recognized in children. One of the main differences that seems to exist between ADHD and childhood bipolar disorder is aggression. Kids with bipolar disorder are thought to be more prone to fighting and irritability in general. Also, their moods seem to be somewhat cyclic. However, one type of bipolar disorder called *rapid-cycling* can show changes in mood and activity levels on a daily or even hourly basis.

Bipolar patients can have all the characteristics of ADHD. Screening tools often don't have the diagnostic nuances needed, and an in-depth interview about their personal history is necessary to make an astute differential diagnosis.

Depression

Depression is a very common disorder — more common, in fact, than ADHD. Depression has the following basic symptoms:

>> Depressed mood

>> Lack of interest in everyday activities

>> Profound sadness

>> Excessive guilt

>> Fatigue

>> Sleep problems, such as insomnia or the need for excessive sleep

>> Loss of appetite or weight

People with depression also have the following symptoms that are common in ADHD:

>> Inattention

>> Loss of concentration

>> Forgetfulness

>> Social isolation

>> Restlessness

>> Distractibility

Distinguishing between depression and ADHD can be easy with some people and very difficult with others. That's partly because the conditions share many similar symptoms but also because the *co-occurrence* (coexistence) of ADHD and depression is very common. Depression occurs 2.7 times more frequently in adults with ADHD than in adults without it. Anywhere from 18 to 53 percent of adults with ADHD may experience depression in their lifetime.

Pervasive developmental disorders

Pervasive developmental disorders (PDD) is a term that encompasses autism, Rett's disorder, childhood disintegrative disorder, and Asperger's syndrome. Children with these conditions show delays in communication and social interaction, and they have repetitive behavior patterns and restricted interests, among other symptoms.

These conditions can be confused with ADHD because someone with PDD may also have symptoms of inattention, hyperactivity, restlessness, and impulsivity.

At the risk of gross overgeneralization, one way to tell the difference between people with ADHD and those with PDD is that the ADHD-like symptoms in PDD aren't as pronounced as those symptoms are in children with ADHD. As well, the developmental delays in children with PDD tend to largely overshadow the symptoms that overlap with ADHD.

Learning disorders

Because ADHD affects your ability to learn, one of the first things a professional looks for when assessing whether you have ADHD is the presence of a learning disorder. Twenty percent of people with specific learning disorders have ADHD, and approximately 50 percent of people with ADHD also have specific learning disorders. Distinguishing between the two requires using educational testing methods (see Chapter 5), as well as looking at how the ADHD-like symptoms relate to the level of intelligence in the person.

Academic achievement tests and other tests of specific processing functions assess several different types of learning disorders. For more details, see Chapter 5.

Oppositional defiant disorder/ conduct disorder

Oppositional defiant disorder (ODD) and *conduct disorder* are very similar to ADHD, but they're characterized by defiant behavior that can range from disobeying rules to using violence. A person with one of these disorders often acts out in socially inappropriate ways. The problem is that many people with ADHD, especially the hyperactive/impulsive type, also act out in socially inappropriate ways. The co-occurrence of ADHD and ODD is considerable; for someone to receive both labels isn't at all uncommon.

Specialists have recognized a common progression from ODD to conduct disorder to antisocial personality disorder (which we discuss in the following section). This progression seems to occur as the person gets older.

Antisocial personality disorder

Someone with an *antisocial personality disorder* (APD) often disregards the feelings of others, lies, defies authority, is aggressive and irresponsible, and lacks remorse. People with antisocial personality disorder also show some of the symptoms of ADHD, such as recklessness, impulsivity, and irritability.

REMEMBER

A person has to be at least 15 years old to get a diagnosis of antisocial personality disorder. Children who have these behaviors are often diagnosed with oppositional defiant disorder (see the preceding section) and can be diagnosed with APD later.

Sleep disorders

Sleep disorders come in various forms, including the following:

>> **Narcolepsy:** *Narcolepsy* is characterized by sleep attacks during the day, *cataplexy* (sudden loss of muscle tone), and *sleep paralysis* (not being able to move at night).

>> **Insomnia:** This disorder involves not being able to fall asleep, waking frequently at night, or not getting quality sleep and feeling tired and unrested afterwards.

>> **Obstructive sleep apnea:** *Obstructive sleep apnea* is disrupted sleep due to a blocked airway while you're asleep, which causes numerous arousals during the night. This poor quality of sleep leads to daytime drowsiness.

>> **Primary hypersomnia:** *Hypersomnia* is defined as having excessive sleepiness. You sleep for long periods of time or often during the day, but the extra sleep doesn't make you feel more rested.

Regardless of the type, all sleep disorders produce levels of daytime sleepiness that can result in many of the symptoms of the inattentive type of ADHD. These symptoms include

>> Trouble concentrating

>> Forgetfulness

>> Distractibility

>> Spacing out

>> Disorganization

These symptoms can also be present in people who have periods of disrupted sleep cycles but don't meet all the criteria for a sleep disorder. As we discuss in Chapter 3, many people with ADHD also have problems with sleep. Some people may be diagnosed with both ADHD and a particular sleep disorder.

Tourette's syndrome

Tourette's syndrome and other tic disorders are characterized by involuntary motor movements (called *tics*), such as blinking, grimacing, or jerking the head, arms, or legs. Older people with Tourette's sometimes develop vocal tics, such as involuntarily saying insults or profanities. People with Tourette's syndrome also experience symptoms similar to ADHD, including the following:

>> Attention problems

>> Impulsivity

>> Restlessness

Tourette's and ADHD are commonly linked; as many as 40 percent of people with Tourette's syndrome also have ADHD. *Note:* Not all tics are necessarily tied to a tic disorder. OCD and autism spectrum disorders also can cause tics and repetitive movements.

Medical Conditions: Making a Physical Connection

We feel a little strange separating these conditions from the ones in the preceding sections, as though the mental conditions we describe aren't also medical conditions! They certainly are. What follows is a discussion of several conditions that can be directly traced to a specific physical disorder or condition and can produce the same symptoms as ADHD.

Allergies and sensitivities

Allergies and sensitivities to toxins can cause some of the symptoms people with ADHD display, including the following:

>> Poor concentration

>> Distractibility

>> Restlessness

>> Forgetfulness

>> Fuzzy thinking

Your family physician or an *allergist* — a doctor who specializes in treating allergies — can test for this issue. People who are allergic may show signs of ADHD even if they don't have it. In addition, people with ADHD who are also allergic to certain foods or chemicals may see their symptoms get worse in the presence of the allergen. If you show symptoms of ADHD but don't have ADHD, your symptoms should disappear after the allergen is dealt with.

Epilepsy

Epilepsy is a condition that causes you to have repeated brain seizures. These seizures can vary in severity from full-body convulsive seizures (*grand mal* seizures) to simply spacing out for a few seconds (*petit mal* seizures). Because some types of seizures aren't very noticeable, they can often be confused with the symptoms of inattention and spacing out common in ADHD.

REMEMBER

Epilepsy is diagnosed by a neurologist; however, as with ADHD, it has no definitive physiological test. Often, the person having the seizures doesn't remember them, so an eyewitness usually has to confirm that a seizure happened. Getting confirmation can be difficult with the petit mal seizures because no dramatic outward sign indicates that a seizure is happening; usually an eyewitness just sees a blank look on the person's face and possibly fluttering eyelids.

Thyroid dysfunction

Your *thyroid* is a gland located in your neck that releases hormones that help determine the level of metabolic activity in your cells. An overactive thyroid (*hyperthyroidism*) or an underactive thyroid (*hypothyroidism*) can cause some ADHD-like symptoms. These symptoms vary depending on whether your thyroid is over- or underactive:

- >> **Hyperthyroidism often includes symptoms of hyperactivity and inattention.** Other symptoms of hyperthyroidism include hand tremors, irritability, anxiety, diarrhea, erratic behavior, and intolerance to heat, among other things.

- >> **Hypothyroidism often includes symptoms of lethargy and inattention.** Other symptoms include feelings of sadness, lethargy, fatigue, muscle and joint pain, and intolerance to cold, to name a few.

Thyroid problems can be diagnosed by your family physician, often starting with a simple test that measures your level of thyroid stimulating hormone (TSH). For more information about your thyroid and its impact on your body, check out *Thyroid For Dummies* by Alan L. Rubin, MD (Wiley).

Brain conditions

Injury to the frontal lobe of the brain can cause the same symptoms you see in ADHD. (In Chapter 2, we talk extensively about the role of the frontal lobe in ADHD.) Trauma or disease to other parts of the brain can cause these symptoms as well. Some possible causes of brain problems include the following:

- >> **Traumatic brain injury:** This type of injury is a fall or blow to the head that causes damage to the brain.

- >> **Frontal lobe disease:** A number of relatively rare conditions affect the frontal lobes. A neurologist can tell you which ones affect different age groups.

- >> **Brain tumor:** A tumor in the brain can cause many of the same symptoms as ADHD, depending on its exact location and size. Brain tumors are quite rare, so don't start worrying about this cause as a very likely possibility.

- >> **Infections:** Lyme disease, parasites, fungal diseases, bacterial and viral encephalitis, and meningitis can all cause a variety of symptoms, including ones that mirror ADHD.

A neurologist can explore these conditions, which aren't usually the first place to look for the cause of your ADHD symptoms. However, damage to the frontal lobes of the brain is more common than most people would expect. If your ADHD symptoms seem to come out of nowhere — especially after a fall — your doctor should check to see whether you sustained any damage to the frontal lobe.

Sensory Processing Disorders Overlapping with ADHD

Some disorders that can cause symptoms similar to ADHD aren't classified as either mental or medical conditions. Therefore, they may receive too much or too little attention, depending on who's doing the looking (see Chapter 4). For the purposes of this book, we refer to these conditions as *sensory processing disorders*. The two most common are central auditory processing disorder and visual processing disorder.

REMEMBER

One key to recognizing a particular sensory processing problem is that a person who has one usually has more difficulty doing things that rely heavily on using that sense.

Central auditory processing disorder

Central auditory processing disorder (CAPD) is a condition that causes you to have a problem understanding speech. Your ear hears someone talking just fine, but for some reason your brain can't completely make sense of the speech.

One of the distinguishing features of CAPD is that understanding speech is more difficult in noisy environments. You may be able to understand someone talking to you just fine in a quiet room, but in a noisy restaurant, very little may make sense. Another symptom of CAPD is confusing similar-sounding words, such as *air* and *hair* or *coat* and *boat*. CAPD also shares some of the same symptoms as ADHD, including

>> Forgetfulness

>> Distractibility

>> Inattention

>> Failure to follow directions

>> Disorganization

CAPD and ADHD sometimes occur together, and distinguishing between the two can be very hard. To find out whether you have CAPD, the best professional to see is a speech–language pathologist or an audiologist who's well versed in CAPD.

Visual processing disorder

Many people experience vision problems that cause them to see words on a printed page differently. The words may seem to fade away or to move as the person tries to read. This difficulty is called *scotopic sensitivity syndrome* (SSS) or the *Irlen syndrome*, named for the psychologist who first discovered the disorder. (Chapter 13 has more details about this disorder and how to fix it.) People with the Irlen syndrome sometimes have the following symptoms similar to ADHD:

>> Loss of concentration

>> Inattention

>> Forgetfulness

Diagnosing this disorder requires seeing an Irlen syndrome diagnostician. To find someone, go to irlen.com.

Other types of visual processing problems may exist that haven't even been discovered yet.

Pseudo-ADHD and Environmental Influences

The symptoms of ADHD (and other disorders we discuss in this chapter) lie on a continuum. In other words, people without ADHD may have the same behaviors and cognitive features of ADHD, but these symptoms and features don't significantly impair their ability to function in the world. *Pseudo-ADHD* is a condition that features the same symptoms as ADHD, except these symptoms are less profound and tend to vary in severity depending on your environment.

Unfortunately, today's society breeds pseudo-ADHD in a variety of ways, including the following:

>> **Digital media, including Internet, video games, and social media:** Having multiple visual and auditory stimuli leads many children to expect that level of stimulation all the time. They don't get that type of stimulation in school, and they end up being restless or hyperactive or not paying attention.

A 2023 study ties excessive screen time in a child's first year to lower cognitive skills later in life. The research shows children exposed to screen time for an average of two hours a day perform worse on attention and executive functions at age 9.

A 2018 study funded by the National Institutes of Health found a correlation between the time teenagers spent on screens and ADHD-like symptoms. Research has shown that social media usage can affect self-esteem and increase anxiety, especially for teenage girls. In addition, many social media platforms are designed to trigger the reward circuit system and release dopamine in your brain.

>> **Sound bite mentality:** In a world where so much gets boiled down to blink-and-you'll-miss-it video stories and 140-character posts, you aren't typically asked to focus for a long time — which means you become unaccustomed to doing it. Attention is like exercise: If you don't practice focusing, you lose some of your skill in doing it.

>> **Multitasking:** Many people have to divide their attention among several things at once. Because most people are short on time, they have to multitask. The problem is that doing so further breeds a short attention span and distractibility.

>> **Sedentary lifestyle:** Lack of exercise tends to create many of the symptoms of ADHD, including inattention, distractibility, and forgetfulness.

TIP

One of the best things you can do for your pseudo-ADHD symptoms is to exercise. Exercise increases blood flow to the brain and raises serotonin levels, which helps your brain function at its best. We cover this topic in more detail in Chapter 15.

Each of these aspects of society increases the ADHD–like attributes in people who don't have ADHD. And for people with ADHD, these things make the symptoms much worse. In Chapters 15, 16, and 17, we talk about strategies to improve your functioning in the world. Minimizing the impact of these attributes of society can go a long way toward decreasing your ADHD symptoms.

REMEMBER

Some people are more susceptible to environmental influences than others; you don't need to cut social media, TV, and video games completely out of your life unless they seem to be creating problems for you.

3
Treating ADHD

Chapter **7**

Choosing the Best Treatment Options for You

You have no shortage of possible ways to address your ADHD symptoms. You can follow the conventional route of medication, counseling, coaching, and behavior modification; explore using vitamins, herbs, and supplements; and consider emerging methods designed to change your brain through experiential, sound, vision, or balancing therapies.

Digging through all the options, even within this book, can be overwhelming. And chances are you'll want to explore many of them. This chapter can help you get off on the right foot in experimenting with these various approaches and help you stay on track as you try to get your symptoms under control. We cover many of these treatment methods in more detail in the rest of Part 3.

In this chapter, we introduce you to the core levels of ADHD treatment: biological, psychological, and social. We help you develop a plan for using the therapies that resonate with you and assist you in keeping tabs on your progress so you can make changes as needed. We also provide resources that can keep you informed on new treatment options as they emerge.

Understanding the Three Levels of Treatment

Treating ADHD involves looking at ADHD from three levels: biological, psychological, and social. The most effective treatment strategy is the *biopsychosocial model* (shown in Figure 7-1), which explores therapies and strategies that address all three. Make sure that whatever treatment plan you develop contains at least one strategy from each category in the following sections.

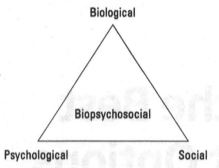

FIGURE 7-1:
The biopsychosocial model of treatment is the most effective.

Biological treatments

Biological treatments change the way your brain works. This change can be accomplished in several ways and can be temporary or permanent, depending on the approach you take. The options we cover in this book include the following:

>> **Medication:** In Chapter 8, we take a detailed look at the different types of medication commonly used to treat the symptoms of ADHD. We also describe the best way to go about working with your doctor to find the right drug, dosage, and schedule for you.

>> **Diet:** Certain types of foods work well for people with ADHD, and certain food groups can make your symptoms worse. We cover diet in-depth in Chapter 11.

>> **Vitamin supplements and herbal remedies:** Using vitamin supplements and herbal remedies is becoming more common for people with ADHD. Few controlled studies have been done or replicated, but quite a bit of anecdotal support exists for using these methods to help reduce the severity of your symptoms. Head to Chapter 11 for more on these treatments.

>> **Experiential and neuromodulation therapies:** These therapies are designed to help facilitate a change in the way your brain functions over time. We explore several approaches in Chapter 12, including the following:

- **Neurofeedback:** Also called *EEG biofeedback* or *neurotherapy,* this approach uses an EEG machine and specific exercises to help you learn how to change your brain activity over time.

- **Auditory brain stimulation:** *Auditory brain stimulation* therapies use sound to impact brain function. This approach includes rhythmic, binaural, and modulated frequency.

- **Electric brain stimulation:** *Electric brain stimulation* uses a mild electrical current through electrodes attached to the scalp. It has several forms, including transcranial direct current stimulation (tDCS).

- **Magnetic brain stimulation:** In *magnetic brain stimulation,* magnetic pulses stimulate brain activity. This approach comes in a several forms, including Magnetic e-Resonance Therapy (MeRT), transcranial magnetic stimulation (TMS), and Personalized repetitive Transcranial Magnetic Stimulation (PrTMS).

>> **Rebalancing therapies:** *Rebalancing therapies* work to help you create a more balanced nervous system. In Chapter 13, we discuss several therapies that use this approach, including the following:

- **Acupuncture:** In this ancient Chinese technique, practitioners place small needles in specific points of your body to help correct the regulation and flow of *qi* ("chi"), also known as *life energy.*

- **Homeopathics:** *Homeopathy* has been around since the 18th century and consists of using very diluted amounts of substances that in stronger amounts can actually cause your symptoms. This practice uses the principle "like cures like" to influence a variety of symptoms, including some of the symptoms of ADHD.

- **Manipulation therapies:** These therapies include osteopathy, chiropractic, and CranioSacral Therapy. They're concerned with the flow of cerebrospinal fluid and the alignment of the spine.

- **Sensory integration therapies:** These approaches are designed to help your sensory system to better process stimuli.

- **Vision therapy:** With *vision therapy,* you do visual exercises (with or without a computer) that are designed to help improve visual processing. You can find out about this type of therapy from a behavioral optometrist.

Psychological treatments

Psychological treatments are therapies that help you deal with the feelings that come from your symptoms — most often, the secondary symptoms that rise out of the core symptoms (see Chapter 3) — and help you understand ways you can change how you think and act to improve your life. In this book we cover the following psychological treatment strategies:

>> **Counseling and psychotherapy:** These approaches take many forms, including talk therapy, cognitive-behavioral counseling, and play therapy. In Chapter 9, we present some of the most common approaches to ADHD counseling and therapy, including the following:

- **Insight-oriented therapy:** This approach helps you understand what you do and why you do it.

- **Supportive therapy:** Because people with ADHD and their family members experience problems in many areas of their lives, *supportive therapy* can help you get perspective and allow you to feel, well, supported.

- **Couples or family therapy:** Because ADHD is a family affair, getting specific treatment for either your primary relationship or the entire family can be very beneficial. We cover ADHD and the family extensively in Chapter 15.

- **Cognitive-behavioral therapy (CBT):** Here's a buzzword for you: CBT. *Cognitive-behavioral therapy* involves using conditioning and association to change the way you think and act.

- **Play therapy:** Life without play is meaningless, and many children with ADHD have little fun. More importantly, many children with ADHD have difficulty realizing what they feel and think. This type of therapy uses play — in a planned way — to help children express feelings indirectly and to work with the negative emotions that accompany ADHD.

- **Psychoeducational counseling:** This approach is designed to educate you on the effects of ADHD, and it teaches you how to better handle the difficulties by offering strategies for coping with your symptoms and their effects.

>> **Coaching:** Coaching focuses on helping you navigate the everyday issues that you may have with ADHD. This approach shares a lot of common ground with skills training and psychoeducational counseling, but it's a discipline all its own.

>> **Training:** Several types of training are available that can help you develop specific skills to improve your life with ADHD. These include the following:

- **Skills training:** ADHD often manifests in disorganization, procrastination, poor listening abilities, and similar difficulties. Skills training can help you develop some tools for improving these areas of your life.

- **Parent training:** This type of training is like a combination of supportive therapy, skills training, behavioral therapy, and psychoeducational counseling. It helps parents deal with their children with ADHD in ways that improve the kids' chances of growing up with fewer problems.

» **Behavior management:** Behavior management is an important part of treatment for people with ADHD. In Chapter 10 we offer several common approaches that can help you manage behavior:

- **Behavior modification:** *Behavior modification* is the most widely used method of managing behavior among children. It involves a consistent use of rewards and consequences to encourage positive behavior and discourage problem behaviors.

- **Cognitive-behavioral therapy:** We introduce CBT earlier in this section.

- **Awareness training:** *Awareness training* involves discovering how to increase your awareness of yourself and your environment with the goal that you'll be more aware of how you act in certain situations. By developing this awareness, you can figure out (among other things) how to stop and think before you act.

You can use each of these approaches for improving your ability to deal with your ADHD. Some help you reduce the impact of the main symptoms, while others allow you to get out from under the grip of the secondary symptoms.

Social treatments

To function effectively in the world, you need certain skills that are often lacking in people with ADHD. After you're dealing with the biological issues of ADHD, you need to focus on developing the social skills and adding to your toolbox of coping mechanisms.

We cover many life strategies in this book, primarily in Part 4. We focus on the following areas:

» **Home:** ADHD affects the entire family. Therefore, everyone needs to be involved in developing strategies to make family life more harmonious. These strategies — which we cover in Chapter 15 — include, but aren't limited to, the following:

- **Developing healthy family relationships:** These strategies focus on skills and techniques you can use within your family to reduce the conflict that's often part of everyday life when a family member has ADHD.

- **Parenting a child with ADHD:** You can use these strategies to increase your child's self-esteem and help them learn to act more appropriately.

- **Living with an adult with ADHD:** Whether the adult is you or someone else in your household, we cover topics that can help, such as working together and taking time for yourself.

- **Developing good habits:** We also offer some strategies that can make everyday life a little bit better, such as getting enough sleep and doing aerobic exercise.

» **School:** Without a doubt, school is the biggest challenge for children with ADHD. Being able to handle the issues that school creates takes some specific skills, which we discuss in Chapter 16. Strategies we cover in this chapter include the following broad categories:

- **Understanding your legal rights:** Being able to navigate the legal process in school to ensure that your child gets the education they deserve isn't easy. We explore the civil rights laws IDEA and Section 504 and let you know what you can expect from them.

- **Working well with your child's teachers:** Your child spends a lot of time with their teachers, and teachers' attitudes about ADHD can have a big impact on how well your child does in class. We offer you some ideas for cultivating a positive relationship with your child's teachers to help you recruit them as advocates for your child.

- **Finding the best school situation for your child:** Many types of schooling options are available, and understanding them is crucial so you can find the best place for your child to learn.

- **Dealing with the tough times at school:** Certain environments can pose extra challenges for a student with ADHD. We explain many of these instances and offer suggestions for getting through them as easily as possible.

- **Working with your child at home:** You can use many strategies at home to make your child's experiences in school more positive. These strategies deal with the obvious homework issue but also others, such as supporting your child's self-esteem.

» **Work:** Life at work can greatly improve when you discover the skills we discuss in Chapter 17. The areas we cover include the following:

- **Understanding your legal rights:** The Americans with Disabilities Act offers you some protections in the workplace. We explain what this law applies to and what it doesn't, and we help you make a decision regarding whether to tell your boss or coworkers about your ADHD.

- **Managing your behavior:** We offer suggestions to help you manage your behavior so that you can conduct yourself professionally at work.

- **Developing healthy work relationships:** Because many people with ADHD have problems with social relationships, we provide some strategies you can use to maximize your work relationships.

- **Creating daily success:** Many people with ADHD have problems with day-to-day activities, such as getting and staying organized or effectively managing time. We offer strategies to develop the skills that help you tackle these particularly troublesome areas.

- **Following a career track:** Finding the right career and developing a long-term strategy for climbing the ladder of success are often problematic for people with ADHD. We help you look at the big picture so you can find work that's satisfying to you.

Trying Multiple Treatments Together

The best way to treat ADHD is to use a *multimodal* approach. In other words, you use several different treatments that augment one another to give you the greatest reduction in your symptoms. For one person, this plan may be a combination of medication, diet, exercise, and behavior modification. For someone else, it may mean herbs, homeopathics, talk therapy, and neurofeedback. In addition, you may use some therapies for a short time and others for a long time. If you use medications, you may switch from one to another or change dosages over time.

REMEMBER

Finding the right treatments and managing them take some research, planning, organization, and persistence. To make life easier, we recommend you choose a medical professional who's very familiar with ADHD to manage your treatment with you. If you use medication, you'll automatically have a professional to work with, and they may be a good person to help you with the rest of your treatment options. If you choose to go without medication, try to find a professional who's attuned to the types of treatments you want to use. This person may be your doctor or any of the professionals we list in Chapter 4.

Developing Your Plan for Treatment

To effectively treat your symptoms, you need to first develop a plan. This process involves doing the following:

1. Determining the areas where you struggle

2. Understanding what you want to accomplish

3. Discovering the best approaches to improve those areas

4. Making a list of the various treatments you're interested in trying

5. Deciding which treatments to do and when

6. Being judicious about combining therapies

7. Monitoring your progress to determine how well you're doing

Figure 7-2 shows how this process works, and the sections that follow walk you through the steps.

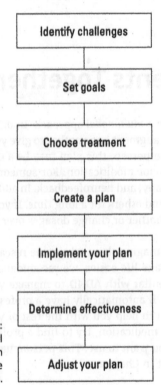

Identify challenges

Set goals

Choose treatment

Create a plan

Implement your plan

Determine effectiveness

Adjust your plan

FIGURE 7-2: A successful treatment plan consists of these steps.

Naming your challenges

If you have ADHD, you may have a hard time seeing your challenges clearly; many people with ADHD don't recognize their own symptoms. We recommend getting the input of a professional (or at least a family member who can be honest with you) to identify areas where you struggle. This person may be able to help you better understand the impact of your symptoms on your life. Work with that individual and make a list of your symptoms.

If your child or another loved one has ADHD, you can help them make a list of the challenges they face.

REMEMBER

In most cases, treating ADHD involves at least one professional. If you're working with more than one person, choose one of them to help manage your care. Having the guidance of a professional is essential to getting the best possible improvement in your symptoms. That professional can also prevent you from getting involved in treatments or combinations of treatments that can make your symptoms worse or that can be unsafe.

Identifying your goals

After you've pinpointed your challenges (see the preceding section), consider each one and make a list of the changes you want to see. Again, a professional can help you develop realistic goals. Optimism is great, but you don't want to be unrealistic about the progress you expect to see.

TIP

On the other hand, you don't want to assume that you can't get better. Many people with ADHD have taken hits to their self-esteem for such a long time that they may not be able to envision much progress at all. A professional can help you realize that you can make significant progress in a short time if you choose your treatment approaches well.

Sifting through the options

In Chapters 8 through 13, we present a variety of treatment approaches that are commonly used to help people with ADHD. We cover a lot of ground, but our discussion certainly doesn't exhaust all the possibilities. Don't feel as though you need to look into absolutely everything available.

Do some research into the general categories of treatment approaches — medication, counseling, behavior management, coaching, vitamins and diet, repatterning therapies, and balancing therapies, for example — and figure out which ones resonate with you.

Once again, a well-versed professional can come in handy when sorting through your options, as can a network of other people who deal with ADHD. Talking to people who have either professional or personal experience with the treatment you're considering can help you understand the results you can expect.

Prioritizing which treatments to do when

When you have a list of treatment approaches you want to try, you need to develop a plan to implement them. Doing so requires understanding the type of commitment you need to make for each one to be successful. A good first step is to discuss your treatment options with your peers or a professional to get a good idea of how long each approach will last.

Some treatments, such as diet, require an ongoing effort and a period of time before you start to see results. Others, such as medication, can produce results almost immediately, but you still need to use them for an extended term.

Some treatments are used for a finite period of time — for example, magnetic brain stimulation techniques, which take between 1 and 10 weeks. In these instances, you know in advance how long you're committing yourself to the course of treatment for. The course for some other time-limited treatments, such as neurofeedback, can't be determined exactly from the start. With neurofeedback, your progress determines the final length of the program, so you must be flexible.

As you create your treatment plan, you must decide when you want to do each treatment you've chosen, and you must understand the implications of doing two or more treatments at the same time. (We discuss the safe combination of treatments in the following section.) You need to make sure that various treatments are compatible and know whether combining them creates the potential for problems. Your ADHD professional should be a good resource.

TIP

Don't be in a rush to try everything at once. Combining too many treatments may be unsafe, and it certainly makes keeping track of what you're doing difficult. Even the best treatment doesn't work if a patient doesn't do it properly. For example, if you take medication, you need to make sure you take the pills when you're supposed to. If you choose neurofeedback, you need to show up at your appointments and practice regularly at home.

Combining approaches safely

Some ADHD treatments, such as neurofeedback and Rhythmic Entrainment Intervention (see Chapter 12), are perfectly safe to use in combination with any other treatment approaches. But biological treatments, such as medications (see Chapter 8), herbal remedies, or supplements (see Chapter 11), need to be monitored carefully by a professional who knows all the possible side effects of combining treatments.

WARNING

Careful monitoring is required because biological treatments interact within your body. Although most combinations are perfectly safe, some aren't. However, we strongly encourage you to do your own research — and consult a professional who's well versed in the biological treatments you intend to use — to make sure that what you take doesn't interact in a negative way

Following your progress

Most people with ADHD try a variety of different treatment programs in the hopes of finding the right balance of symptom control. If you choose to take this approach, you need to be committed to keeping a log so you can follow the progress of your efforts and understand the outcomes of the various treatments. This task can be daunting. This section lays out some suggestions for keeping tabs on what you're doing and how each treatment is working. Also, check out the appendix for sample forms to use to help with this process.

REMEMBER

If you use more than one treatment at a time (which includes each of the vitamins you may take), knowing which part of your combination is providing which effects can be very difficult. In fact, it can be virtually impossible. We strongly recommend that when you make modifications to your treatment plan, you limit the changes to one or two strategies at a time and take careful notes.

Here are some suggestions for following your treatment plans and their effectiveness:

>> **Get a good calendar with enough room on each day to enter notes.** A business appointment planner may work, or look for a planner specifically created for following your health status, which is often called a *personal health journal.* You can also use apps to track progress and keep track of medications.

TIP

Because journaling can be an effective treatment, you may not be able to tell whether the other treatments are having an effect or whether you're just benefitting from the discipline required to keep track of your treatments. Either way, journaling is a valuable activity.

>> **Write down all the specifics about the treatment.** Include the time a treatment takes and the amount of treatment you use, take, or undergo.

>> **Record your observations of your ADHD symptoms for the day.** Include any changes you see throughout the day. This step is especially important in the case of medication because the drug's effects change over time.

>> **Do a quick review of your status once a week.** Pick the same day every week to do a quick assessment of your plan. Make sure that you're following the proper protocol for each treatment and that you don't have any serious side effects that are making your life more difficult than it already was.

>> **Once a month, do a more careful analysis of your progress.** Compare where you are to where you were a month ago and to where you thought you'd be given the plan you drafted for yourself. Be honest with yourself about the results of what you're doing to treat your symptoms, and adjust your plan based on what you see.

REMEMBER

If you're the one with ADHD, you may find accurately assessing your progress (or lack thereof) difficult. In this case, get someone else's input to help you see how you're doing. This person may be a family member or a professional. Make an appointment with them every month to discuss your progress.

>> **Adjust your plan as needed.** After you do your weekly review or monthly assessment, if you see things you don't like, don't be afraid to adjust your plan. If a medication isn't working, meet with your doctor and discuss changing it. If the diet you're trying makes you feel worse, change it.

REMEMBER

Don't just a drop a treatment from your plan if things aren't happening as fast as you want. Change takes time. So before you stop — unless the side effects are getting in the way of your life — consult the professional you hired to help you with that treatment. If the treatment is something you decided to try on your own based on a recommendation or some research, talk to people or do more research into the treatment to see whether you're doing something wrong. Look for ways to adjust the treatment before you give up on it.

Keeping Up-to-Date on New Therapies

We can guarantee one thing about ADHD treatments: change. The available treatments will evolve, and new approaches will be developed. As the professional community learns more about the causes of ADHD, it also discovers better ways to deal with the symptoms. The sections that follow show you how to keep up with the pace of change.

Attending conferences

ADHD conferences can be an excellent way for you to discover more about ADHD and get a chance to talk to ADHD professionals and other people with the condition. These conferences cover topics such as treatment options, life strategies, and current research findings.

For the most part, conferences by each sponsoring organization are held once a year. They occur across the country, and many have online attendance options. The most prominent are the conferences sponsored by the groups ADDA and CHADD. You can find out about these conferences and discover other useful information on the ADDA and CHADD websites:

» **ADDA:** ADDA stands for Attention Deficit Disorder Association. ADDA is a *clearinghouse* (a fancy name for a central distribution channel) for ADHD information and resources. You can find ADDA at add.org.

» **CHADD:** CHADD stands for Children and Adults with ADHD. You can contact CHADD at chadd.org.

You may discover that your local area hosts a chapter of CHADD. If that's the case, you may want to participate in local meetings, which can serve as a resource for information as well as support.

TIP

You may find that conferences on autism or learning disabilities include sessions that have valuable information for you. To find such a conference, type "autism conference" or "learning disabilities conference" into your favorite search engine.

If you have a child with ADHD, you may want to look into special education conferences. Most states have at least one of these conferences each year. They're often geared toward educators, but they can offer parents some useful information as well. If you live near a college or university, contact its special education program and ask whether it sponsors a conference. Even if it doesn't, someone in that program may know about conferences being organized in your area.

Browsing the Internet and social media

The Internet and social media can be great sources for information on ADHD. The only problem with the Internet and social media as research tools is that dodging all the junk that's floating around in cyberspace can be tough.

As a starting point, check out the ADDA and CHADD websites we list in the preceding section. Each site has a list of informative links. You can also try the following:

>> **ADDitude Magazine (www.additudemag.com):** ADDitude Magazine has been around since 1998 and offers a lot of information beyond its paid subscriptions.

>> **National Institutes of Mental Health (www.nimh.nih.gov):** NIMH is the U.S. government's official mental health website.

>> **Reddit forums:** Reddit has a lot of activity on ADHD, with the most popular community (r/ADHD or www.reddit.com/r/ADHD/) having almost 2 million members.

Reading professional journal articles

Many journals in specialty fields such as psychiatry, psychology, neurology, genetics, social work, and special education have articles about research and advancements in both the causes and treatment of ADHD.

TIP

Perhaps a better resource to know about is medical search databases. By using these online databases, you don't have to subscribe to professional journals in hopes that you'll find an article or two on ADHD throughout the year. (However, you may have to pay to access a particular article.) With these websites, all you have to do is enter a search term — such as "ADHD" — and articles from a variety of publications appear. Following are some of the best websites we've found for this purpose:

>> **U.S. National Library of Medicine (www.nlm.nih.gov):** This site, sponsored by the U.S. government, has links to several databases, such as MedlinePlus, one of the best medical databases available.

>> **MedBioWorld (www.medbioworld.com):** This site has links to thousands of medical journals and articles.

>> **PubMed (pubmed.ncbi.nlm.nih.gov):** This site is a free search engine and has millions and millions (more than 36 million as of this writing) of citations for literature from MedlinePlus, life science journals, and online books.

You can also just do a search for articles on your favorite search engine. In addition to (possibly) locating professional journal articles, general search engines may turn up newspaper and magazine articles on your topic. However, if you go this route, you increase the chances that you'll get a bunch of unrelated hits. We suggest you do a narrow search — for example, "ADHD homeopathy study" — to reduce the volume of responses. Be mindful of the sites you search, because many so-called studies have been neither replicated nor peer-reviewed.

Participating in support group meetings

Support groups can be very helpful for a variety of reasons. They not only offer much-needed moral support but also can be great sources of information. You can talk with people who have ADHD and have tried or heard about new treatments. We offer some advice for finding or starting a support group in Chapter 20.

Chapter **8**

Managing Medication

edication intervention is often the first line of defense against the symptoms of ADHD, although it isn't always the best solution for everyone. This chapter helps you examine whether drug treatments are the right option for you or your child, lets you know about the types of medications commonly used in treating ADHD symptoms, and shows you how to work with your doctor to find the best drug or combination of drugs for your situation.

Considering Whether Medication Is Right for You

If you consult a medical doctor about ADHD, medication will most likely be part of your initial treatment plan. With the right drug and optimal dosage, the success rate of medication is high: It can work for at least 80 percent of people with ADHD. Starting a medication treatment program requires more involvement from you than simply taking a pill.

Before you embark on the pharmacological path, here are some things to consider:

>> **Finding the right medication, amount, and dosage schedule can take a while.**

>> **Every medication has side effects.** Balancing them with the positive effects of the medication is an art and may take time to perfect. (See the section "Singling out side effects" later in the chapter.)

>> **You must keep in communication with your doctor and follow their advice (or let them know if you're doing something different).** If you don't communicate with your doctor, they can't help you get the most out of your medicine.

>> **Medication can be a quick way to help you out of a crisis and give you time to develop life strategies to lessen your symptoms and their impact.** You still want to undertake other aspects of a varied treatment plan, which we describe in Chapter 7.

>> **A pill is not a skill.** However, medication can help you use skills more effectively.

>> **Medication isn't a magic bullet.** Medication helps manage the symptoms of ADHD; it doesn't cure ADHD.

REMEMBER

Periodically, ADHD medication gets a bad rap — you may hear or read some scary things. But be sure to evaluate the source before determining how much credence to give the negative reports. Most of the medications used for ADHD are safer than the majority of medications used in modern medicine.

Understanding How ADHD Medications Work

Medications for people with ADHD focus on affecting brain chemicals called *neurotransmitters* (see Chapter 2). This section explores the types of neurotransmitters involved in ADHD and how medications can change the levels of these chemicals in your brain.

The medications that work for ADHD generally impact either the norepinephrine-containing *neurons* (nerve cells) or the dopamine-containing neurons. (Norepinephrine and dopamine are brain chemicals called neurotransmitters.)

These medications tend to work by increasing the amounts of these neurotransmitters in the *synapses* — the areas between transmitting and receiving neurons. The increase allows the brain to rebalance the activities of these two systems and, consequently, the activities of other transmitter systems. Dopamine is responsible for the strength of signals coming into the brain and for the filtering capacity of the areas that select what you pay attention to. Norepinephrine is responsible for your arousal level (how awake or drowsy you are) and the clarity of your brain processes. Both increase your level of motivation.

Exploring Medication Types

A veritable smorgasbord of medication options is available to help with your ADHD symptoms. The trick is to know which types of medication work for which types of symptoms. Although you obviously need to consult with your doctor, that discussion may be more effective if you have a general idea of what the different medications are and how they work. This section provides you with that information.

TIP

Because many of the medications we discuss in the following sections share similar side effects, we discuss those effects *en masse* in the later section "Singling out side effects." If a medication has an unusual potential side effect, we note that in the discussion of that substance.

Stimulants

Stimulant medications are the most popular and effective drugs for treating ADHD. There are more brands of stimulants than any other class of medications. The big difference among the brand names is the delivery system — how the drug is released in the gastrointestinal tract, and how long it lasts in the body. Some people find that one brand works for them, and the others don't.

TECHNICAL STUFF

Stimulants work by causing more dopamine or norepinephrine (or both) to be released into the synapses and by causing more of the transmitter(s) to be retained in the synapses for a longer time. Other neurotransmitters may be affected directly or indirectly. Stimulants increase blood flow to the brain, especially those areas involved with attention, motivation, and task-engagement.

You find two main types of stimulants: methylphenidate and amphetamine.

Methylphenidate

Methylphenidate has been FDA-approved to treat ADHD since 1955, and it's very widely used. It isn't quite as potent as amphetamine, but in most studies, it is as effective. It also stimulates a serotonin receptor thought to reduce anxiety and depression.

Formulations of methylphenidate include, but aren't limited to, the following:

» **Ritalin (methylphenidate hydrochloride):** Ritalin is the oldest and best-known ADHD medication. You can find Ritalin in both standard and extended-release tablets.

» **Concerta (methylphenidate HCl ER):** Concerta is available as a unique extended-release capsule.

» **Metadate (methylphenidate hydrochloride):** Metadate is available in both standard and extended-release forms.

» **Focalin (dexmethylphenidate hydrochloride):** Focalin has a slightly different structure than Ritalin. Focalin is available in both standard and extended-release forms.

» **Azstarys:** (dexmethylphenidate): Combination immediate release and prodrug (converted to dexmethyphenidate in the body, giving a smoother release)

» **Jornay PM (methylphenidate hydrochloride):** Jornay PM is a delayed and extended-release formula designed to be taken at bedtime. The medication begins activating 10 to 12 hours after ingestion and continues throughout the day.

» **Daytrana (methylphenidate hydrochloride):** Daytrana is a *transdermal* patch that you apply to your skin and wear for up to nine hours.

» **Aptensio XR and Cotempla XR (methylphenidate hydrochloride):** Aptensio and Cotempla are available as extended-release capsules.

» **Quillichew (methylphenidate hydrochloride):** Quillichew is available as chewable extended-release tablets.

» **Methylin (methylphenidate hydrochloride solution):** Methylin is available as a standard-release tablet.

Some of the chewable medications like Quillichew and some liquid medications are very useful for children who cannot swallow pills or capsules.

Amphetamine

Amphetamine has been FDA-approved to treat ADHD since 1996. The main difference among the various amphetamine-based stimulants is in the delivery system and release time.

Here are some common amphetamine stimulants:

>> **Adderall (amphetamine/dextroamphetamine):** Adderall is available in extended and standard-release forms.

>> **Vyvanse (lisdexamfetamine):** Vyvanse uses an inert substance (called a *prodrug*) that your body metabolizes into its active form. It has the smoothest release. It's also used to treat binge eating.

>> **Xelstrym (dextroamphetamine):** Xelstrym is available as a transdermal patch. It takes about two hours to begin taking effect, and you must remove it after nine hours.

>> **Dexedrine, Zenzedi, and Procentra (dextroamphetamine sulfate):** Zenzedi and Procentra are available as standard-release formulas. Dexedrine and Zenzedi are tablets, whereas Procentra is a liquid.

>> **Provigil (modafinil):** This drug is prescribed mostly for narcolepsy. It isn't FDA-approved for ADHD, and insurance companies don't cover it. However, it has shown some success if providers prescribe off-label.

Provigil and Nuvigil

Provigil (modafinil) and Nuvigil (armodafinil) are stimulants prescribed mostly for narcolepsy and fatigue due to sleep apnea or shift work. The exact mechanism of action is not known. They are not FDA-approved for ADHD, and insurance companies will not cover them. However, they have shown some success if providers prescribe off-label. Armodafinil is the mildly more active form of modafinil.

Nonstimulant ADHD medication

Not all ADHD medications are stimulants. The most popular of the nonstimulant medications are norepinephrine reuptake inhibitors (NRIs). NRIs are typically used to treat depression by increasing the amount of the neurotransmitter norepinephrine in your brain. A few NRIs are FDA-approved to treat ADHD, including these:

>> **Strattera (atomoxetine):** Strattera was the first NRI used for ADHD. It directly increases the brain's norepinephrine, increases dopamine in the frontal lobes,

and it may exert its beneficial effect via glutamate blocking, which in turn increases dopamine elsewhere in the brain. It's available in both standard and extended-release capsules.

» **Quelbree (viloxazine):** Quelbree is available as an extended-release capsule that many people open and sprinkle on their food. It directly increases norepinephrine, dopamine in the frontal lobes, and it may directly affect some serotonin receptors.

Non-SNRI antidepressants

Some antidepressants beyond SNRIs (see the preceding section) are often used for people with ADHD, though they aren't approved for that purpose and your insurance may or may not pay for it. These include the following:

» **Wellbutrin (bupropion):** This medication modestly increases dopamine and norepinephrine. It is indicated for treating depression and has fewer sexual side effects than SSRIs. It can be quite helpful in treating ADHD, especially for impulsivity and motivation.

» **Desyrel (trazodone):** This mild antidepressant is often used when people have sleep problems, which is not uncommon in ADHD.

Antihypertensives

Psychiatrists use these medications to treat some anxiety conditions, and they're sometimes used to control hyperactivity or anger. They can also be helpful with treating *rejection sensitive dysphoria* (a condition that affects your emotional response to failure and rejection).

Antihypertensives used for people with ADHD include the following:

» **Catapres (clonidine):** This medication is somewhat sedating and short-acting. Catapres is sometimes used to induce sleep in children and adults and is also helpful for hyperactivity and impulsivity.

» **Tenex (guanfacine):** This medication is similar to Catapres but is longer-acting and less sedating.

Monitoring Your Success with Medication

As we explain earlier in the chapter, a lot of different medications are used to treat ADHD and associated conditions, so finding just the right one and just the right dose for your symptoms can be tricky. Just to make it more interesting, many people often need to use more than one medication. You may also need a medication to treat a coexisting condition like depression, anxiety, or bipolar disorder. With a good doctor on your side — one who has experience in working with a variety of people with ADHD — your chances of finding the right fit increase. You can read more about choosing a professional to work with you in Chapter 4.

REMEMBER

Often the medication doesn't last for the entire day. Even the long-acting formulas often fade in six or eight hours. Some people take multiple doses throughout the day or combine a long-acting with a shorter-acting medication in the evening to get complete coverage.

Because the effects of different medications can vary and the side effects can run from mild to severe, you need to make sure you're diligent in following your progress. Your doctor can only know how well your medication is working if you provide feedback on your experiences. The best way to do that is to understand the positive results you're looking for and to be aware of the potential side effects that can accompany them.

This section gets you up to speed on potential positive and negative results of your medication trials. We offer some guidelines to help you follow your progress with each medication you try so that your doctor has the information they need to find the right combination of drug and dosage.

REMEMBER

Even the best medication at the perfect dose does you no good if you don't take it when you're supposed to. People with ADHD are notorious for forgetting their medication, and many children and adolescents with ADHD resist taking medication at all. Before you write a medication off as not working, make sure you give it its due by strictly following the doctor's instructions on how and when to take your pill(s) and then discussing the results with the doctor.

Recognizing positive results

Many people don't know what constitutes a positive result with medication. Obviously, you're hoping to see changes in your symptoms, but what exactly does that mean? Some of the results you should see when a medication and dosage level are working for you include the following:

>> **Better control over attention.**

>> **Decreased distractibility.**

>> **Better ability to remember things.**

>> **Decreased hyperactivity or restlessness.**

>> **Improved ability to control emotions.** Irritability, impatience, and moodiness are common symptoms. The proper medication can reduce these effects considerably.

>> **Improved motivation level.** This change can be as simple as being able to start and finish projects that you couldn't before, or it can be an increase in your desire to do something.

>> **Increased ability to think before acting.**

>> **Improved school or job performance.**

REMEMBER

For some people, these effects can be hard to see right away; for others, they can be immediate. Also, a medication may improve some symptoms without touching others. Keeping a log of your daily experiences can help you see how well your medication program is working for you. (See the later section "Charting your progress.")

WARNING

When you get positive results, you may think that you should try to minimize the amount of medication you take. Becoming your own doctor is a common mistake. You do know your body, but you and your physician need to work in tandem. You may be one of those people who has a fine tuning point of medication that gives you optimal results. That is, if you take just a little less or more than you should, you don't function nearly as well. You don't know that unless you allow the doctor to try different doses (and maybe different medications).

Singling out side effects

If you take medication to treat your ADHD, you may experience side effects. They may be so mild that they don't discourage you from taking your medication, or they may outweigh the benefits you see from the drug. Still others may be downright unhealthy for you even if you can stand them long enough to give the medication a fair trial.

Some of the most common side effects of ADHD medications include the following:

>> **Loss of appetite:** Most of the time, stimulant medications cause a brief decrease in appetite, which then returns to normal. (Flip to the earlier "Stimulants" section if you're unsure whether your medication is in this category.) Working your meals around your medication schedule can help you get the food you need throughout the day. Because medication is scheduled to wear off before bedtime, you can usually plan an evening snack — or even a full dinner. Another good solution is to plan a healthy protein-rich meal in the morning before you take your first dose for the day.

Children seem to be more prone to the appetite suppression so make sure they eat a good breakfast prior to taking the medication and a hearty dinner when it's wearing off.

>> **Insomnia:** Difficulty falling asleep or winding down at night is fairly common in ADHD, even when medication isn't in the picture. If your medication causes sleep problems, sometimes adjusting either the strength or the timing of the last dose of the day can sometimes reduce them. Some hyperactive people need a dose right before bed to help them calm down, while other people without hyperactivity respond to a lower afternoon dose or even an elimination of it.

TIP

If these changes in medication don't work, or don't work well enough, try practicing good sleep *hygiene* (habits). We cover sleep hygiene in Chapter 15. Occasionally, the doctor needs to prescribe something to induce sleep.

>> **Rebound symptoms:** Some ADHD patients who take stimulants experience rebound effects as the medication wears off. The rebound symptoms can be moodiness, irritability, increased distractibility, or other increased ADHD symptoms that last for half an hour to an hour. This effect is usually worst when the medication is wearing off before the evening meal because that's a low point in most people's days anyway. You can reduce the rebound symptoms in a variety of ways, such as adjusting the dosage timing or taking a small dose later in the day. People may not mind the increase in ADHD symptoms at the end of the day, when less attentiveness is required. Sometimes difficulty falling asleep (see the preceding bullet) is a rebound symptom when the medication wears off in the hour or two before bedtime.

>> **Stomach upset:** Taking your medication with food usually cuts down on the incidence of stomachache or nausea.

>> **Headaches:** For most people, ibuprofen or acetaminophen alleviates the pain until this side effect disappears.

>> **Increased heart rate or blood pressure:** The symptoms are generally mild, but if your heart rate is very high or if you experience chest pains or a fluttering feeling in your chest, call your doctor immediately.

>> **Anxiety:** Too high a dose of stimulants can cause anxiety, which can usually be alleviated by lowering the dose, or switching to an extended-release formulation, which doesn't cause blood level peaks. Frequently, stimulants reduce anxiety in people with ADHD by improving overall functioning and by allowing one to focus on what is relevant.

REMEMBER

Don't let the list of side effects frighten you; in most cases, you won't have to tolerate any side effects at all. And if you do, you and your doctor can eliminate most side effects by changing either the dosage or the medication itself. Work with your doctor closely to find the optimal combination of the medication, the dosage level, and the time of day that you take it.

TIP

Sometimes side effects decrease after a week or two of taking a medication. Talk with your doctor, and try to stick with your planned medication for a few weeks before making a change based on side effects.

REMEMBER

Sometimes too much of a good thing can be a problem. When you take your medication, look for signs that the dose is too strong, such as these:

>> Feeling anxious, jittery, or overly drowsy

>> Developing symptoms that you didn't have before

>> Experiencing mood changes

Charting your progress

To get the most out of medications, you need to keep track of your progress and create a log that you can review with your doctor. Although keeping a log does take some time and organization, it makes getting the right drug, dosage, and schedule much easier and keeps you from retracing your previous steps.

Here are the things to keep track of when you try a medication:

>> **Medication name:** Use the name on the label of your medication if you're uncertain of the brand or generic name. You can also check out the earlier section "Exploring Medication Types" for help connecting the dots between brand and generic names.

>> **Dosage amounts and schedule:** Make sure you note whether you remembered to take your dose when you were supposed to.

>> **Observed positive effects:** This list includes any of the bullet points we list in the "Recognizing positive results" section earlier in the chapter. Also include when these effects start (how soon after taking the medication) and when they stop.

>> **Side effects:** Note any negative effects you feel from the medication and include when they appear and disappear. These negative effects consist of both the side effects we list in the preceding section and any worsening of your symptoms over the course of the day.

>> **Comments from other people:** If you're the one taking the medication, you may not be able to see some of its effects. We recommend you have a loved one make notes regarding your symptoms and behavior. We suggest that you write down any comments you receive from other people throughout the day as well, such as praise you get at work.

TIP

You can find a medication log in the appendix at the back of this book. We provide a copy online as well at www.dummies.com; simply search for "ADHD For Dummies Cheat Sheet."

Knowing when to call it quits on medication

Finding the right medication, strength, and dosage schedule is a trial-and-error process. Unfortunately, hitting just the right combination can be frustrating for some people, especially if side effects come into play. In this case, you have a few options:

>> **Stick it out.** You have a lot of alternatives for medications, strengths, and time schedules, so if you don't see success right away, chances are you'll find it eventually. Don't get discouraged if your first attempt (or second or third) doesn't work. The odds are in your favor for finding the right medication.

>> **Take some time off and try again later.** Sometimes just giving your body a break can do wonders. Take a few weeks or months off from using medication and try it again later. New drugs come out all the time, one of which may be just right for you.

>> **Look for other alternatives.** Medication is effective for most people, but it's not the only way to treat the biological side of ADHD. We cover lots of options in the other chapters of Part 3.

>> **Find a new doctor.** Sometimes a new professional with a fresh perspective can help you find the right medication (and dosage) for your symptoms. If you go this route, make sure you take all your notes about what you've tried, when, and what your experiences were. Be sure to include the medication types, dosage times and amounts, and when you tried them.

REMEMBER

You can take other avenues to treat your ADHD symptoms. Don't give up if medication doesn't work for you. We can confidently say that at least one treatment option we present in this book will have a positive impact on your life.

IN THIS CHAPTER

» Considering what therapy and counseling bring to your treatment

» Breaking down types of counseling and therapy

» Examining ADHD coaching

» Discovering training options

» Locating a professional to work with

Chapter 9

Queuing Up Counseling, Coaching, and Training

Counseling, coaching, and training are parts of the core treatment strategy for many people with ADHD. Combined with biological treatment approaches (see Chapters 8, 11, 12, and 13), they can do wonders in helping you develop the necessary awareness and skills to handle the symptoms of ADHD and the other conditions that occur along with ADHD.

In this chapter, we examine the roles of counseling, coaching, and training in treating ADHD. We discuss many of the types of counseling that are commonly used for people with ADHD, such as insight-oriented and cognitive-behavioral. We introduce you to the discipline called *ADHD coaching* and present several types of training to help you develop essential life skills. This chapter also guides you through the process of finding the right therapist and presents some other options, such as group therapy and ADHD support groups.

Thinking about How Counseling Can Add to Your Treatment Plan

Even though ADHD is a biological disorder (see Chapter 2), counseling can do a lot to help you deal with the symptoms that accompany the condition. It can help you develop skills to deal with many of the primary and secondary symptoms (which we discuss in Chapter 3), although it doesn't eliminate the symptoms altogether.

REMEMBER

People often use the terms *counseling* and *therapy* interchangeably, but they are different. In rough terms, *counseling* refers to help in the form of conversation and discussion with someone who has general training in problems of emotions, behavior, and relationships. A counselor may or may not have detailed, specific training in a particular set of therapeutic techniques and usually doesn't have as much advanced training as a clinical psychologist or social worker. *Therapy*, in this context, usually refers to the application of specific theories or techniques by someone who has advanced training in those theories and techniques.

Counseling comes in many different forms and, as a result, can offer differing levels of success for someone with ADHD. To choose the right type of therapy for you and your goals, you must understand how counseling fits into your ADHD picture. Here are some things to consider:

>> **Understand that you'll need to make adjustments.** Chances are that before you ever got a diagnosis, you developed coping strategies to deal with problems caused by having ADHD. With a diagnosis in hand, you may need to replace your original coping strategies with skills that will work better in the long run. Even if medications help you substantially (see Chapter 8), you probably need to adjust the way you live. Counseling can help a lot.

>> **Manage the label.** For many people with ADHD, putting a label on their symptoms is complicated. On one hand, having an explanation for why you act the way you do is nice. On the other hand, identifying too much with the label can cause problems of its own, such as feeling limited in what you can do because you have a "disorder." That's why many people benefit from examining with a professional what being labeled with ADHD means.

>> **Recognize the biological basis for the condition.** When you understand a bit about the cause of ADHD — the fact that ADHD has a biological basis (see Chapter 2) — you can begin to look at your symptoms differently and remove some of blame and shame that you may have about the way your brain works.

>> **Examine your attitude about therapy.** Some people still associate the word *therapy* with psychiatry and psychology and thus with being mentally ill.

Luckily, the validity of mental health and treatment are much more widely talked about and acknowledged than ever before, and the climate around getting help is more accepting. Are you working with past prejudices and stigma, or have you updated your own attitudes toward getting help with problematic emotions, thoughts, and behaviors?

>> **Deal with denial.** Some people with ADHD want to deny their condition or the severity of their symptoms. Part of the difficulty is that ADHD is a neurobiological condition, and research indicates that many people with neurobiological conditions have a limited understanding of their problems. The stigma that we discuss in the previous bullet is obviously another factor.

In order to find the best type of counseling, you need to understand the areas you want to work on and your views and feelings about different types of therapy.

Exploring Counseling and Therapy Options

Many options for counseling and therapy are available to help you with your ADHD. (For more on the difference between these terms, head to the preceding section.) Each type has its strengths and weakness, and not all are right for every person. In the following sections, we break down many of the common types of counseling and therapy and offer a realistic view of what each type can and can't do for you.

Understanding yourself through insight-oriented therapy

Insight-oriented therapy is one of the oldest forms of psychotherapy. Basically, you have a long, extended conversation with a knowledgeable therapist to help you better understand what makes you tick. Insight-oriented therapy helps you uncover your unconscious motivations so you can understand why you do what you do and make better choices about how to behave.

Bringing the unconscious to light

Insight-oriented therapy works on the belief that your actions have many causes, some of which you're aware of and some of which you aren't. For example, as a person with ADHD, you may procrastinate because putting something off until the last minute adds external pressure that gives you motivation (stimulation) to do the work. Or maybe you procrastinate because you don't like the job you have to do and want to avoid it as long as possible. Or maybe both factors (and some others) are at play. By knowing what causes you to wait until the last minute to do your job, you can develop ways to stop procrastinating. For example:

>> If you unconsciously want or need the stimulus of a tight deadline to get to work, you can set up several interim deadlines for yourself. You can use the pressure of each deadline to avoid having to do the entire project at the last minute.

>> If your unconscious motivation for procrastination is that you really don't like the job you have to do, you can change your relationship to the work and avoid having to suffer at the last minute and end up doing a bad job. In this case, you can set up a system of small rewards to encourage yourself to get a little bit of work done each day.

REMEMBER

The bottom line is that by understanding your motivations, you can design ways to work through the problems. Without a clear idea of why you act the way you do, finding a way to change is like shooting in the dark. You may hit on a solution by chance, but the odds are much better if you turn on the light and take aim first.

Realizing the limitations

One of the problems of using insight-oriented therapy for ADHD is that some of your behaviors are not only unconscious but also hard-wired into your brain. Because you don't learn these behaviors in the usual ways — they're biologically determined — this type of therapy may not help with all your symptoms.

TIP

Don't take on responsibility for something you really can't control. Just because you know why you act a certain way doesn't always mean you'll be able to change your behavior. For example, you may not be able to change your impatience with standing in lines if that's part of the pattern of your ADHD. However, you can learn to recognize it and effectively manage it.

BUT THERAPY DIDN'T WORK FOR ME

Many people with ADHD try therapy before they even discover they have the condition. And many of them experience few, if any, positive benefits. We can also safely say that nearly everyone (okay, everyone) we've worked with has tried self-help strategies and been disappointed with the results.

If you're one of these people, you're probably ready to just skip over this chapter because you didn't see any results before. We encourage you to try counseling and therapy again even if they didn't seem to do much for you before you knew you had ADHD. The knowledge of having ADHD can help you identify areas where counseling and therapy can help. But more importantly, by addressing the biological end of things (through one or more of the biological treatments we present in this book), you'll more than likely find that you're able to make some real headway with the right therapy or combination of therapies.

Digging deep

The process of identifying your hidden motivations obviously involves looking within yourself. When you take on this process with the help of a skilled therapist, it can uncover a lot of things that are painful to deal with, such as the near-constant feelings of shame and the defenses against it that go hand-in-hand with having ADHD. That's why you must work with a good therapist who can help you cope with the emotions that emerge.

This type of therapy can help you deal with the grief of having missed important parts of your youth or with the difficulties of accepting the realities of being "different." (Supportive therapy, which we discuss in the following section, can do the same.) Insight-oriented therapy can be useful for alleviating *co-occurring* (coexisting) conditions, such as depression and anxiety; working through trauma; and coping with secondary symptoms of ADHD, such as low self-esteem.

Benefiting from supportive therapy

Think of supportive therapy as your personal cheerleader. *Supportive therapy* not only offers you encouragement but also often helps you keep a healthy perspective on your progress.

The purpose of supportive therapy is to help you see your life in perspective and get better at using your internal resources to help yourself. (Because many people with ADHD have low self-esteem, they can't see their strengths or abilities objectively.) Supportive therapy can also help you find solutions to problems you're having. One thing that supportive therapies don't emphasize is substantially analyzing what you can't immediately see or know about yourself — that's why insight-oriented therapies exist. (Check out the earlier section "Understanding yourself through insight-oriented therapy" for more on this topic.)

Most integrated programs of treating ADHD include some aspects of supportive therapy. You're unlikely to find a therapist who uses *only* supportive therapies, so the best way to find out whether a particular therapist incorporates this approach is to ask. If your therapist describes their practice as "humanist psychotherapy," you can bet they have supportive therapy in their repertoire.

Considering cognitive-behavioral therapy

Cognitive-behavioral therapy (CBT) is a systematic approach to helping you change your behavior. The cognitive aspect of this approach consists of figuring out what your internal dialogue is and how it relates to your moods and actions. Cognitive therapists look at these as *metacognitions* (the process of thinking about your own thinking). The behavioral aspect involves using various methods of manipulation to change your behavior.

CBT focuses on identifying thought and behavior patterns and using techniques to change them. Proponents of CBT believe changing your thoughts and behaviors also changes your underlying beliefs. The point is that you learn your behaviors through a combination of thought processes and conditioning, so you can alter them by using the same methods.

Doing cognitive-behavioral therapy usually involves some type of homework (but don't worry; there won't be a quiz). Here's what's involved in the traditional form of cognitive-behavioral counseling:

>> **Record your thoughts.** You write them down as they appear. (Well, not always right at the moment, but as soon as you have time.) The key thoughts are the ones that occur before a negative behavior.

>> **Record your behaviors.** What you're trying to do is create a record of how many times your behavior is a problem, how your behavior relates to your thoughts, and what exactly happens from moment to moment as a behavior unfolds.

>> **Qualify and scale your emotions.** You may associate certain behaviors with particular emotions or experience certain emotions more frequently than others. Keep track of the types of emotions you experience and their intensity. Use a 100-point scale, with 100 being the most intense, and assign a level to each of your emotions. Doing so usually helps you understand how strong the motivation is for a particular behavior and makes seeing how what you think relates to what you do easier.

>> **Look for connections.** The information you've collected so far should lend itself to finding patterns of relationships among your thoughts, feelings, and behaviors. Identifying these patterns prepares you to figure out how to change them.

>> **Create alternative ways of thinking to change the behavior.** This step involves replacing the negative thoughts with positive ones and using conditioning principles to change your behavior.

If you're a left-brained, intellectual type of person, these steps aren't too cumbersome. But for many people, especially disorganized people with ADHD, these steps can represent a challenge. Fortunately, most cognitive-behavioral therapists use a more organic, dynamic approach to this process that makes discovering your thoughts and changing your behavior much easier (and faster).

TIP

For the most part, cognitive-behavioral therapy is a good fit for people with ADHD. For adults especially, it's much more effective than behavior modification (which you can read about in the following section). In fact, we believe in the cognitive-behavioral approach so strongly that we cover it in more detail in Chapter 10.

Changing it up with behavior modification

Behavior modification is the most common type of behavior therapy, especially for children with ADHD. This type of therapy involves using a structured environment to provide rewards to reinforce positive behaviors and consequences to minimize the possibility for negative behaviors. Behavior modification is particularly helpful for children who have discipline problems and for children with ADHD under the age of 12. Because of the need for consistency and structure, behavior modification for your child with ADHD often requires modifying your *own* behavior as much as your child's.

As we explain in Chapter 10, you apply behavior modification differently to address ADHD than you do to address other problems. Like most of the other approaches to counseling and therapy we discuss in this chapter, the best results come when you combine behavior modification with other types of therapy (see Chapter 7).

Expressing yourself through play therapy

Play therapy uses structured play to help children express their feelings. It's basically a children's version of the insight-oriented therapy we talk about earlier in the chapter. Many people with ADHD struggle with knowing how they feel; if this describes your child, play therapy can help them get in touch with their emotions in a nonthreatening way.

REMEMBER

Play therapy doesn't seem very effective at helping people reduce the actual symptoms of ADHD, but it works very well for children with emotional problems who are cut off from their inner worlds or their abilities to express their emotions.

Adding to your toolbox with psychoeducational counseling

Psychoeducational counseling educates you on the effects of ADHD and teaches you how to better handle the difficulties by developing strategies for coping with your symptoms and their effects. This type of counseling is all about helping you understand your condition and giving you skills and strategies to work with it.

TIP

Psychoeducational counselors are essentially teachers; they instruct you about ADHD and give you coping strategies and problem-solving skills. When you leave a good psychoeducational session, you should take away new tools for dealing with your ADHD and a better understanding of why you do the things you do.

This counseling approach is very practical, focusing on education and skills rather than on underlying emotions or beliefs. Psychoeducational counseling is often helpful for people who like to gather information and need new skills but don't need or want to dig deeply into their emotions.

Bringing everyone together for family therapy

ADHD and its associated behaviors are a family problem. The person with ADHD may have the symptoms, but the people they live with are all affected by them. It can be the elephant in the living room: Everyone is bumping into it, but no one is acknowledging its presence. For this reason, you may want to get your entire family involved in therapy.

For example, if you have a child with ADHD, therapy can help you discover how to best interact with them to promote the types of behaviors you want to encourage and reduce the behaviors you want to avoid. If your spouse or partner has ADHD, going to therapy with them can help both of you deal with communication, with recognizing the role ADHD has played in your lives, and with the workarounds you've come up with to bandage over the real issue.

Like individual therapy, family therapy can take many forms. But the basic goal of each is to try to clear up communications between family members and to balance influence and power so everyone can get more of what they need. A therapist with specific experience in ADHD is, obviously, the best choice.

TIP

Families often go into therapy together after a crisis, but we encourage you to take advantage of family therapy before things get to the boiling point.

Getting into group therapy

We're big fans of group therapy, particularly for adults with ADHD. In *group therapy*, a group of people with similar issues meet (usually regularly and for a set period of time) under the guidance of a therapist. Group therapy often focuses on helping you develop specific skills and allowing you to share your experiences with other people who have ADHD. This type of therapy can take many forms, including the following:

>> **Ongoing:** Some therapists facilitate an ongoing group that may have members who cycle in and out. The constants are the therapist and the overall structure they provide.

>> **Time-limited:** Some groups are scheduled to meet for a specific amount of time, possibly with a set agenda for each session. Many therapists find that having a group that lasts ten weeks, say, is beneficial because each member is likely to attend each session. This consistency helps members feel comfortable with each other and create bonds. Obviously, this setup has real advantages, especially if establishing and maintaining relationships is part of the group's focus.

>> **Skills-based:** Sometimes a therapist sets up a group to address specific areas of struggle and focus on problem-solving or skills training. For example, a group may work specifically on social skills or financial management.

>> **Supportive:** As the name implies, these group sessions generally focus on sharing experiences and offering support. This type of group may or may not emphasize learning coping skills or problem-solving techniques.

Of course, a single group can combine two or more of these approaches. If you're interested in group therapy, look for a group that's structured in a way that matches your wants and needs.

Beefing up your treatment with support groups

If you're looking for an informal way to meet with other people with ADHD, a support group may be the answer. ADHD *support groups* give you a chance to commiserate with other people who face some of the same challenges you do. Doing so can help you get a healthy perspective about both your struggles and where you excel. These groups are generally open to anyone and scheduled to meet every week or so.

To get the most out of a support group, you need to understand what it can and can't do for you. Here are some facts about support groups to help you keep their role in perspective:

>> **Support groups are often informal organizations created by nonprofessionals — usually people with ADHD.** That means some groups don't have an ADHD professional facilitating the discussion. The risk here is that you may end up getting some questionable ideas and misinformation from someone else in the group. (A lot of misinformation about ADHD is still floating around.)

>> **People can come and go as they please, which means that the membership of the groups changes often.** Some may welcome the novelty of new people, but others may struggle to feel comfortable in a constantly changing group dynamic.

>> **There's no commitment; you can choose to attend only when you want or need to.** This flexibility can be an asset, considering how busy most people's lives are. On the other hand, it means that the group can fall apart for lack of support. Support groups are often very dependent on the few stalwart people who found them and make the effort to keep them going.

Chapter 20 contains suggestions for locating support groups in your area.

Adding an ADHD Coach to Your Treatment Team

An *ADHD coach* is, among other things, part cheerleader, part taskmaster, part personal assistant, and part teacher. Coaches come from a variety of backgrounds, including psychology, counseling, and teaching. The main attribute a coach brings to the table is specialized knowledge about the challenges facing people with ADHD and the skills that help overcome those challenges.

Keep in mind that becoming an ADHD coach requires no specific training, and coaches aren't officially licensed (though at least one organization does provide some criteria for legitimate coaches).

Working with a coach can be very useful if you have ADHD. A coach may use techniques related to counseling or training approaches, such as psychoeducational counseling, supportive therapy, or skills training (all of which we discuss in this chapter), but their goal is to help you improve your life. A coach may help you do the following:

>> Develop structures for organizing your life

>> Make plans and set goals

>> Deal with mundane tasks, such as paying bills

>> Get and stay motivated

>> Develop time and money management skills

REMEMBER

A good ADHD coach works with you to identify the areas where you struggle and helps you find ways to improve on them. A coach wants to see you succeed, and they root for you every step of the way.

The way an ADHD coach works varies depending on the coach and your wants and needs. Some coaches meet their clients only occasionally and stay in frequent contact by phone or video chats. For example, this type of coach may schedule 15-minute calls with you each day to check on your progress and guide you along your way. Other coaches focus more on face-to-face contact; some even come into your home to help you with specific tasks, such as organizing or working on social skills.

Looking at Training to Help You Develop Important Skills

Training approaches focus on helping you develop specific skills that you may be missing or areas where you can stand some improvement. Training covers many areas and isn't necessarily specific to people with ADHD. By the same token, a variety of professionals offer training, from teachers to psychotherapists to coaches.

Keeping awareness training in mind

Awareness training consists of developing skills to gain a greater awareness of who you are and of the world around you. (Makes sense, huh?) Awareness training can take many forms, but the most common is meditation. By meditating and exploring your inner life, you can gain insight into why you act the way you do and how you can change your behavior.

If you have ADHD and think you could never sit still or quiet your mind long enough to meditate, don't despair! This type of training can take many forms, and some of them (for example, Kundalini yoga or Sufi dancing) are much more active than the Zen-like practice that many people imagine.

We believe that awareness training can have huge benefits for people with ADHD. That's why we spend some time in Chapter 10 exploring this approach in more detail.

Putting yourself in parent training

If your child has ADHD, *parent training* combines therapies we discuss in this chapter — such as supportive therapy, skills training, behavior modification, and psychoeducational training — to help you work with your child effectively and reduce the problems they have to deal with. The skills you learn in this type of training are particularly important if you (or your partner) have ADHD as well; parents with ADHD often have difficulty with self-discipline and organization, and they may have been poorly parented themselves if their parents didn't know much about ADHD.

Parent training can take many forms — small classes run by a psychologist; commercial curriculums; one-on-one study sessions to workshops led by traveling professionals; and so on — and so can the content. Some programs can be very basic, teaching young parents how to take care of their children, while others may be targeted at particular problems or types of children (or parents). If this type of training interests you, you need to do some research to determine what's available in your area that offers the information and skills you need.

TIP

Before you sign up for a training program, make sure it focuses specifically on parenting a child with ADHD — not any other condition. Also keep in mind that you may need to take more than one class to get all the information and skills you need.

Improving yourself through skills training

If you have ADHD, you may lack some basic skills, like social, organizational, or academic skills, to name a few. *Skills training* can help because it focuses on the areas where you need to develop your abilities rather than on your emotions.

For someone with ADHD who doesn't want to do talk therapy, skills training can be a valuable approach. With this type of training, you focus on improving your weak areas without having to dig deeply into your motivations for why you may act a certain way. Also, this approach is very practical in that you focus only on skills you want to work on.

Skills training doesn't address the emotional challenges you may have, except the skills of recognizing and expressing what you feel. It also doesn't necessarily result in changing your behaviors; then again, you may find that having new skills to deal with what you have to do may change the way you go about daily life.

Finding the Right Counselor, Coach, or Trainer for You

The single most important aspect of counseling, coaching, and training — even more important than the type of approach you choose — is the professional you work with. A good professional who understands the issues facing someone with ADHD and who can help guide you through the many difficulties you face can do wonders for your ability to function successfully in the world.

You may have to work hard to find the right professional for you. In Chapter 4, we discuss how to find a healthcare professional and how to work with one to get your needs met. These suggestions are also valid for choosing a counselor, coach, or trainer, so we encourage you to flip to that chapter.

In addition, here are some ways to go about finding a good professional:

>> **Ask your other healthcare professionals for a referral.** Most healthcare professionals have referral lists and are happy to make recommendations to their patients.

>> **Ask other people you know who've been dealing with ADHD.** Referrals from friends can be very helpful, but keep in mind that a therapist, coach, or trainer who's a good fit for your friend may not be the best person for you. If you know several people with ADHD, ask each of them for suggestions.

>> **Attend a support group.** If you don't know many other people with ADHD, a support group is a great place to meet people who can offer suggestions for professionals such as therapists, coaches, or trainers. Head to the section "Beefing up your treatment with support groups" earlier in this chapter for more on these groups.

>> **Check with your insurance company.** If you rely on insurance to pay for your care, your choice of professionals may be limited. You may also have restrictions on the number of times you can see a therapist in a year.

>> **Search the Internet.** In your favorite search engine, type in the approach you want to try (such as "cognitive-behavioral therapy" or "ADHD coach") and your location, and you should find some leads. Make sure professionals are really who they say they are and not just posing as an ADHD expert to get clients.

TIP

The Internet can be helpful in other ways as well. If you find an article about ADHD written by a therapist whose ideas resonate with you, try contacting the author and asking whether they have suggestions for therapists in your area.

REMEMBER

Finding a good counselor, coach, or trainer requires the same combination of networking, tenacity, and luck as finding a good professional of any sort. Don't get discouraged if you don't find the right person right away; the up-front effort will pay off.

IN THIS CHAPTER

» Exploring the role of behavior in treating ADHD

» Using behavior modification

» Implementing cognitive-behavioral therapy

» Incorporating awareness training into your life

Chapter **10**

Managing Problem Behaviors

Without a doubt, the main aspect of ADHD that you're going to deal with — whether in yourself, your child, or another loved one — is the behaviors that accompany the symptoms. Since the beginning of ADHD treatment, these behaviors have been targeted with specific approaches. By far the most popular and long-standing approach is behavior modification, but other techniques have been developed that work well for most people. These alternatives include cognitive-behavioral therapy (CBT) and awareness training.

This chapter explores all three techniques and gives you some insight into how they're used for people of all ages in treating the many problem behaviors that are part of ADHD. We offer suggestions for using these approaches and for finding a professional who can help you fit them into your overall treatment strategy.

REMEMBER

The treatment strategies we discuss in this chapter can't alleviate every ADHD symptom and should be just one part of a complete treatment program that involves biological, psychological, and social approaches. See Chapter 7 for ideas of how to approach treatment from a variety of angles.

Taking Behavior 101

We're going to get theoretical for a minute: One traditional psychological theory hinges on the belief that behavior is simply a mechanical process of connecting reflexes together. According to this model, learning involves conditioning, and teaching involves setting up situations that encourage desired behaviors and eliminate undesired behaviors (through conditioning). The methods this model promotes are the stock-in-trade of behavior modification.

Another way of looking at your behavior is to see it as the result of motivation and the connections between what you think and feel about yourself and your world. Several processes shape and refine behavior over time, including *cognitive* study (intentional teaching and learning through language) and the more subtle and mostly unconscious activity of *modeling* (copying other people's behaviors). Treating behaviors involves using teaching techniques, such as the ones in this chapter, and other types of techniques that are based on the way science thinks our (and other animals') brains work.

Association

The internal mechanisms of the brain are largely based on *association* — connecting one thing with another. These connections occur both in the wiring of the brain and in the meanings you assign to things in your mind. If two things happen at the same time, for example, you tend to associate them with each other, and that creates a weak connection. If they happen at the same time on a regular basis, the connection becomes stronger; their happening together becomes a pattern.

The pattern can be modified to varying degrees by using the same methods of association that caused it to develop. Usually this task involves connecting an *intrinsic motivation* (something you naturally want to do anyway) with a desired behavior. The mechanisms involved in accomplishing this connection are probably more complicated than we describe here, but if you're familiar with Pavlov's dog, that's a great example to keep in mind. In human terms, by connecting a behavior you want with a specific reward — for example, getting to play video games after completing homework — you encourage the behavior you want.

Feed forward/feedback

Behavior occurs as a process called *feed forward/feedback*. *Feed forward* is making a plan and executing it. *Feedback* is seeing how your plan works and making corrections. It may sound complex, but the process is fairly simple and involves the following steps:

1. **Make a plan.**

   You decide on a course of action. For example, if you hear a sound, you want to see what's going on. You plan to move your eyes to look. This is the first part of the feed forward.

2. **Execute your plan.**

   Your eyes move to look in the direction of the sound. This is the second part of the feed forward.

3. **Evaluate the outcome.**

   You get feedback. For example, you see whether you're looking where you meant to look.

4. **Make adjustments.**

   You try a new feed forward.

5. **Repeat the process.**

For people with ADHD, the feed forward/feedback system doesn't work very well. The prefrontal lobes of the brain use this system, and that same part of the brain is affected by ADHD, as we discuss in Chapter 2.

In particular, the feedback part of the process doesn't work properly. You may be able to formulate a plan and execute it, but you probably struggle to see the effects of your actions and make adjustments. In addition, you may lose track of your plan (because of distractibility) and make a new one instead of modifying the old one. This breakdown makes learning new behaviors difficult. That's why many ADHD people find that they make the same types of mistakes over and over, even though the feedback is a costly penalty or some other painful outcome. Because the feed forward/feedback process isn't working as it should, and correcting your actions is difficult, you may struggle to create a practice of correct behaviors.

Behavioral therapy basics

The purpose of behavioral therapies, such as those we describe in this chapter, is to help you gain skills to develop better behaviors and help you become better able to learn from the results of your actions. In the simplest sense, behavior modification attempts to accomplish these goals by creating a very structured environment with specific *motivators* (rewards and punishments) to help you learn to behave a certain way in a certain situation.

The other two approaches we present in this chapter — cognitive-behavioral therapy and awareness training — support an internal process of understanding your motivations and responses (behaviors) and helping you change the results of those motivations into more desirable behaviors.

By consciously working on understanding the process your brain uses to create behaviors, you can develop skills to help you improve the feedback, which then helps you determine how to adjust your behaviors as they occur.

Looking at Behavioral Treatment Strategies

Behavioral treatment strategies consist of specific techniques designed to correct misbehavior and support positive behavior. No single approach can work for everyone, every time (even though some experts claim it can). In this section, we present three common (and often effective) approaches, describe each one, and offer our views on when and where each can work best.

Behavior modification

Behavior modification is one of the standard treatments for ADHD, usually used by parents or teachers working with children. (It's used in other conditions — such as eating disorders and drug abuse — in both children and adults.)

REMEMBER

Because of the possibilities for abuse, we recommend behavior modification only in instances when a very structured environment is required — for example, in children or teens who also have oppositional defiant disorder (see Chapter 6) and are out of control. In this case, a very rigid form of behavior modification is often used, such as a token system that regulates all facets of the person's behavior (see the nearby sidebar "The token system").

Covering behavior modification basics

Behavior modification is a system of rewards and consequences. It involves directing the child's behavior by doing the following:

>> **Creating an environment conducive to good behavior:** By reducing the possibility of misbehavior, you make it easier for your child to act the way you want them to.

>> **Reinforcing positive behaviors:** Positive feedback for good behavior is the surest way to perpetuate it. By praising and rewarding your child when they

behave the way you want, you both reinforce their self-esteem and encourage more of this positive behavior.

>> **Providing consequences for misbehavior:** Having clear consequences for misbehavior discourages that behavior. The consequences need to be logical to the situation, and your child must clearly understand them.

>> **Being consistent:** You need to apply the rewards and consequences as consistently as possible. As we discuss in the earlier section "Feed forward/feedback," people with ADHD have trouble making the connections (associations) you want them to make. If you're inconsistent about your expectations and the consequences for good and bad behaviors, you add to the confusion. At the same time, you can't expect yourself to be perfect, which is fine because the rest of the world isn't perfectly consistent, either.

Making behavior modification a success

Behavior modification has been around awhile, and no shortage of experts claim to have the best method to implement it. Here are some effective approaches we recommend for getting the best out of behavior modification:

>> **Use both rewards and consequences.** Some behavior modification plans use either rewards or punishments, but you really need both to get the best possible results.

>> **Act quickly.** Studies have shown that if the reward or consequence is delayed, even for a short time, it doesn't work as well. Make sure you provide the feedback (reward or consequence) for your child's behavior as soon as that behavior happens.

>> **Keep it going.** Behavior modification takes a long time to be effective. Don't expect to see lasting improvements after just a few weeks or even months. Keep up the program for the long haul and adjust as you need to. Which brings us to the next suggestion . . .

>> **Change the rewards and consequences as needed.** Your ADHD child will get bored with the rewards and consequences quickly. (After all, people with ADHD need change.) If you don't change them before boredom sets in, your child will lose interest in following the program.

>> **Use positive reinforcement.** As much as possible, try to reward desired behaviors. Sometimes just a word or two to show you noticed your child doing the right thing is enough.

>> **Use positive phrasing.** For example, if you ask your misbehaving child to write a statement about their misbehavior, make it a positive statement, such as "I will leave other children's things alone" rather than "I won't take Johnny's toy."

>> **Use concrete reinforcements.** People with ADHD have a hard time with abstractions, so instead of putting a star on a chart for a positive reward, give the child a poker chip or penny. Providing something tactile can make the reinforcement more real.

REMEMBER

Behavior modification is as much about changing *your* behavior as it is about changing your child's. In fact, you may very well end up doing the most changing. Take another look at this list and notice that it places most of the burden on you — the parent — to make this system work. You need to make sure you act in a certain way if you want your child to respond as you expect.

Many teachers — especially in special education — have training in using behavior modification in the classroom. Your therapist should also be able to help you tailor-make a plan that works for your family.

Being aware of possible downsides

For many ADHD professionals, behavior modification has become the standard behavioral treatment and is often considered flawless. In our opinion, it isn't. Behavior modification is only as good as the people involved in it and can be applied too rigidly if you're not careful.

WARNING

Here are some things to be careful of when you use behavior modification:

>> **Power struggles:** Some experts advise parents and teachers to make sure they always win power struggles. We think avoiding these struggles by thoughtful preparation and creative adjustments is better. Although you create and enforce the rewards and consequences, their effectiveness relies on your child's agreeing to abide by them. If your child doesn't want to obey your rules, what do you do? The only way to avoid this situation is to set up your rewards and consequences so that they're agreeable to both you and your child. Consider involving your child in the process of deciding rewards and consequences for their behavior.

>> **The idea that ADHD is a disorder needing external correction:** This mindset is the main problem that behavior modification can create. By its nature, this approach suggests that to behave correctly, a person with ADHD needs to have their behavior controlled (modified) externally. This assumption implies that without the rewards and consequences, the person has little chance of learning to act properly. If you accept this idea, you set up a scenario where you must be there all the time to make your child perform correctly. (This situation is called *negative reinforcement.*)

>> **Coercion:** Some see using rewards and consequences to control someone's behavior as a form of coercion. Even at its most benign, behavior modification models coercive, manipulative behaviors through its external control. But the degree to which behavior modification is coercive and oppressive depends on the degree and range of modifications you're trying to make and the level of control you try to have over your child.

TIP

To minimize the possible problems, consistently reevaluate the goals and objectives of your behavior modification plan and your child's progress. By being mindful of the dynamic between you and your child, you can make adjustments to keep these problems from occurring. If problems develop in spite of your vigilance, you may find that cognitive-behavioral therapy is better suited to your situation (see the next section).

REMEMBER

If you're going to undertake behavior modification with your child, make sure you do it with compassion. Set up a system that's clear and fair and doesn't control to the point of not allowing your child to make some decisions on their own. You want to be authoritative without being an authoritarian. The goal is to help your child develop self-discipline and behavioral competence. Adjust as your child grows and improves their behavior and allow more freedoms. Try to keep the rewards more prevalent than the consequences. (In other words, catch your child doing things right as often as possible.)

THE TOKEN SYSTEM

Parents of children with serious behavioral issues, such as those with oppositional defiant disorder (see Chapter 6), may use a strict interpretation of behavior modification that involves issuing tokens for every positive behavior and taking some away for every negative behavior, including rudeness and resistance. If the child doesn't comply with a parent's request promptly, the cost for misbehavior goes up — they lose double or triple tokens.

When using this system, your child earns tokens by fulfilling their responsibilities, such as doing homework and chores. If they want to do anything beyond those tasks, they must pay for the privilege with their earned tokens. For example, in order to go to the movies, they have to have earned enough tokens (through positive behavior) to pay for it.

Cognitive-behavioral therapy

In Chapter 9, we introduce *cognitive-behavioral therapy* (CBT), a systematic approach to helping you change your behavior. It involves changing the way you think and is based on the idea that the way you feel and act is related to the way you talk to yourself. CBT uses techniques of conditioning, association, and environmental control.

REMEMBER

The *cognitive* aspect of this therapy consists of figuring out what your internal dialogue and thought patterns are and then understanding how they relate to your moods and behaviors. The *behavioral* aspect consists of using conditioned responses to these internal dialogues to change your behavior. Unlike with behavior modification, where your behavior is essentially controlled by external rewards and punishments, in CBT you moderate your behavior by understanding your thoughts and using preconditioned approaches. (Check out the earlier section "Behavior modification" for more on that therapy.)

CBT is more cooperative than behavior modification and is very effective for older children and adults. (Less so for very young children — those who are unable to articulate their thoughts and feelings — and people who need a much more structured approach, such as those who are exceptionally defiant and unwilling to cooperate in managing their behaviors.)

Understanding how cognitive-behavioral therapy works

Usually, in cognitive-behavioral therapy, a therapist works with you to find your problem behaviors — your motivations and the circumstances under which they appear — and develop strategies for changing these behaviors. The basic setup of CBT involves the following steps:

1. **Choose a behavior.**

   You examine only one behavior at a time because each behavior is complex, and diving into more than one confuses your understanding of motivations and circumstances.

2. **Explore a situation where this behavior manifests.**

   This step involves getting into two key elements, motivations and circumstances:

   - **Motivations:** By understanding what your thoughts and feelings are before and during your behavior, you can better find a way to change the behavior by using strategies that diffuse the emotions and change the thoughts that cause it.

- **Circumstances:** Taking a look at when a behavior happens can help you understand the motivations for it.

3. **Develop strategies.**

   After you understand when a behavior happens (or at least think you do) and what your thoughts and feelings are during this time, look for ways to change your behavior. Create a list of these possible strategies.

4. **Implement a strategy.**

   Use one of your strategies when you're in a situation where the behavior tends to happen.

5. **Assess your results and make adjustments.**

   Chances are that you won't be completely successful in eliminating a behavior with the first strategy you try. By evaluating the results of your strategy, you can adjust how you approach a behavior until you end up with a strategy that works. You may end up with several different approaches to the same behavior depending on the circumstances that bring that behavior forward.

Checking out CBT in action

REMEMBER

The bottom line is that cognitive-behavioral therapy involves looking for the pattern in your behavior and finding ways to change this pattern. The tricky part of this behavioral approach is finding the best ways to change the behavior. As you can see in the following example, you may need significant time to explore and experiment.

Suppose that you are constantly late. Using cognitive-behavioral therapy can help address three areas:

» What happens in your mind when you hear that you're late again — what do you hear, feel, and think?

» What are you thinking about on your need to be on time? What do you think about your own relationship to time? For example, do you think you can just keep doing more things? Do you think you need to get more done in a day?

» How do you approach this issue for you and your family? For example, do you use your phone for a reminder? Do you set your watch 15 minutes early? Do you yell at people to stop nagging at you? What do you do?

As you can see, finding the best ways to deal with the behavior may require a lot of digging.

The answers to these questions determine what type of strategy can help. For example, say that you are generally on time but find yourself anxious or uneasy if you have a lot to do during the day or that requires many appointments. Are you concerned that people will be disappointed in you when you're late? Are you angry that people will cancel your appointment if you are late or start a meeting without you? At this point, the strategy may be threefold:

>> **You may benefit from some deep breathing techniques when you are running late**. You may even be able to do this in your car as you are driving to your appointment. You may also need to work on creating an internal dialogue where you tell yourself that you did the best you could and not make it worse by shaming yourself.

>> **Gently remind your family or boss that telling you to try harder isn't exactly what you need to hear.** This trap is a classic one, and even though people are trying to motivate you, trying harder isn't the answer for many people with ADHD.

>> **Let people know you are taking responsibility for this problematic aspect of your ADHD.** They can still have a goal of helping you be on time, but they can offer you more support or praise for showing up on time rather than shaming you for being late.

The advantage with this approach is that after you get some experience with it and have some successes, it becomes pretty easy to get to the heart of the matter. And when you find the right way to change a behavior, you see significant results.

Awareness training

In *awareness training*, you learn how to increase your awareness of yourself and your environment. The goal of this approach is to help you pay attention to how you think, feel, and behave. It's a bit like cognitive-behavioral therapy except that you're examining what's happening in your head at this very moment rather than analyzing your thoughts, feelings, and behaviors after the fact. You monitor them all the time and make conscious decisions about how to behave as a result. For many people, a combination of cognitive-behavioral therapy and awareness training can be very effective. Head to the earlier section "Cognitive-behavioral therapy" for details on that method.

TIP

A simple way to illustrate how awareness training works is to imagine you build skyscrapers for a living. To do your job and not fall off, you need to be constantly aware of where your body is and how each of your actions is going to affect your ability to stay on the building. You need to know whether reaching too far to your right means you'll fall off balance. You can see that it isn't just a process of thinking, "I can't fall off! Don't step there! Watch out!" It involves paying attention, not just thinking and talking to yourself.

Through constant attention, awareness training tries to fix the feed forward/ feedback mechanism (which we discuss earlier in the chapter) that's spastic in people with ADHD. In the example of the skyscraper, the sheer level of physical danger is enough for most people with ADHD to maintain their attention on not falling. However, when your environment isn't so dangerous, you need to apply techniques that help you develop the awareness and keep your attention where you want it. That's where awareness training comes in.

Many approaches to awareness training exist, and more are being developed every year. This approach holds a lot of promise for people with ADHD, both because the techniques are varied (you can find an approach to fit just about everyone) and because the techniques can benefit anyone.

Here are a few ways to develop your awareness:

>> **Mindfulness meditation:** Mindfulness meditation training comes in several forms, but the easiest one for most people with ADHD is a *walking meditation*. This approach consists of the following steps:

1. **Find a quiet place free of distractions where you can walk quietly.**

   This place can be your backyard or a park.

2. **Stand up straight.**

   Keep your back straight, your shoulders back, and your head looking down at a point a few feet in front of you.

3. **Breathe deep, slow breaths.**

   Breathe in a relaxed manner from your stomach.

4. **Slowly take a step.**

   Focus on the sensation of lifting your foot, moving it forward, and putting it down. In this meditation, you focus on your walking rather than your breath. Follow each foot as you lift and place it in front of you.

5. **Release your thoughts.**

   As you walk, let go of any thoughts other than the moving of your feet. Release any thought that comes into your mind by thinking "Lift, move forward, and put it down." Watch, listen, feel, taste, and smell. Don't talk to yourself about what's going on as you're walking.

>> **Martial arts:** Many types of martial arts, such as aikido, can help you become aware of your body and keep your mind in the present moment.

>> **Tai chi and certain forms of yoga:** These techniques are useful for helping people become more aware of themselves and their surroundings.

>> **Sensory integration:** Sensory integration techniques vary, but at their core they involve helping you become more aware of your body in space. We cover this approach in detail in Chapter 13.

Most of these techniques focus on developing body awareness, but one of the main aspects of awareness training is to help you learn to be in the present moment and be aware of more than just your body. Ultimately, you want to figure out how to focus your attention on how you feel, what you think, and how you act. Knowing these things can help you see where your behavior comes from and help you develop ways to change it.

TIP

Awareness training is much easier to do with the help of a coach (see Chapter 9). A coach can not only show you techniques and make sure you do them correctly but also offer gentle reminders to keep you on track.

Chapter **11**

Considering How Nutrition, Supplements, and Your Environment May Impact ADHD

Many people find that making changes to their diets and using vitamins, herbs, and combination supplements called nutraceuticals judiciously go a long way toward reducing the symptoms of ADHD. Although definitive research doesn't exist to demonstrate the effectiveness of many of these supplements, anecdotal evidence suggests they may work for some people.

In this chapter, we cover the many ways that people are using diet, vitamins, and herbs to manage the symptoms of ADHD. In addition, we discuss how controlling your physical environment may impact ADHD. We try to stay as objective as possible, presenting the various options available to you and explaining potential benefits and risks. But we admit that sometimes we get a little biased: After all, eating a balanced diet, drinking enough water, and avoiding allergens are just good common sense whether you have ADHD or not!

For treatments that are more complex, such as taking vitamins or herbs, we strongly suggest spending time up front finding qualified professionals to help you. Frankly, these treatments can get involved, and we simply don't have space in this book to go into the detail you need before deciding to ingest one or more of these substances.

We see some similarities between the treatments we discuss in this chapter and treatments that involve medication (which we cover in Chapter 8). Changing your diet, or taking vitamins, herbs, or nutraceuticals, changes the chemical makeup of your body and brain. And just as you must be careful how you're using medications, you must be careful how you use vitamins, herbs, and nutraceuticals, or else you can throw your system further out of whack and worsen your symptoms.

WARNING

Just because something is natural doesn't necessarily mean it's safe. And a substance that may be helpful at a low dosage may cause problems in a higher dose. Likewise, one herb or supplement may be safe by itself but toxic if taken in combination with something else. Be aware of potential effects by seeking professional help before you start any of these treatments.

Digging Into a Healthy Diet

So much information is tossed around about diet these days that figuring out what the words *healthy diet* actually mean is becoming nearly impossible. Should you focus on reducing fat? Eliminating carbohydrates? Following the food pyramid?

Part of the confusion stems from the fact that everyone has different dietary goals. Maybe you want to lose 20 pounds, your brother needs to reduce his cholesterol, and your best friend wants to bring their blood pressure down. The best diet for you may not be the best diet for your brother or best friend.

In the sections that follow, we discuss diet strategies that seem to make sense for everyone and may have a particularly positive effect for people with ADHD.

REMEMBER

One of the main challenges that people with ADHD have is eating well. Many people with ADHD eat fast food or snack foods to get by and never get around to eating a balanced meal. For some people, the organization required to buy all the necessary groceries in advance and prepare and cook them into a good, nutritious meal is too difficult. No matter what the causes of unhealthy eating are, everyone can use some reminders of what constitutes a healthy diet.

Drinking more water

About two-thirds of your body is made up of water. The body uses this water for everything from metabolizing food to eliminating wastes to hydrating your cells (every last one of them). Many people don't drink enough water. For healthy adults, the average daily water is about 15.5 cups for men and about 11.5 cups for women. That may mean you need only four to six cups of plain water per day, depending on other fluid sources such as plant milk, juice, fruits, and vegetables.

TIP

Most people wait until they're thirsty to take a drink, but the problem is that if you feel thirsty, you're probably already dehydrated. Earlier in the chapter we promise to try to be objective here, but we have to step out of that role for a minute. We strongly recommend that you consider how drinks such as coffee and soft drinks affect you and consider replacing them with water. You may have been told that caffeine can improve your symptoms if you have ADHD. But research hasn't proved this effect, perhaps because people develop tolerance to the stimulating effect of caffeine, which is true for the majority of people with ADHD.

Alcohol is another issue: It may make you feel relaxed, but alcohol has been shown to make the symptoms of ADHD worse. It also tends to dehydrate you and can produce changes in sleep.

TIP

If you're used to flavored drinks, you may find water a little, well, tasteless at first. Try a squeeze of lemon or lime, or cucumber to add some flavor. After you get used to how it feels to be hydrated, you'll probably actually enjoy drinking water and have fewer cravings for sugary, caffeinated drinks.

Adding essential fatty acids

Essential fatty acids are fats that help your brain function properly. Research is showing that a proper level of fatty acids can help with the symptoms of a variety of neurological and mental conditions, including ADHD.

Essential fatty acids come in two forms: omega-6 and omega-3. You need some of each in your body, but you can't manufacture these fats yourself; you have to ingest them. You can find omega-6 fatty acids in the following foods:

>> Fruits

>> Nuts, such as pine nuts and pistachios

>> Grains

>> Seeds, such as sunflower, flax, pumpkin, and hemp

You can find omega-3 fatty acids in the following foods:

>> Fish, such as salmon, mackerel, sardines, anchovies, and tuna.

>> Flax, sesame, and pumpkin seeds.

>> Walnuts and Brazil nuts.

>> Avocados.

>> Some dark leafy green vegetables, such as kale, spinach, mustard greens, and collards.

>> Some oils, such as canola oil, soybean oil, and wheat germ oil. The oils need to be *cold-pressed* and *unrefined* (check the label for these terms that relate to how the oil is manufactured).

TIP

Cooking with oils such as the ones we note here doesn't add essential fatty acids to your diet because these fats are very unstable and break down under heat. For the same reason, you must eat nuts and seeds in their raw form — not roasted.

You need more omega-6 than omega-3 in your diet — two to four times as much, in fact. But most people have no trouble getting enough omega-6; where they struggle is with omega-3. Adults need about 1.5 grams of omega-6 a day and anywhere from one-third to three-quarters of a gram of omega-3. This amount isn't a lot, but the foods we list in this section don't contain a large amount of these fats.

WARNING

While you're working on taking in enough essential fatty acids, be sure you aren't counteracting their effects. Certain foods you eat — primarily simple carbohydrates, such as junk food and sugar — make using the omega-3 and omega-6 fatty acids difficult for your body. You can read more about simple carbs in the later section "Cracking down on simple carbohydrates."

Research has suggested that getting enough omega-3 fatty acids can help protect people against the recurrence and worsening of a variety of psychiatric and neurological problems, including ADHD.

Being alert to food allergies and sensitivities

Many people with ADHD find that certain foods make their symptoms worse. For example, many people with a gluten sensitivity have a hard time concentrating after eating foods such as bread or pasta that have gluten in them.

Following are some ingredients that people with ADHD may be sensitive to:

» The aforementioned gluten, found in wheat products including breads, pasta, flour, and baked goods

» Dairy products, including milk, cheese, butter, yogurt, sour cream, cottage cheese, whey, *casein* (a protein found in milk), and ice cream

» Corn products, including corn chips and tortillas, popcorn, and any product containing corn oil, vegetable oil, corn syrup, or corn sweetener

» Eggs and any products containing eggs, including almost all baked goods

» Citrus fruits (and foods containing them), such as oranges, grapefruits, lemons, limes, and tangerines

» Artificial ingredients, preservatives, and dyes

REMEMBER

Identifying the foods or ingredients that create a negative reaction in you or your child may take a while. You may have to hunt around and experiment to see exactly what part of the food is causing the reaction. For example, some people react strongly to the dyes in foods, while other people react strongly to a whole category of foods, such as dairy products.

When you pinpoint an offending food and stop eating it, you may find that you can later add a small amount of that food back into your diet. Just be sure to watch closely for any reaction to that food and be prepared to cut it from your diet again if necessary.

TIP

Here are some suggestions for figuring out what foods may be giving you grief:

» **Elimination diet:** You can find out whether you have sensitivities to particular foods by performing an elimination program. This approach isn't easy because some types of triggers can be *additive,* meaning amounts of different substances that wouldn't trigger a reaction by themselves can add together to cause a reaction. So you must start with an extremely limited diet in order to try to get rid of your symptoms. *Remember:* Consult with a professional dietitian or your physician before taking this step; you don't want to waste your time on a halfhearted or poorly designed elimination diet.

» **Special tests:** A variety of tests are available to check for allergies or sensitivities, with names like the RAST, skin prick, and VEGA tests. Each can be useful for finding the foods that you may be allergic or sensitive to, but to be honest these tests can't check for everything. The substance you're sensitive or allergic to may not be on the list of things these tests check for.

The most surefire way to determine whether a food creates a reaction in you or your child is to monitor your diet closely and take deliberate steps (preferably under the guidance of a professional) to find and eliminate the culprit(s).

Cracking down on simple carbohydrates

Not all carbohydrates are bad, but unfortunately people with ADHD (and people without ADHD, for that matter) often go for the kind of carbs that can cause problems: the simple carbohydrates. *Simple carbohydrates* include white flour, pasta, potatoes, corn, white rice, and other refined foods. Junk snack foods, which many people seem to live on these days, are simple carbohydrates as well.

Eating these foods can trigger an overproduction of insulin, which tends to produce exactly the types of symptoms that appear in ADHD. These symptoms include

>> Inattention

>> Tiredness

>> Scattered thinking

For people with ADHD who already experience these symptoms, the effects often get worse after the person has eaten refined foods, either immediately or within an hour or so.

To prevent creating or worsening these symptoms, the solution is simple: Eat complex. Carbohydrates, that is. You want to eat complex carbohydrates rather than simple carbohydrates as often as possible. Whereas simple carbohydrates are refined foods, *complex carbohydrates* contain all the fiber and nutrients of the whole food, so they take a lot longer to convert into energy in your body. This slower process offers a sustained level of energy that doesn't create the quick burst followed by the crash. Table 11-1 shows examples of simple and complex carbohydrates.

TABLE 11-1 **Examples of Simple and Complex Carbohydrates**

Simple Carbohydrates	Complex Carbohydrates
White bread	Whole-wheat bread
Pasta	Lentils
White rice	Brown rice
Potatoes	Beans
Processed cereals	Whole grains

Providing plenty of protein

As you get rid of simple carbohydrates (see the preceding section), you may want to add some more protein to your diet. Not only are proteins important to the structural integrity of your body, but the amino acids that make them up are also the raw materials for *neurotransmitters* (chemicals that transmit nerve impulses). Some people with ADHD find that eating meals rich in protein can help with their ability to concentrate and to sit still.

Good quality proteins include the following:

>> **Lean meats, such as chicken, turkey, and lean cuts of beef:** Preparation counts: Opt for baking or grilling over frying as often as you can.

>> **Rice and beans.**

>> **Soy products, such as tofu (unless you're among the unfortunate who have an allergy or sensitivity to soy).**

>> **Fish.**

>> **Protein powders:** Be careful with these, though, because some are made with pea protein that can cause an allergic reaction if you're sensitive to peanuts.

>> **Dairy products, such as milk or cheese:** Again, some people have sensitivities to dairy products, so be cautious. Also, you don't want to make dairy products the number-one source of your protein because they often have high fat content.

FINICKY EATERS: TASTE OR TEXTURE?

Quite a few people with ADHD are picky about what they eat. This fussiness has less to do with stubbornness or cravings for junk food than it does with the textures of certain foods. If you or your child is bothered by food textures, a sensory integration issue may be at play. To avoid having a limited diet, you have to work at providing yourself or your child with a good variety of nutritious foods with enjoyable textures. Or you can undertake a sensory integration therapy program to help reduce the aversion to the bothersome textures. For details about sensory integration therapies, check out Chapter 13.

Saying goodbye to sugars

Because sugars are simple carbohydrates and they metabolize fast, they can give you what's often called a *sugar rush*. (You can read about this food category in the earlier section "Cracking down on simple carbohydrates.") This rush is often addicting to people with ADHD because it can help them have increased energy for a (very short) while. The problem is that this increased energy is short-lived, and after it fades the person's concentration is even worse — sometimes much worse.

Many people benefit from cutting sugar out of their diets. But to do so successfully, you need to be a good detective because sugar is in almost all processed foods in one form or another. For example, you want to avoid foods that list any of these ingredients:

>> Sucrose

>> Glucose

>> Dextrose

>> Corn syrup or corn sweetener

>> Fructose

>> Maltose

Balancing your body's yeast

Yeasts are single-cell organisms that live on the surfaces of all living things, such as fruits, vegetables, grains, and the human bodies. They're one of many tiny organisms that contribute to the health of their host. One particular yeast, called *Candida albicans*, lives in your digestive system and, along with the bacteria called *Bifidobacterium bifidum* and *Lactobacillus acidophilus*, creates a healthy system that helps you digest your foods better.

Sometimes the delicate balance between the yeast in your body and the friendly bacteria is thrown off by something such as the following:

>> **Taking antibiotics:** Antibiotics kill the bacteria in your body, including the good ones.

>> **Taking birth control pills:** These pills often encourage yeast growth.

>> **Eating sugar-laden foods:** Yeast feeds off sugars and can grow out of control if you have too much sugar in your body.

>> **Eating junk food:** Simple carbohydrates convert into sugars very quickly in your body. This sugar feeds the yeast.

>> **Consuming alcohol:** Alcohol converts to sugar in your body, which feeds the yeast.

An imbalance between the yeast and the friendly bacteria in your digestive system creates a condition called *dysbiosis*, which for some people seems to result in symptoms similar to those in ADHD, including fuzzy/scattered thinking and inattention. This imbalance also tends to cause the following symptoms:

>> Athlete's foot

>> Allergies and food sensitivities

>> Bloated stomach

>> Constipation

>> Diarrhea

>> Fatigue

>> Jock itch

>> Vaginal or genital infections

To ensure that you keep a healthy balance of microorganisms in your digestive system, follow these guidelines:

>> Eat a well-balanced diet like the one we recommend throughout the preceding sections.

>> Avoid alcoholic beverages and sugary foods.

>> Eat yogurt with live *Lactobacillus acidophilus* cultures in it.

If you get an imbalance, or if you suspect one, you may want to try one of the following treatments:

>> **Take probiotic supplements.** The most commonly recommended and studied probiotics contain lactobacillus acidophilus or bifidobacterium. These supplements can be found in health food stores, some supermarkets, or pharmacies.

>> **Go on an anti-candida diet.** Several types of anti-candida diets exist; most of them restrict candida-friendly foods such as breads, simple carbohydrates, and alcohol. The length of time you need to follow this diet depends on your symptoms. If you want to go this route, we suggest consulting a good book on eating an anti-candida diet, such as the classic *The Yeast Connection: A Medical Breakthrough* by William G. Crook (Vintage) or *Is This Your Child?: Discovering and Treating Unrecognized Allergies in Children and Adults* by Doris Rapp, MD (William Morrow & Co).

>> **Take candida remedies.** Many remedies — homeopathic and herbal — claim to kill the overabundance of candida yeast in your digestive tract. Check with your healthcare professional to find the best remedy for you.

>> **Consult a healthcare provider who has experience with *systemic candidiasis*.** Be aware that many doctors don't recognize this condition, so you need to talk to one who is familiar with its diagnosis and treatment. Ask your family practitioner if they know anyone specializing in this area.

Viewing Vitamin and Herb Supplements

Adding vitamins to your diet may be worth considering simply because most people don't eat as well as they should. If you have concerns about the quality of your diet, a daily multivitamin can help make up for some vitamins you don't get from the foods you eat.

But aside from using a multivitamin, some people take specific vitamin supplements with the hope of reducing their ADHD symptoms. In this section, we examine the most commonly used supplements and categorize them as either supportive or specific. *Supportive* supplements are those that support your overall health; *specific* supplements are more focused in their effects on your body's nervous system and neurotransmitter system.

REMEMBER

Scientists have conducted very little research on the effectiveness of vitamins and herbs for treating symptoms of ADHD. We strongly suggest that you discuss their use with your doctor and/or another professional, such as a nutritionist or herbalist, before starting to take any of them.

WARNING

Some people react strongly (and negatively) to even the most common dietary supplements. If you start taking one or more of these substances and suspect you're experiencing problems as a result, stop the treatment immediately and consult your doctor. And although you want to be cautious about deciding to ingest any of these substances, you must be especially careful about giving them to your child.

With many of the herbs we discuss, results build up over time. You may need to take them consistently for a month before you see any real benefit. However, because the amount of the active ingredients found in herbal remedies varies so widely, and because many of the ingredients in these herbs aren't very well understood, you assume a risk (even if slight) in taking them for extended periods of time. We can't recommend strongly enough that you talk with your doctor or consult a qualified herbalist to help you find the herbs and dosages for you.

You can find the supplements we discuss in the following sections at most health food stores.

Make sure you get your supplements from reliable sources. Not all companies go to the same lengths to ensure their products are free from toxic contaminants or consistent in their active ingredients. With all supplements your best bet is to seek out a competent professional to help you find the best product.

Considering supportive supplements for better overall health

People with ADHD use some supplements to help support their bodies and overall health. We list such supplements in this section.

Blue-green algae

Blue-green algae is a plant that grows naturally in water and is very high in a lot of nutrients, including amino acids (the building blocks of protein), minerals, vitamins, and essential fatty acids (which we cover in the following section). Because of the concentration of nutrients in blue-green algae, some people take it to try to reduce the symptoms associated with ADHD.

Several species of blue-green algae exist, and each has slightly different components and characteristics. Certain types may have potentially harmful effects on some people; we strongly recommend reading about the experiences people have had with each type before deciding to take one.

Essential fatty acids

As we explain earlier in this chapter, essential fatty acids are, well, essential to life. And your body doesn't produce them, so you need to get them from the foods you eat. Because many people don't eat a diet with foods high in these nutrients, you may want to consider taking a supplemental form of omega-3 and omega-6. Many supplements are available that contain these fats, including the following:

- » Flaxseed oil
- » Blue-green algae
- » Evening primrose
- » Fish oils
- » Borage oil
- » Grapeseed extract

TIP

Because omega-3 and omega-6 are inherently *unstable* (they break down easily in the presence of light and oxygen), you want to look for products that are stored in a refrigerator or freezer and sold in opaque containers. Also, keep in mind that these oils don't keep very long even in a cool, dark place. If you don't ingest them within a few months of purchase, they may go rancid. If it smells bad, don't take it!

Calcium and magnesium

Calcium and *magnesium* are minerals that help your body absorb B vitamins. Some researchers have suggested that many people with ADHD have a deficiency in these minerals. By adding calcium and magnesium to the diets of people with ADHD, some researchers have reported an increased ability to those people's focus and a decrease in their hyperactivity.

Both minerals come in several different forms, not all of which your body can effectively absorb. The most easily tolerated types of calcium are these:

>> Calcium bisglycinate

>> Calcium citrate

>> Calcium chelate

Avoid the calcium carbonate formulas. Calcium can reduce the absorption of medications, so check with your prescriber.

The most easily tolerated types of magnesium are

>> Magnesium citrate

>> Magnesium gluconate

>> Magnesium sulfate

Avoid magnesium oxide.

Choline/lecithin

Choline is a substance that's essential for brain function. People with various cognitive problems often are found to have choline deficiencies. Choline is believed to have an effect on memory and concentration, mostly through its contribution to the synthesis of *acetylcholine*, one of the neurotransmitters.

You find choline in foods such as egg yolks, lean beef, fish, liver, oatmeal, soybeans, cauliflower, and kale, but many people take additional choline to give their brains a boost. Several forms of choline are available in supplements, but the form most often used is phosphatidylcholine, also known as lecithin.

Ginseng

Ginseng is often touted as an energy enhancer. This root has been used for ages to help reduce stress and improve physical performance. You can find ginseng in a variety of formulations, from dried powders to teas to capsules to unprocessed roots.

WARNING

Ginseng can increase the stimulant effect and side effects of stimulant medication used to treat ADHD. They should NOT be taken together. It also can interfere with other medications and herbal products so please check with a healthcare professional or pharmacist before using it.

Maritime pine (Pycnogenol)

This antioxidant comes from extracts of the bark of a European coastal pine tree (*Pinus pinaster,* or maritime pine) and has been used for decades in Europe. Pycnogenol is a proprietary name for a concentration of the chemical proanthocyanidin. You can also find maritime pine sold as oligomeric proanthocyanidins (OPC).

Antioxidants are considered important in deactivating free radicals, and Pycnogenol has 20 times the antioxidant properties of vitamin C and 50 times the antioxidant properties of vitamin E.

Some researchers have suggested that Pycnogenol may support and improve the function of the neurotransmitters *dopamine* and *norepinephrine* (which we discuss in Chapter 2).

Taking specific supplements to support your nervous system

Some people with ADHD use specific supplements to support and possibly enhance nervous system function. We list the most commonly used specific supplements in this section.

Vinpocetine

Vinpocetine is a substance derived from the periwinkle plant. In Europe, it has been used to help protect people who experience strokes and other brain injuries from having more extensive brain damage.

This substance has two interesting properties that relate to ADHD: It increases blood flow in the brain (especially in the frontal lobes), and it increases dopamine levels (which we discuss in Chapter 2).

Melatonin

Melatonin is a hormone that helps regulate sleep. Some people find melatonin supplements useful if they have sleep problems along with ADHD. Melatonin may be helpful for people who have a hard time winding down at night and falling asleep and for those who wake up several times during the night.

TIP

If you choose to try melatonin, you may want to start with a small dose. Some people report that larger doses make them feel groggy and tired the next day, as if they have the type of hangover often associated with sleeping pills.

L-tyrosine

L-tyrosine is an amino acid and a building block for the neurotransmitter dopamine. (In Chapter 2, we discuss dopamine and its relationship to ADHD.) L-tyrosine seems to increase the level of a brain stimulant called phenylethylamine (PEA), as well as improve attention and concentration for some people.

WARNING

Unfortunately, L-tyrosine can also contribute to health problems, such as high blood pressure, including if it's taken in combination with certain medications. Talk to your healthcare professional before you take this supplement.

5-HTP

The substance *5-hydroxytryptophan* (5-HTP) is extracted from the seeds of a West African shrub called *Griffonia simplicifolia*. Your body makes 5-HTP from *L-tryptophan*, an amino acid found in most protein-rich foods. (You may relate to the spacey, sleepy feeling you get after eating Thanksgiving turkey.) Some research indicates that 5-HTP increases levels of the neurotransmitter serotonin, which is instrumental in regulating sleep, feelings of anxiety and aggression, and the ability to perceive pain, among other things.

Some people take 5-HTP to improve their sleep and overall mood and to decrease aggressiveness.

Because this substance can cause an upset stomach, take it with food to help avoid this problem. Most people start with a small dose and increase the dosage over time, which helps with stomach upset as well.

Talk with your prescriber before taking 5-HTP in combination with prescribed antidepressants, because they may not play well together.

St. John's wort is made from the flowers of the *Hypericum* plant. This herb is used most often for depression, insomnia, and anxiety because it increases serotonin levels in the brain. It enhances the activity of dopamine and norepinephrine as well (see Chapter 2).

Some people with ADHD find that St. John's wort can help them feel more emotionally balanced, especially if they also suffer from depression or anxiety.

As with 5-HTP, which we discuss earlier in the chapter, don't take St. John's wort with any prescription antidepressants without first checking with your friendly psychopharmacologist. Because St. John's wort can accelerate the breakdown of many medications, always check with your doctor before starting it.

Valerian root

Valerian root is an herbal extract that has been used for a very long time to create a feeling of calm. People with ADHD often use valerian to help initiate sleep. Unlike melatonin, which is also used to help people get to sleep, valerian can sometimes be more effective for people who wake up early and can't get back to sleep. And it doesn't create grogginess in the morning.

Nutraceuticals: Combining Vitamins and Herbs

Many vitamins and herbs are reported to help with some ADHD symptoms. Even if you read this whole chapter, which presents just some of your options, you may not have any idea where to start using them in your life. To make things easier, many products are available that combine some of the vitamins and herbs we describe here with the specific goal of aiding people with ADHD. These prefab combinations of vitamins and herbs are called *nutraceuticals*. (*Note:* The term *nutraceuticals* refers to any food substance that's used to treat illnesses, but we limit our use of the term to these combination compounds.)

Nutraceuticals have become all the rage in a variety of areas, from people with ADHD and autism to people with insomnia and depression. You can find these formulated combinations of vitamins and supplements for ADHD by talking to your nutritionist or herbalist.

Little scientific research has been conducted to support the reported effects of many of the vitamins, minerals, and herbs that we discuss in this chapter. We want you to know they exist because each one seems to be anecdotally effective for some people with ADHD. But we don't have room in this book for an exhaustive treatment on each nutraceutical, so we strongly advise that you get more information, talk with healthcare professionals, and give these treatment options serious consideration before trying them.

Addressing Possible Aggravators in Your Environment

When you have ADHD, even your everyday environment can exacerbate your symptoms. (In fact, the environment can create ADHD-like symptoms in people without ADHD, as we discuss in Chapter 6.) Many environmental factors can make your symptoms worse. In the following sections, we discuss two categories of these factors: allergens and chemicals.

Allergens

Allergens are things in your environment that can cause you to have an allergic reaction if you're sensitive to them. Allergens come in many different forms, but the most common are dust, dust mites, mold, pollens, and animals. In this section, we offer advice for controlling allergens in your environment.

Your doctor can test your sensitivity to these allergens to help you understand whether these things are causing or exacerbating some of your ADHD symptoms. Many people feel at least ruling out these allergens as a cause of symptoms is worthwhile. However, keep in mind that you may be sensitive to one or more of these allergens without showing a positive result on a test because these tests aren't 100 percent accurate.

If your ADHD symptoms get worse in the presence of any of the allergens we discuss in the following sections, talk to your doctor about ways to get your allergies or sensitivities under control. A variety of medications and natural remedies exist that seem to help a lot of people.

Dust

Dust is everywhere. No matter what you do, it's going to build up in your house. Unfortunately, regular household dust can be very toxic to sensitive people. This dust can contain everything from pieces of dead skin to residues from toxic chemicals. The best way to deal with dust is to eliminate it.

TIP

Here are some tips for getting dust (which we discuss in the next section) under control:

>> **Vacuum often — at least once a week.** Vacuuming your house can help, but you need a decent vacuum cleaner or else you're just moving the dust around rather than getting rid of it. Buy a vacuum with a good filter system, or use a whole-house vacuum system that exhausts outdoors.

>> **Eliminate carpeting.** This step may not be practical for you, but, if possible, get rid of your wall-to-wall carpeting and opt for any non-toxic hard floor instead. Carpeting tends to hold onto dust, and even the best vacuum cleaner may not get it entirely clean. Sweeping and mopping wood floors results in a cleaner house.

>> **Clean regularly.** This task is often easier said than done, especially when a family is dealing with the stress of ADHD. But make it a priority so the dust doesn't accumulate.

>> **Make sure to keep the bedroom clean.** People spend almost a third of their lives in bed, so if you only have time to get one room in your house dust-free (or at least dust-minimal), make it your bedroom. For example, by washing your sheets and pillowcases often (at least every other week), you cut down on your exposure to dust.

>> **Get an air cleaner.** A good air cleaner can catch the dust before it settles down on your stuff; we recommend a HEPA filtration system. If you use an air cleaner, make sure it's a high quality product and that you maintain it properly. A poorly working air cleaner is worse than no air cleaner at all.

Dust mites

Dust mites are nasty little critters, from the same family as spiders and ticks, that eat the dust in your house. (Well, not just *your* house — everyone's.) Dust mites themselves aren't so much a problem, but their droppings are. Some researchers have suggested that dust mite droppings are the leading cause of asthma around the world.

You can't tell the number of dust mites in your house by how clean it is; rather, your dust mite population depends on how moist your house is. People who live in warm, moist climates tend to have more dust mites than those who live in drier or cooler climates.

TIP

Here are some suggestions to help you get rid of dust mites (or at least minimize their impact). Unsurprisingly, some of them overlap the advice on eliminating dust in the preceding section:

>> **Get rid of your carpeting.** If you can, removing carpeting is the single best way to reduce the mite population in your house. Replace the carpeting with wood or tile so you can give it a good cleaning often.

>> **Use an allergen spray on carpeting.** If you can't replace your carpeting, at least treat it with an allergen spray made to kill dust mites.

>> **Use a good, sealed vacuum.** To control dust mites, you must have a vacuum that doesn't spew dust everywhere. If you can afford it, look for a good HEPA filter system on a vacuum cleaner. Vacuum often, particularly if you must have carpet.

>> **Use protective bed coverings.** Because dust mites tend to be a real problem in the bedroom, get protective coverings (called *dust mite covers*) for your mattress and pillows to seal the dust mites out. Wash the covers in hot water before you put them on. These covers come in many styles but usually consist of tightly woven fabric that dust mites can't penetrate.

>> **Optimize the humidity in your house.** Mites grow best in environments that have 75 to 80 percent relative humidity, but they can't live in areas with less than 50 percent humidity. You can achieve this lower level by using a dehumidifier when necessary.

>> **If you have a forced-air heating system, install filters.** Filters prevent the mites from flying all over your house with the heat. You can also turn the heating vents off in your bedroom to reduce the chance that the dust and mites in your bedroom will blow around.

>> **Wash your bedding often in hot water.** Water temperatures over 130 degrees Fahrenheit kill the mites on your bedding.

>> **Keep your clothes in a closet, and keep the door closed.** This strategy at least keeps any mites that get on your clothes away from you when you sleep.

Mold

Mold has received a lot of attention lately. More and more houses are turning out to be breeding grounds for molds, especially in wetter climates. Mold is everywhere; about 100,000 types of mold exist. Most are relatively harmless, but a few (24 by some accounts) can cause some serious problems. Molds are known not only to make asthma worse but also to cause problems with cognition (your ability to think). People who have a mold allergy or sensitivity often have ADHD symptoms, and people with ADHD who have these sensitivities see their symptoms get worse in the presence of molds.

Mold needs moisture to grow, so to control mold in your house you need to make sure you don't have any water leaks. If you do, fix them immediately. You can also install an air cleaner in your house — look for a HEPA or UV filter — to reduce the airborne mold spores.

Animal dander, fur, and feathers

Animal dander, fur, and feathers can cause allergic reactions in some people. If you're allergic to your furry (and feathered) friends, all you can really do to minimize the allergy's effects on your life is to not have a pet and to avoid homes that do have them.

REMEMBER

You may not even know a pet makes your ADHD symptoms worse because you may not display the classic symptoms of a runny nose, sneezing, coughing, and so on. You may just feel tired or have scattered thinking.

If you suspect that your beloved pet is making your ADHD symptoms worse, board it at a kennel or have a friend take it for a few days while you clean your house. If your symptoms improve and then get worse when your pet comes home, you may have a difficult decision to make.

Pollens

Pollens are a common cause of allergies. As springtime rolls around, some people are hit with such a bad reaction that they don't get to enjoy the outdoors in the good weather. If you have both seasonal allergies and ADHD, your ADHD symptoms may get worse while you're dealing with a runny or stuffed-up nose, labored breathing, headaches, and other allergy symptoms.

Even if your pollen allergies and your ADHD symptoms don't have a direct link, you may find your sleep is disrupted enough to make concentrating difficult. The solution is to safeguard your sleep by taking medication or a natural remedy to help with your allergy.

Chemicals

As if the typical allergens aren't enough to worry about, most people's home environments are riddled with chemicals that can make ADHD symptoms worse for a person sensitive to them. Potential offenders include, but aren't limited to, the following:

>> **Cleaning products:** Many cleaning products contain chemicals that are derived from petroleum, which can impact ADHD symptoms. With cleaning products, just inhaling these chemicals may worsen your symptoms.

- >> **Scented products:** If you look around your home, you'll probably notice a long list of products, such as toilet paper, soaps, and deodorants, that contain fragrances. Many children and adults are allergic to these products or have adverse reactions, such as brain fog and difficulty concentrating, which can exacerbate ADHD symptoms.

  Perfumes and colognes: Personal fragrances are big business. Unfortunately, the smell of these products can make some people sick. As with other chemicals, some perfumes and colognes contain petroleum-based fragrances that can make ADHD symptoms worse.

- >> **Plastic food storage containers:** Some plastics used for food storage can leach chemicals into the food. These substances include bisphenol A (BPA), polyvinyl chloride (PVC), and polystyrene (PS). BPA is especially concerning because manufacturers use it in the production of a variety of plastics used for food storage (polycarbonate no. 7).

- >> **Plastic toys, furniture, and appliances:** Certain plastics, namely PVC, give off gases that are a problem for some people. Unfortunately, most hard plastic toys, furniture, and appliances are made at least in part from PVC.

TIP

  If you read labels, you may find some young children's plastic toys that aren't made with PVC; if PVC wasn't used, the product label usually says so. (If the label doesn't say, the toy is probably made from PVC.) Furniture and appliances aren't yet labeled so you may want to avoid plastic altogether if you're concerned about the gas given off by PVC.

- >> **Building materials:** Building materials can contain toxic chemicals that continue to give off gas for quite a while. (That's what creates the "new carpet smell.") For example, formaldehyde is used in making plywood.

  If you build a new house, consider all the materials that go into it. If you live in a fairly new house, be aware that it may be giving off chemicals that make your ADHD worse. A good HEPA air filter system can help, but the only real solution is to remove either yourself or the offending materials from your house.

- >> **Synthetic fabrics:** Petroleum is a component of so many products that it can be hard to comprehend. Polyester fabric is one such product. People with sensitivities should wear only natural fiber clothing, such as cotton, wool, or silk.

REMEMBER

For most people, the chemicals we discuss in this section aren't a problem. But for people with sensitivities, even a little exposure can make their ADHD symptoms much worse. If any of these products seems to make your symptoms worse, get rid of it.

Chapter **12**

Examining Neuromodulation Therapies

As we explain in Chapter 8, the mainstream biological treatment for ADHD is medication. Although medication successfully provides symptom control for most people with ADHD, it can also have serious side effects for some people. For this reason, some emerging therapies are being explored that can offer benefits for people with ADHD without the same level of side effects.

In this chapter, we look at therapies that are designed to modulate brain activity to improve the symptoms of ADHD. This approach is called *neuromodulation* and includes neurofeedback, auditory brain stimulation, electrical brain stimulation, and magnetic brain stimulation.

REMEMBER

These therapies aren't often part of the more conventional ADHD professional's therapy options and don't have the extensive research that pharmaceuticals have to back them up. For that reason, we offer a little more technical detail in describing these therapies than we do with the medications in Chapter 8 so you can go in armed with the information you need to make a decision. We also encourage you to look deeper for studies on these approaches and for professionals who may be able to offer them to you. To help you, we include a section for each therapy on finding a provider. The resources we suggest can also provide information on the results of studies on the approach in question.

REMEMBER

We say this many times in this book, but it bears repeating: The most effective way to treat ADHD is to use a multipronged approach. Ideally, you want to use treatment approaches that cover the biological, psychological, and social aspects of the condition. The treatments in this chapter are biological — they alter the way your brain functions. If you choose to try one of these treatments, you should combine it with psychological treatments, such as those described in Chapters 9 and 10, and social approaches, such as the ones we present in Chapters 15, 16, and 17.

Altering Brain Activity Through Neurofeedback

Neurofeedback (also called *neurotherapy* or *EEG biofeedback*) is a therapy that helps you change your brain activity by using specific exercises and watching how your brain wave states change as you do them. Neurofeedback is essentially an exercise program for your brain. As we discuss in Chapter 2, people with ADHD experience lower activity in certain areas of the brain from what people without ADHD do. With neurofeedback, you can increase this activity by actually seeing it and then using techniques to change your brain patterns.

Getting some background on neurofeedback

Neurofeedback has been around since the 1960s and has been studied extensively for many years. This therapy relies on the idea that by changing the level of activity in the brain you can improve the symptoms associated with ADHD.

In order to understand how neurofeedback works, you first need to understand the concept of brain waves. Brain activity can be measured as brain waves at different *frequencies* (speeds) and *amplitudes* (levels). The brain wave states indicate how active a particular part of the brain is, which relates to your overall level of awareness. Five basic brain wave levels exist:

>> **Delta:** *Delta* is the sleep state and exists at a frequency between 0 and 4 hertz (Hz, or cycles per second).

>> **Theta:** *Theta* is the meditative state of consciousness, which consists of brain wave frequencies between 4 and 8 hertz. Many people with ADHD have too much of this activity in their brains. This represents a lower-than-normal level

of activity and, as we talk about in Chapter 2, may have something to do with the symptoms of ADHD.

>> **Alpha:** *Alpha* is a relaxed yet alert state. It encompasses frequencies between 8 and 12 hertz. Some people with ADHD have too much of this rhythm in the wrong locations in their brains, which can interfere with the communication between different areas of the brain.

>> **Beta:** *Beta* is a normal wakeful state of consciousness with frequencies between 12 and 30 hertz. The goal with neurofeedback is to try to increase the level of this activity in the brain areas that have too much theta. In many cases, the area in question is the frontal lobes.

>> **Gamma:** *Gamma* is the fastest brain wave state, existing between 32 and 120 hertz. Gamma waves are often associated with conscious perception, working memory, attention, and some forms of meditation.

REMEMBER

The goal with neurofeedback is to train you to be able to change your brain wave patterns at will. This process involves doing learning exercises, which usually means playing specific video games on a computer (as we describe in the following section). By repeatedly achieving the desired balance of different types of brain activity, the brain learns to establish the conditions that support those new states, thus making a different way of functioning more likely. (In other words, your brain learns how to get what it needs.)

Although researchers don't have much direct evidence about the biological changes that take place in neurofeedback, quite a bit of evidence exists that this procedure does change the brain. For example, many people whose ADHD is improved by neurofeedback are able to maintain their improvements over a period of years without further training.

Exploring the neurofeedback process

Neurofeedback usually starts with an intake process that may involve many of the psychological and neuropsychological tests that you went through when you were diagnosed with ADHD. You're also hooked up to an EEG device, usually with 19 electrodes attached to your scalp, to have a baseline evaluation done. (Don't worry; it doesn't hurt.) This evaluation gives the practitioner a clear picture of what your brain activity looks like.

They compare this data to information about what "normal" brain activity looks like in a person your age. From this comparison, the practitioner selects appropriate exercises that can help you correct the areas where your brain functions differently from that of someone without ADHD. These exercises usually involve a computer program that responds to the changes you make to your brain wave patterns. For example, one program uses a Pac-Man–like game where the movement of the figure depends on your producing certain brain waves. Another program uses an airplane that flies based on your brain activity.

By using these programs, you discover how to consciously change your brain activity over time. Like any new activity, it can initially be frustrating. However, within a few sessions most people get the hang of it and can make the object move.

Generally speaking, the neurofeedback process involves between 25 and 50 sessions that last for about 40 minutes. These sessions are often done at least once a week, and assessments along the way determine exactly how many sessions are needed.

Some computer-based programs are available that you can do at home, but they don't account for the way your brain works. In other words, with at-home treatment you don't get a baseline evaluation and have exercises tailored to you. Instead, you do standardized exercises that may or may not help you.

Knowing what to expect from neurofeedback

Neurofeedback is being used for people with a lot of different conditions, including many that often occur along with ADHD, such as depression and anxiety disorders (see Chapter 6). The ADHD symptoms that are often improved by neurofeedback include the following:

>> Impulsivity

>> Hyperactivity

>> Attention

>> Sleep

>> Mood regulation

TIP

A significant additional benefit for people with ADHD is the improved self-esteem that comes from learning how to control your brain activity.

The effects of neurofeedback are generally long term, assuming you go through enough sessions, and there don't appear to be any serious side effects. The side effects that can occur include these:

>> Irritability

>> Trouble getting to sleep

>> Anxiety

>> Fatigue

>> Feeling spacey

These side effects are often short-lived and disappear within a few weeks. Most of the time, negative side effects indicate a transition period, but they can be a sign that the training program needs to be modified.

While neurofeedback shows promise for people with ADHD, well-designed research studies using sham treatment (placebo) have not supported its effectiveness, while other studies have. It is best to say that it can be effective for some people. The biggest drawback is its cost, which is often not covered by insurance, and the time investment required for making up to 50 office visits.

Finding a neurofeedback provider

Generally, neurofeedback practitioners are mental health professionals, such as psychiatrists, psychologists, and counselors. However, you may find other healthcare providers who are qualified to administer neurofeedback. To find a qualified neurofeedback professional, check out one of these organizations:

>> The International Society for Neuronal Regulation (isnr.org)

>> The Association for Applied Psychophysiology & Biofeedback (aapb.org)

You can also ask your primary healthcare provider for a referral or do an Internet search for "Biofeedback professionals."

Using Auditory Brain Stimulation to Ease ADHD Symptoms

Music and sound have been used therapeutically for thousands of years. Music as therapy is arguably based on a psychological response to the music and the result of association (familiar feelings and connections to past events) to change the listener's perception. This means that you choose music that you like and that makes you feel a certain way.

Auditory brain stimulation techniques, on the other hand, rely on a physiological response to the sound. This means that you don't have to like the sound for it to work (and you won't with most of these treatments). Auditory brain stimulation therapies — Rhythmic Entrainment Intervention (REI), Tomatis-based approaches, and binaural beats — stimulate brain activity by using musical sounds, including drumming rhythms, modulated and filtered classical music, and specific tone frequencies.

Auditory brain stimulation therapies rely on two basic concepts:

TECHNICAL STUFF

>> **Brainwave entrainment:** Not to be confused with entertainment, *entrainment* is simply the synchronization of two or more rhythmic cycles. Mathematician Christian Huygens first discovered this phenomenon in the 17th century.

When Huygens was perfecting the design of the pendulum clock, he placed one clock on the wall and started it; he then placed another clock next to it and started that one. He observed that the clocks would start by ticking in their own time and would eventually synchronize and begin to swing in unison: One clock would shift its cycle to match the rhythm of the clock next to it. You can find examples of entrainment throughout nature. (Use "entrainment" as your keyword in your favorite search engine to see what we mean.)

Certain types of sound are able to influence brain wave activity; research has shown that external rhythmic stimulus can entrain the brain. A direct correlation exists between the speed of a rhythmic pulse and the ensuing entrained brain patterns. This process is known as *brainwave entrainment.*

>> **Neurostimulation:** Your brain likes *novel* stimuli, meaning new or unrecognizable things. This point is especially true for people with ADHD. When you hear novel sound patterns, your brain is stimulated in ways that result in improvements in many of the symptoms of ADHD.

As we note in Chapter 2, many people with ADHD have lower activity in one or more parts of their brains than people without ADHD do. To increase the activity level, many treatments use some sort of stimulus. (As we explain in Chapter 8, many medications used for people with ADHD are stimulants.)

The following sections explore REI, Tomatis-based therapies, and binaural beats in more detail.

Rhythmic Entrainment Intervention (REI)

Rhythmic Entrainment Intervention (REI) is a therapy that uses musical rhythm in the form of hand drumming to stimulate the nervous system. Created by coauthor Jeff Strong, REI is based on the concept that your nervous system is rhythmically organized and can be influenced by externally produced auditory rhythms.

TECHNICAL STUFF

While majoring in percussion at LA's Musician's Institute in the 1980s, Jeff found that his ability to focus improved after playing nonrepetitive, syncopated rhythms. He then began experimenting to figure out whether playing the rhythms was necessary or whether just listening to them provided the same results. By 1993, he was convinced listening was sufficient and began clinical research into this approach for people with developmental disabilities, including ADHD.

Since then, research has consistently shown that using auditory rhythm can have a positive impact on people with ADHD. (You can see some of this research at www.stronginstitute.com or brainstimaudio.com.)

REI employs both the brainwave entrainment and neurostimulation aspects of auditory brain stimulation.

Exploring the REI process

REI is a home-based therapy consisting of three basic approaches:

>> **Immediate, *episodic* (temporary) effects:** You can listen to personalized playlists as often as you like and receive an immediate short-term change.

>> **Supporting sensory processing:** You can achieve support for sensory processing designed to be listened to with or without a sensory professional. (Chapter 13 has more on sensory processing and ADHD.)

>> **Custom stimulation for long-term improvements:** The REI Custom Program is a personalized therapy consisting of a comprehensive online questionnaire and custom-made 22- to 26-minute audio sessions that you listen to once a day. This program can last for several weeks or more, depending on your challenges and goals.

REI doesn't require you to use headphones (though you can use them if you want). Just play the music quietly as background stimulus.

REI is pleasant to listen to because it uses hand-drumming rhythms, sometimes in conjunction with mixtures of ambient instrument sounds.

Knowing what to expect from REI

For most people, the first couple of weeks of REI produce improvements in anxiety and sleep. For ADHD symptoms, REI's most significant impacts start occurring after a few weeks of listening. At this point, you may see one or more of the following changes:

>> Improved attention span

>> Less distractibility

>> Less impulsivity

>> Less hyperactivity or restlessness

>> Improved learning abilities

>> Increased ability to regulate mood

>> Improved social abilities

>> Increased language abilities — both expressive and *receptive* (understanding)

As long as you follow the directions for the program (entering feedback to receive new tracks according to your unique schedule), you shouldn't experience any side effects. People who don't follow the program exactly — by playing the music more often than recommended or by skipping feedback — may experience agitation, irritability, or minor sleep problems. You can eliminate these effects by taking a few days off from the music and reaching out for a new music track.

Finding an REI provider

The easiest way to find out more and start the program is to go to either of these websites:

>> **Brain Stim Audio (brainstimaudio.com):** This site contains all forms of REI, including personalized playlists, the sensory processing player, and the REI Custom Program.

>> **Strong Institute (www.stronginstitute.com):** This site contains training programs and the REI Custom Program.

Tomatis-based approaches

Tomatis-based approaches include the Tomatis Method, Auditory Integration Training (AIT), and other "listening" therapies. These sound-based therapies are intended to change the way you hear sound. The Tomatis Method was created in France in the 1950s by Dr. Alfred Tomatis, while AIT was developed by Dr. Guy Berard — also a French physician — based on his work with Dr. Tomatis. AIT became popular in the United States starting in 1992.

Both AIT and the Tomatis Method use specific types of frequency modulated and filtered music to try to correct problems with auditory processing. We cover both techniques in this section even though AIT has become much more popular and has been the subject of more research than the Tomatis Method.

Tomatis-based therapies employ the neurostimulation technique and don't use brainwave entrainment to influence brain activity.

Exploring Tomatis-based processes

Tomatis-based therapies vary depending on whether you choose the Tomatis Method, AIT, or home-based listening therapies. The Tomatis Method and AIT in their pure forms require office visits according to a specific schedule, whereas other Tomatis-based therapies may not, depending on your goals.

>> **Tomatis Method:** The Tomatis Method usually consists of two or three 13-day sessions with four to eight weeks between sessions. Each session begins with an assessment, *audiogram* (hearing testing consisting of a graph of your hearing ability across the frequency spectrum), and consultation lasting between 1½ and 2 hours. Depending on the provider, you can complete the listening sessions at home or in your provider's office.

>> **AIT:** Berard's AIT is a more condensed form of Tomatis's approach and includes twenty 30-minute listening sessions conducted over ten consecutive days (two sessions per day). Depending on your provider, these sessions can be performed in an office or at your home.

>> **Other Tomatis-based approaches:** Other Tomatis-based approaches, including the Listening Program (TLP), Integrated Listening Systems (ILS), and Therapeutic Listening each have their own schedule, though most require daily listening for a period of anywhere from a few weeks to a year or more.

All Tomatis-based approaches require listening with headphones, and some use specialized devices.

The sound of the filtered and modulated music generally isn't pleasant to listen to, and you can't mask the sound and have it still be effective (sorry).

Knowing what to expect from Tomatis-based approaches

AIT, the Tomatis Method and other listening therapies all seem to produce similar results. Although most of the research on these approaches has focused on their impact on autism, people with ADHD often experience one or more of the following improvements:

>> Improved receptive and expressive language

>> Decreased sensitivity to sounds (painfulness or discomfort)

>> Reduction in noise (such as ringing) in the ear

>> Improved ability to talk at a normal volume

>> Less hyperactivity

>> Increased attention span

>> Less distractibility

These results often appear within a few weeks of starting either program. Jeff's observation is that beyond improvements in sound sensitivity and language abilities, the effects are often subtle and vary considerably from person to person. (This range may occur because many practitioners use random frequency modulation instead of tailoring the music to the client.) Generally, the results last for the long term, but we've heard of instances where the results slowly disappear over several months. Reintroduction of the sound therapy often helps gains reappear.

Side effects are usually mild and temporary and can include anxiety, irritability, sleep disturbances, and aggressiveness.

Finding a provider for Tomatis-based approaches

You can find no shortage of Tomatis-based therapy providers. The following have been around long enough to have documented some success with ADHD:

>> **AIT — berardaitwebsite.com:** This website offers information and a list of providers of Berard's AIT.

>> **Integrated Listening System (ILS) — integratedlistening.com:** Part of Unyte Health, ILS programs integrate Tomatis-based music protocols with sensory integration (SI) techniques.

>> **The Listening Program (TLP) — try.advancedbrain.com:** TLP is a home-based program created by Advanced Brain Technologies.

>> **Therapeutic Listening — vitallinks.com/therapeutic-listening:** Created by an occupational therapist, Therapeutic Listening is optimized to be used in conjunction with sensory integration exercises. You can often listen at your practitioner's office or at home.

>> **Tomatis — www.tomatis.com/en:** This site offers comprehensive information on the Tomatis Method, including a list of practitioners.

REMEMBER

Many variations on AIT and the Tomatis Method are being used for people with ADHD. Some practitioners use different types of music, and several different devices can create the frequency modulation effect these approaches rely on. The provider you choose may have their own way of doing things that differs from our description here. Providers also have different levels of effectiveness, so do your homework and choose the best provider for you (which may not be the person closest to you).

Binaural beats

Binaural beats are artificial pulsations your brain creates when you hear one sound frequency in one ear while hearing another frequency in the other ear. The result is a subtle pulsation that equals the difference between the two sound frequencies. For example, a frequency of 400 hertz heard in the left ear and a frequency of 408 hertz in the right ear produces an 8-hertz pulsation. This difference has the ability to entrain the brain to an 8-hertz state — the low end of the alpha state of consciousness.

Heinrich William Dove first discovered this phenomenon in 1841, and Robert Monroe popularized it in the 1970s. This approach has been researched for meditation, relaxation, sleep, and attention.

Because of the regularity of the binaural beat entrainment process, this approach doesn't engage the neurostimulation aspect the other auditory brain stimulation therapies use.

Exploring the process of binaural beats

Because binaural beat approaches are less organized than either REI or Tomatis-based approaches, the ways they're used for ADHD depend on where you listen and the provider you choose, if you use one. Binaural beats are designed to be used for immediate, episodic effects. Listening as you need results, knowing that they'll last only for the time you're listening, is the most common way to use binaural beats. Generally, you choose a delivery source and play the beats for 20 to 30 minutes at a time.

Binaural beats require using headphones and being able to hear in both ears because each ear needs to hear its unique frequency clearly. You can find some variations on binaural beats using what are called isochronic tones/beats that some people believe don't require headphones.

Binaural beats aren't pleasant to listen to by themselves; therefore, many creators add nature sounds, such ocean waves or rain showers, to mask the beats' frequencies.

Knowing what to expect from binaural beats

The results you can expect from binaural beats can vary. Many areas this approach is useful for, such as sleep and anxiety, aren't part of typical ADHD symptoms. The most common ADHD areas binaural beats are known to help include

» Increased attention span

» Improved memory

Because binaural beats influence your brain through brainwave entrainment and don't include any level of neurological stimulation, your results will be episodic, requiring you to listen each time you want their effects. Like with the other auditory brain stimulation techniques, side effects are generally mild and temporary and can include sleep disturbances, anxiety, and agitation.

Finding a binaural beats provider

If you do an Internet search, you can find a mind-boggling number of binaural beat options, including dedicated websites, YouTube channels, and streaming playlists on sites like Spotify. They're widespread largely because creating binaural beats is easy if you have audio recording software. The downside to this cornucopia is that many people create binaural beat tracks that aren't well grounded in the latest research (or any research at all).

With so many options coming and going over time, finding the best ones can be hard. We suggest trying some options to see what works for you. We also caution you to avoid producers who promise binaural beats as a cure-all or who promote binaural beats as an alternative to recreational drugs.

Using Electrical Brain Stimulation to Dim Your ADHD Symptoms

Transcranial electrical brain stimulation (tEBS) techniques use a mild electrical signal — 1 to 2 milliamps — delivered to the brain through electrodes attached to your scalp (that's what makes them *transcranial*).

Electrical brain stimulation comes in a few varieties, but these three are the most common:

>> **Transcranial direct current stimulation (tDCS):** tDCS delivers a constant electrical current to either excite or suppress brain activity. This approach is generally focused on a particular region in the front of the brain (the left and right dorsolateral prefrontal cortex, or DLPFC).

>> **Transcranial alternating current stimulation (tACS):** tACS consists of an alternating current to stimulate the brain. Like with tDCS, the DLPFC area is generally the focus of this stimulation for people with ADHD.

>> **Transcranial random noise stimulation (tRNS):** tRNS delivers an alternating current at variable frequencies to stimulate brain activity. Because of the variable nature of the stimulation, tRNS produces a similar effect to the auditory neurostimulation techniques we described in the earlier section "Using Auditory Brain Stimulation to Ease ADHD Symptoms."

tDCS, tACS, and tRNS are generally available in office visits with a trained professional. You may find some tDCS devices for home use, but their effects on ADHD are unknown as of this writing because these items are mostly used for general wellness and depression.

Tracing electrical brain stimulation to its start

The use of electrical current to stimulate the brain goes back centuries. In the late 1700s, Luigi Galvani and Alessandro Volta began using low-level electrical current for brain stimulation. In 1801, Galvani's nephew, Giovanni Aldini, successfully treated a patient with depression (then known as "melancholy") by using a mild electrical current. Britain recently approved this approach for depression; however, in the U.S. the FDA approved this approach as safe in 2019 without giving it the nod for any particular condition.

tEBS has been explored for use for a variety of other conditions, including ADHD, though the FDA hasn't approved it as of this writing. Regardless of its lack of official approval, you can find quite a few research papers and professionals who find good results with tEBS in people with ADHD.

Keeping current on electrical brain stimulation processes

The process for electrical brain stimulation varies depending on whether you use tDCS, tACS, tRNS, or another form and whether you see a professional or use a home device.

Generally speaking, the therapy process includes daily 20-to-30-minute sessions three to five times per week for between four and eight weeks, depending on your needs and the professional you see.

Knowing what to expect from electrical brain stimulation

According to studies, tDCS, tACS, and tRNS seem to produce similar results, though some more-recent research suggests tRNS may produce better overall improvement than the others because of the variability of the stimulation. Studies with people with ADHD show one or more of the following improvements:

» Increased attention

» Less impulsivity

» Improved cognitive flexibility

» Improved memory

These results often appear within a few weeks of starting one of the programs. As of the time of this writing, provider-administered treatments in office or at home tend to offer better, longer-term results than devices that you buy and use on your own at home. You can expect this discrepancy to change as these therapies mature.

Side effects tend to be mild and include headaches, scalp discomfort, minor scalp burns, and an itching or tingling sensation on the head.

REMEMBER

Some studies have suggested that combining tEBS, particularly tRNS, with cognitive–behavioral therapy (CBT) provides better, longer lasting results than when using either alone. (You can read more about CBT in Chapters 9 and 10.) This connection makes sense to us because combining biological, psychological, and social approaches works best for ADHD.

Finding a transcranial electrical brain stimulation provider

You can locate transcranial electrical brain stimulation therapists by doing an Internet search for the stimulation type you're interested in. For example, depending on where you live, doing a search for "tRNS in my area" will likely bring up a variety of professionals. We suggest looking for reviews of these professionals and calling some to get a feel for how comfortable you feel with them and their approach. Also, don't be afraid to ask to talk to some of their recent clients for insight to help you decide if a certain therapist may be a good fit for you.

Your research will get results with other types of brain stimulation not listed in this chapter. You'll also likely find some inexpensive devices available for home use. While inexpensive in-home devices may be tempting, the results you can expect from them is generally less than visits to a professional because a professional can tailor the stimulation to your needs.

REMEMBER

As we write this, the broad category of transcranial electrical brain stimulation is in its infancy, and a lot of companies are coming and going. Finding the best ones can be hard, so we suggest reading reviews and doing your own research into the effectiveness of the options that appeal to you.

Making Sense of Magnetic Brain Stimulation

Transcranial magnetic stimulation (TMS) delivers a mild electromagnetic signal through the skull by using a magnetic coil to stimulate the brain. This approach is different from electrical brain stimulation (tEBS, which we cover in the earlier section "Using Electrical Brain Stimulation to Dim Your ADHD Symptoms") in that the magnets used can be more focused to a specific brain region and can reach deeper into the brain.

Repetitive transcranial brain stimulation (rTMS) is a variation on the basic TMS but adds a repetitive magnetic pulse rather than a single one. Both approaches are used for people with ADHD and may be called by the general TMS name, depending on the provider.

TMS is implemented in a clinical setting and not available for use at home.

Getting some background on transcranial magnetic stimulation

Dr. Anthony Barker created TMS in 1985. The FDA approved it in 2008 for use in treatment-resistant depression and in 2018 for treating obsessive-compulsive disorder (OCD). TMS is also often used for ADHD, anxiety, and post-traumatic stress disorder (PTSD), though it isn't FDA-approved for these purposes.

TECHNICAL STUFF

TMS draws from decades of the use and understanding of the limitations of electroconvulsive therapy (ECT). ECT uses electrical shocks to induce a seizure, "resetting" the brain and stimulating the release of the neurotransmitter serotonin. TMS improves on ECT by targeting specific areas of the brain and using a mild pulse.

Exploring the transcranial magnetic stimulation process

TMS begins with a brain-mapping session to find the area of the brain to stimulate. The practitioner sends magnetic pulses across your head to find the *primary motor cortex*, a part of your brain associated with muscle contraction, among other things. The pulses cause tingling in the scalp and twitching in the right hand when they find this location.

The therapy process includes daily 30-to-60-minute sessions for between one and ten weeks, depending on your therapist and unique needs (though four to six weeks is typical). A newer version of TMS, referred to as *theta-burst-stimulation* (TBS), has a shorter treatment duration, lasting only five days for most patients.

Knowing what to expect when using TMS

Although most of the research on TMS has focused on depression, OCD, PTSD, and anxiety, people with ADHD seem to experience improvements in one or more of the following areas:

>> Improved attention

>> Decreased hyperactivity

>> Reduction in impulsivity

>> Improved symptoms of *co-occurring* (coexisting) conditions such as depression, PTSD, anxiety, and OCD.

Side effects tend to be mild, but may include dizziness, headaches, scalp discomfort, and a tingling sensation in or twitching of the facial muscles.

Finding a transcranial magnetic stimulation provider

Given that TMS requires office visits, you need to find a practitioner in your area or a place you're willing to travel to. The good news is that North America has no shortage of TMS providers. An Internet search for "TMS provider near me" will likely produce quite a few results. Because the number of sessions, and therefore cost, can vary depending on the provider, we suggest interviewing the ones you are drawn to so you can better determine how they would work with you. Also, ask for referrals of their recent clients with similar issues to yours.

IN THIS CHAPTER

» **Exploring acupuncture**

» **Discovering homeopathy**

» **Looking into manipulation therapies**

» **Examining sensory integration treatments**

» **Viewing vision therapy**

Chapter **13**

Getting a Handle on Rebalancing Therapies

As we explain in Chapter 12, many ADHD treatment options exist beyond the established approaches of medication and behavior management. The treatments we discuss in this chapter all have a similar goal: to help you create balance in your body. Some, such as sensory integration, focus on the nervous system itself; others, such as acupuncture, work on trying to create overall balance.

The treatments we present in this chapter aren't the first line of defense against the symptoms of ADHD; most haven't been adequately studied for their effectiveness for ADHD. We include this chapter for two reasons. First, you'll probably hear about one or more of these treatment approaches while trying to find the best way to get your symptoms under control. Second, one of these techniques may make sense as part of your *multimodal* treatment strategy — an approach that covers the biological, psychological, and sociological aspects of ADHD (see Chapter 7).

REMEMBER

Because the therapies in this chapter are considered alternative therapies and their use for ADHD is often not part their focus, they may or may not be covered by insurance. We recommend asking your provider whether they accept insurance and contacting your insurance company to see if the therapy is covered and if your provider is part of their network. Even if the therapy may be covered, keep in mind that it will probably include a copay.

Balancing Energy through Acupuncture

Acupuncture is an ancient Chinese system (several thousand years old) of balancing the flow of subtle energies through the body. It has been studied quite extensively and grown in popularity in the Western world since the 1970s. In fact, according to the Food and Drug Administration, people in the United States make 10 million office visits for acupuncture annually. Overall, acupuncture supports general health, but some people use it to reduce some of the symptoms of ADHD, as well as many of the *co-occurring* (coexisting) conditions such as anxiety and depression.

REMEMBER

If you've seen the word *acupuncture* and immediately gotten nervous (because needles!), we assure you that these needles don't hurt if they're placed properly. They're very small, and they go only a little way into your skin. Most people report only a mild prick when the needles are inserted. When the needles are in, most people don't notice them.

Understanding the practice of acupuncture

Acupuncture is part of the traditional Chinese medicine (TCM) system, along with herbs, meditation, and a host of other techniques. Acupuncture (and the rest of TCM) is based on the concept that all parts of the body and mind are interconnected — every part influences the function of every other part.

The belief is that a vital energy called *qi* (pronounced, and often spelled, *chi* in the West) connects the various parts of your mind and body. This qi flows through the body, and any disruptions in this flow affect your health, resulting in illness. The goal of acupuncture is to keep this flow going smoothly, which keeps you healthy. If you're already sick, acupuncture frees the blockages that are causing your illness.

The qi flows through channels called *meridians*, which connect your internal organs with the surface. TCM identifies 12 primary meridians relating to each of your organ systems and 8 secondary meridians, for a total of 20 meridians. Acupuncture involves placing needles on certain localized points in the skin to direct the flow of qi through each of these meridians.

Many theories on how this system works are available, but two stand out:

>> The meridians lie along main nerve centers in the body, and each acupuncture point stimulates the nervous system in a specific way.

>> The acupuncture points, when stimulated, stimulate the body to produce certain endorphins.

Regardless of the mechanism involved in acupuncture, its longevity alone suggests that it must help some people.

Exploring the acupuncture process

As many as 2,000 acupuncture points exist, and an acupuncturist must figure out which point(s) to stimulate to offer you any benefit. Doing so involves a diagnostic process that usually includes the following:

>> **Questions to determine your symptoms and history:** These questions may involve asking you about your tolerance to heat or cold, your eating habits, and your sleep patterns. Your answers provide a big-picture view of you and your condition.

>> **Examination of your tongue:** According to TCM, a patient's tongue holds a lot of information, so your acupuncturist will likely want to take a look.

>> **A check of your pulse:** Again, according to TCM, your pulse tells your provider a lot about your state of health. Unlike in Western medicine, an acupuncturist is interested in more than just the speed of your pulse; they look for its strength and rhythm as well.

When the intake exam is complete, you lie down while your provider puts needles in different parts of your body. As we note earlier in the chapter, most people don't even notice the needles after insertion. (However, your coauthor Jeff often feels a very slight tingling sensation.)

REMEMBER

If you feel any significant amount of pain from the needles, they aren't put in properly, and you may want to look around for a different acupuncturist. The most you should feel is a slight pricking sensation when the needle is inserted.

After the needles are in, you remain relatively still for up to 30 minutes, at which point the acupuncturist removes the needles and you're free to go.

Knowing what results to expect from acupuncture

Your results from acupuncture are going to depend on your condition. Even though you have ADHD, your acupuncturist may focus on other areas. Remember that the goal of acupuncture is to correct any disruptions in the flow of energy (or qi) in your body, so you should receive a very individualized treatment.

Generally speaking, you need several sessions before you can expect to see any significant changes in your symptoms. Side effects, if any, are minimal. Most often, your acupuncturist is able to give you a clear idea after your initial examination as to the number of sessions you need (and their cost) and whether you'll need to return later for tune-ups.

Finding an acupuncture provider

Many acupuncturists are in practice these days, but finding one who has experience working with people with ADHD may be hard. As with any healthcare professional, your best bet is to get a referral from a family member, a friend, or another healthcare provider. If you can't find any referrals, start with your local phone book (either in hard copy or at www.yellowpages.com) or an Internet search for "acupuncture" or "traditional Chinese medicine." You can also check the bulletin board of your local natural foods market.

Helping Your Body Heal Itself with Homeopathy

Homeopathy is intended to help your body heal itself using the concept that like cures like. Homeopathic remedies, which are designed to stimulate your body to eliminate your symptoms, are being used more and more for people with ADHD. Homeopathy has been around for a couple of hundred years and has gone through several periods of popularity, including now.

Understanding the practice of homeopathy

Developed by Samuel Hahnemann in the late 18th century, homeopathy is based on the *law of similars:* Like heals like. In other words, homeopaths use very diluted doses (we're talking *minute* traces here) of substances that cause the exact symptoms you have. For example, a homeopathic remedy for a sleep disturbance may have a minute trace of caffeine in it to help you get to sleep.

REMEMBER

Homeopathic remedies are made from substances that, if taken in their undiluted form, are toxic. The key to homeopathics is in the preparation and dilution. The process of creating the remedy usually involves mixing alcohol and water with the active substance and diluting the solution substantially. According to Hahnemann, the more diluted the solution, the stronger the effects.

Exploring the process of homeopathy

Effective homeopathy relies on your homeopath's getting a complete picture of your symptoms. Doing so involves a pretty extensive process of asking you about your symptoms, history, and lifestyle. Your provider then consults the homeopathic *materia medica* (the list of more than 3,000 remedies that have been tested) for the best remedy for you.

Your provider prescribes a certain remedy, or group of remedies. These medicines generally come in the form of small pills that you dissolve under your tongue; your homeopath asks you to take them according to a strict schedule (usually something like four pills twice a day) for a certain amount of time. You shouldn't eat or drink anything within about 20 minutes of taking the pills.

In most cases, you have occasional follow-up appointments to see how the remedy is working for you, and your provider gives you different remedies if needed.

Knowing what results to expect from homeopathy

REMEMBER

The effectiveness of homeopathy for the symptoms of ADHD depends on which remedy you use. Determining the best remedy for an individual takes skill and practice, so your choice of provider has a huge impact on whether you end up seeing any significant benefits. We cover locating a homeopath in the following section.

Both of us have seen homeopathy work well for people with ADHD, but you should expect it to take some time to work — as much as several months. The good news is that side effects are often nonexistent. Some practitioners believe in a concept called *aggravations,* where your symptoms get a little worse before beginning to improve; other practitioners don't see this happening.

The cost of homeopathics is very low, but if you take a remedy for months at a time, the cost obviously adds up. How long you end up taking a remedy and how long the results last depend on many factors, including the severity of your symptoms and the appropriateness of the remedies taken.

Finding a homeopathy provider

The best way to look for a local homeopath is the same way that you find any professional: Ask for referrals from people you trust. If you don't succeed at getting a referral, check your phone book (or online equivalent) or do an Internet search for "ADHD homeopathy".

Using Manipulation Therapies

Manipulation therapies — chiropractic, osteopathy, and CranioSacral Therapy — are concerned with the flow of *cerebrospinal fluid* (fluid of the brain and spinal cord) and the alignment of the spine. Manipulation therapies are used to assist those with ADHD because some people believe that a disruption in the flow of the cerebrospinal fluid — caused by misalignment of the bone or soft tissues in the body — can affect nervous system function and may result in symptoms similar to ADHD in some people.

Understanding the practice of manipulation therapy

The idea that manipulation of the body can help improve health goes back a long way. According to the American Chiropractic Association, people were writing about spinal manipulation almost 5,000 years ago in China. Ancient Greeks also used spinal manipulation. In fact, the Greek physician Hippocrates wrote extensively about the benefits of adjusting the spine, saying in one instance, "Get knowledge of the spine, for this is the requisite for many diseases."

Following is a bit of background about each manipulation therapy:

>> **Chiropractic care:** *Chiropractic* focuses on the alignment of the bones, but most chiropractors are also well versed in preventive care, such as nutrition. Many are also trained in CranioSacral Therapy (which we discuss later in this list). You can also find chiropractic neurologists who regularly work with people with ADHD.

>> **Osteopathy:** This field of medicine is also concerned with the alignment of the bones but goes a few steps further than chiropractic. Developed by Dr. Andrew Taylor Still in 1874, *osteopathic medicine* was the first Western form of healthcare to use the concept of *wellness* (preventive care). Still actually drew from Hippocrates's ideas on the spine when he developed the practice. Osteopathic physicians often act as primary care physicians and are trained in *osteopathic manipulative treatment* (OMT), which focuses on your skeletal system and its relationship to your health.

>> **CranioSacral Therapy (CST):** Osteopathic physician John E. Upledger, of the Upledger Institute (www.upledger.com), developed this therapy based on research he conducted starting in 1975, but another osteopath, William Sutherland, did the original work on *cranial rhythms* (the specific flow of the cerebrospinal fluid) about a century before. CST uses very gentle pressure on the scalp to evaluate and improve the functioning of the *craniosacral system,* which consists of the membranes and fluid that protect the spinal cord and brain.

The main idea behind these manipulation therapies is that neurological problems can develop due to misalignment of the bones in your body, and realigning them can improve neurological function. Chiropractic focuses mainly on the spine, osteopathy covers the entire skeletal system, and CranioSacral Therapy concerns itself with the cranial rhythm by adjusting the bones under your scalp. People generally only do one form of manipulation therapy at a time, and it's recommended you not do them within 6 to 8 weeks of back surgery.

Exploring the manipulation therapy process

Each of the manipulation therapies begins with an intake process that evaluates the alignments of the particular area. For chiropractors, the exam focuses on the spine; the osteopathic physician evaluates the skeletal system; and craniosacral therapists look at the cranial rhythm. Most of these professionals also ask a lot of questions regarding your overall health as well as your ADHD symptoms.

When the evaluation is done, you get an adjustment. This process usually isn't painful, and most people find it quite relaxing. (But, in fairness, your coauthor Jeff has always had uncomfortable chiropractic sessions in the past for reasons unknown, so not everyone finds chiropractic adjustments relaxing.) After your adjustment, your professional will likely offer suggestions of things you can do at home to help the process, such as supplements or exercises.

The number of sessions required depends on your health and your professional. In some instances, one session is enough to make a dramatic change. For other people, three sessions a week for several weeks or even months may be required. After your evaluation and first adjustment, your professional should be able to give you a reasonable idea of how many sessions you may need.

Knowing what results to expect from manipulation therapy

Many people describe a feeling of calm after receiving an adjustment. For conditions such as back pain, the effects of the manipulations can be significant and immediate. However, for the symptoms of ADHD you may not see much improvement right away, and the results you do end up seeing may be subtle.

Finding a provider for manipulation therapy

A referral is best if you can get one. If not, do a phone book or web search, or take a look at the websites for these organizations:

>> **The American Chiropractic Association** (https://handsdownbetter.org/find-a-doctor): The ACA is the largest chiropractic organization in the world and through this site offers a listing of chiropractors. (You can find a lot of information about chiropractic in general at the ACA's main site, www.acatoday.org.).

>> **The American Osteopathic Association** (https://findado.osteopathic.org): The AOA is a professional association for osteopaths, and you can use this page to search for an osteopath near you. (The AOA's general website, https://osteopathic.org, has a ton of great general information as well.)

Assisting Your Brain with Processing Sensory Information

The term *sensory integration* refers to the way your brain can process and organize all the sensory information your body receives. Many people with developmental disabilities and learning problems have difficulties with sensory integration, and many (but not all) people with ADHD have some sort of sensory processing dysfunction. Sensory integration therapy is designed to help these people better process and organize (neurologically) what their senses pick up.

Understanding the practice of sensory integration

Occupational therapist A. Jean Ayres, PhD, OTR, developed sensory integration therapy in the 1950s. Dr. Ayres studied the effects that sensory processing and *motor planning* (a process that helps you remember and execute movements for doing tasks) have on learning and behavior. Her research suggested a link, and she spent many years developing ways to improve sensory processing. Since its inception, sensory integration therapy has become a common part of occupational therapists' treatment approaches, with almost 10,000 occupational therapists in the United States making it part of their everyday work.

A breakdown in your ability to process sensory input can result in the following symptoms:

>> Hypersensitivity to touch, movements, sights, or sounds

>> Little or no response to sensory input

>> Unusually high or low overall activity level

>> Problems with coordination

>> Developmental delays

>> Poor motor planning, which can include problems with *fine* (hand and wrist) or *gross* (whole body movement) motor skills

>> Behavioral problems

>> Learning difficulties

>> Not knowing where your body is in space

The purpose of sensory integration therapy is to help your brain make sense of all the sensory information you receive so you can respond better. Improving your ability to handle sensory stimuli reduces many of the symptoms we list here.

Exploring the process of sensory integration

REMEMBER

Just because you have ADHD doesn't mean you have a sensory integration dysfunction; however, sensory integration issues are often a co-occurring condition for people with ADHD.

Your first step is to find out whether processing sensory information is a problem for you. This process usually involves certain standardized tests that evaluate your coordination, posture, balance, and response to stimuli, among other things.

If the occupational therapist determines you have a sensory processing dysfunction, they suggest some exercises and other sensory stimulation techniques to try to improve your ability to process the sensory information that seems to be getting mixed up in your brain.

The exercises look like play and often involve balls, swings, trampolines, and other items that involve sensory stimulation. Because most children with sensory processing dysfunction tend to seek out activities that stimulate them in the way that they need, many occupational therapists let children help choose what exercises to do. This approach lets them have some degree of control over the treatment and makes the process more dynamic for the therapist.

Occupational therapists usually give you exercises to do at home in addition to the exercises and activities you perform with them. Occupational therapy sessions usually occur at least once a week and can continue for several months.

TIP

Some schools have an occupational therapist on staff who can work a sensory integration therapy program into your child's school week. To access these services, you need to receive an official diagnosis of a sensory processing dysfunction from your child's school. You then have to go through the process for determining services under the special education laws, which we talk about in Chapter 16.

Knowing what results to expect from sensory integration

As with the other therapies we discuss in this chapter, results of sensory integration therapy vary from person to person. Generally, you can expect to see some minor improvements within the first few sessions, with greater changes developing over time. Your occupational therapist will tailor your treatment according to the changes taking place and can give you a good idea of the type of progress to expect.

Finding a provider for sensory integration

Your best bet in finding a provider for sensory integration therapy is to look for an occupational therapist (OT) who specializes in this area near where you live. Your other healthcare providers may have a referral for you, but if they don't, you can check with the American Occupational Therapy Association (www.aota.org). This organization can give you a list of licensed OTs in your area who do sensory integration therapy.

Looking Into Vision Therapies

Vision therapy is basically exercise for your eyes. This approach uses training exercises, vision aids, and stimulation techniques to help you process visual stimuli better. Several approaches to vision therapy exist. The two most common are behavioral optometry and the Irlen Method (which addresses what's called scotopic sensitivity syndrome).

Understanding the practice of vision therapy

Vision therapies are regularly used for people with learning problems. The theory behind these techniques is that even though you may see clearly, you may not be able to process visual stimuli properly. Proponents of this type of therapy believe that some people with ADHD have perception problems, which may include the following:

>> **Not being able to get both eyes to focus on the same thing:** This issue is called *convergence insufficiency*. A 2005 study by Dr. David Granet at the University of California San Diego School of Medicine suggests that people with this vision problem are three times as likely to have ADHD as people without convergence insufficiency.

>> **Not being able to track effectively:** This problem often manifests as not being able to follow the words on a page when you read.

>> **Not being able to maintain focus on an object in space:** Focus may come in and out.

>> **Seeing objects moving on the page, or having your eyes fatigue easily:** These effects stem from the focus issue in the preceding bullet and are symptoms of scotopic sensitivity syndrome (SSS).

A 2016 study suggested that these problems make paying attention or completing work on time difficult for people and seem to contribute to symptoms that are common in ADHD, such as inattention, carelessness, disruptive behavior, and distractibility.

Vision therapies often employ techniques such as the following:

>> **Special lenses to compensate:** Many times, certain types of lenses are used to help either reduce the stress on your eyes or correct your vision imbalance. For example, to mitigate the effects of scotopic sensitivity syndrome, the Irlen Method uses specially colored lenses that you can wear either all the time or only when you read. (Some people forgo the lenses and simply use colored plastic sheets placed over their reading material to help them see the printed page better.)

>> **Computer programs:** Some behavioral optometrists use computer-based vision exercises to help improve the areas that cause vision processing problems. These programs are like computer games that require specific visual processing tasks to help you strengthen your ability to process visual stimuli.

>> **Vision exercises:** Behavioral optometrists often have you perform specific eye exercises to help you compensate for the areas that they determine aren't functioning properly.

REMEMBER

Most of these techniques are designed to address specific vision problems, which may or may not contribute to your ADHD symptoms. Regardless, any visual stimulation is going to influence your brain. We believe that this stimulation is precisely the reason some of these techniques may work for people with ADHD.

Exploring the vision therapy process

Both behavioral optometry and the Irlen Method start with an evaluation. In the case of behavioral optometry, this evaluation (called a *developmental vision evaluation*) includes a series of tests to determine your aptitude with specific areas of visual skills. From these tests, the behavioral optometrist sees the areas where your vision may not function as well as it should. They then assign exercises to help you develop these areas. A behavioral optometrist may also recommend certain types of visual stimulation to help your visual processing deficits. These can be in the form of office visits, take-home exercises, or devices that you purchase (such as computer software programs) that you can then use in your home.

For the Irlen Method, the evaluation consists of determining whether you have scotopic sensitivity syndrome and to what degree. This process also involves finding the specific colors or combinations of colors that you can use to alleviate the symptoms. You often choose between using colored lenses or contacts and using colored overlays when you read.

Knowing what results to expect from vision therapy

The results of behavioral optometry and the Irlen Method really depend on which perception problem you have — for example, not being able to get both eyes to focus on the same thing or not being able to track effectively. ADHD-specific improvements from these approaches have been seen in the following areas:

>> Increased attention

>> Improved reading abilities

>> Reduced hyperactivity

REMEMBER

The side effects are minimal, if any, but keep in mind that the results of these approaches are wholly dependent on whether a vision problem is contributing to your ADHD. If you don't have a vision problem, you obviously can't expect to see any changes in your ADHD symptoms when doing one of these therapies.

Finding a vision therapy provider

Providers of vision therapies include behavioral optometrists and sometimes psychologists and other therapists working with people with learning disabilities and ADHD (see Chapter 4).

Many behavioral optometrists are in practice around the country; check your local phone book online under "Optometrist." To locate a behavioral optometrist who specifically works with people with ADHD, check out the website for the Optometrists Network at www.optometrists.org.

To find a provider who specializes in the Irlen Method to deal with scotopic sensitivity syndrome (or to find out more about SSS), check out irlen.com.

4

Living with ADHD

Find your strengths and accentuate them.

Make life at home as low-stress and rewarding as possible.

Know your legal rights at school. Handle Individual Education Plan meetings and work with teachers. Ensure your child does their homework.

Take on the demands of work and determine the type of work that best suits your style.

Chapter **14**

Accentuating the Positive

hen you have ADHD, you receive many negative messages (even in some of the pages of this book). You can easily develop a poor — and limited — view of yourself and your potential. This chapter can help balance your perspective so you can avoid being tarred with negativity.

Although not everyone agrees on whether ADHD has positive aspects, we feel that many advantages exist along with all the difficulties that come with ADHD. For example, many people with ADHD have boundless energy and deep stores of creativity. Some fearlessly follow risky ideas with faith and conviction (which can occasionally backfire but also can often lead to great achievements).

In this chapter, we illustrate the gold you can mine from the neurodiverse brain. We explore many of the areas in which people with ADHD perform as well as — if not better than — people who don't have ADHD. We start by examining the core symptoms of ADHD and how they can positively influence your life. We then discuss the ways these traits can benefit you. Finally, we help you identify the positives in your abilities and determine how to accentuate them in your life.

Seeing the Positive in Your Symptoms

Most of the symptoms that people with ADHD experience can have a positive or useful side as well as a negative or problematic one. For example, consider these primary symptoms and their potential positives:

>> **Hyperactivity:** Many people who are hyperactive have tons of energy that, when harnessed, can help them get a lot done. If an energetic person also has the tendency to hyperfocus, the combination of traits can be a huge advantage in the workplace (although you must beware of becoming a workaholic; see Chapter 17). This energy can also manifest physically in the form of, say, superior athletic abilities. Olympic medal winners Simone Biles, Michele Carter, Shaun White, Nicola Adams, and Michael Phelps have all acknowledged receiving ADHD diagnoses in their childhoods.

>> **Impulsivity:** Impulsivity can be a problem when it results in doing something dangerous to yourself or other people. But when used effectively, this trait can be an asset. For example, what makes someone a successful entrepreneur? Often entrepreneurs are impulsive, which allows them to take chances on ideas that seem outrageous to everyone else. They leap at opportunities while others are still thinking about them.

Impulsivity has also been linked to creativity — specifically to the ability to make connections and pull ideas "out of a hat." (We explore creativity in the following section.) Comedian Trevor Noah, filmmaker Daniel Kwan, and cofounder of Microsoft Bill Gates have all acknowledged having ADHD. Famous actors including Whoopi Goldberg, Emma Watson, and Audra McDonald have used their ADHD to their advantage.

>> **Distractibility:** The positive side of distractibility is the ability to be aware of even the subtlest activity going on around you. For example, you may hear sounds that other people don't hear or notice things that other people don't notice. Tuning into the environment in this way can be useful for certain types of jobs, such as firefighting, working in an emergency room, or running a daycare center. Some experts believe that distractibility contributes to creativity and intuition (which we cover in the following section).

>> **Inattention:** Even though we talk about people having an attention *deficit*, most people with ADHD don't have a deficit as much as they have a problem regulating their attention (see Chapter 2). One advantage of this trait is that you generally don't pay attention to things that aren't worth the effort. Many people with ADHD can focus their attention when something interesting is going on. In fact, they focus so well at these times that everything else around them ceases to exist in their minds. (Just try to get the attention of a kid playing a video game!) This intense focus can be a major advantage when you're problem-solving or working on arduous (but interesting) tasks. The inattentive dreamer can also be a visionary.

Examining Areas of Aptitude

As the preceding section illustrates, the symptoms of ADHD can have a positive side for many people. The way the brain works in people with ADHD can produce some beneficial abilities. Obviously, these abilities vary from person to person, but we cover some of the most prevalent in the following sections.

Capitalizing on creativity

Creativity is a common characteristic of people with ADHD. The aspects of ADHD that may contribute to creativity include the following:

>> **Lots of thoughts coming and going:** Many people with ADHD have very busy minds. Thoughts are constantly springing up, and some of them are bound to result in great ideas.

ADHD: ADVANTAGE, DISADVANTAGE, OR BOTH?

A growing number of people — including health professionals — want to dismiss the troubling symptoms of ADHD and paint the disorder as a gift for the person who has it. These people look at the symptoms and traits of ADHD with respect, and they view people with ADHD as simply being different. The "ADHD-as-gift" group focuses on the things people with ADHD can do well, and it puts less — if any — attention on the struggles these people have. When these people do consider the struggles of ADHD, they often view them within the context of society and place responsibility not on the individual but on the situation they're in.

On the other end of the spectrum, some professionals believe that ADHD is a serious mental disorder with no positive traits. They have difficulty seeing anything but the negative behaviors and the challenges the ADHD person experiences. This viewpoint is based on the belief that the person with ADHD doesn't fit the mold, and fitting the mold is crucial. These people often see all the struggles a person with ADHD goes through and realize how hard they try to fit in.

Most people fall somewhere between these two extremes; they see ADHD as both a liability and a blessing. They recognize that the struggles are real, but so are the positives. Perhaps with ADHD, the need to work outside the box causes a greater dependency on creativity. If you break your dominant hand, you quickly become better at using your other hand; it's not a gift or a blessing but a compensating strategy. Likewise, many people with ADHD develop their strengths to compensate for their areas of weakness.

>> **Uninhibited ideas:** One great gift that highly creative people have is the ability to examine any idea, no matter how absurd. Many creative motivators and teachers focus on this ability to let ideas flow without judgment because they know that doing so is key to coming up with new ideas and solutions to tough problems. Many people with ADHD don't need coaching because this skill comes naturally.

>> **Making connections:** When ideas are flowing freely, seeing connections that other people may miss (or dismiss) is easier. This skill is related to the ADHD symptom of distractibility. When a person doesn't keep focusing on a logical train of thought, they can piece seemingly disparate ideas together.

Capturing chaos

Many people with ADHD can tolerate — and even thrive in the midst of — chaos. For some people, chaos exists in their minds in the form of scattered or constant thoughts. For others, it exists in every aspect of life.

REMEMBER

We talk a lot about organization in this book (see Chapters 15 through 18), but for some people a clean, organized environment is actually counterproductive. For example, consider how your coauthor Jeff writes books such as this one: When he's in the middle of a project, his desk is piled high with books and papers. These are his thoughts and ideas. If he cleans this clutter, he also seems to wipe his mind clear of his thoughts. (Out of sight, out of mind.)

This situation isn't good for him because without these ideas, he can't complete his work. The clutter may look bad, but he knows where everything is (well, almost). He makes it a habit not to clear his desk until all the ideas on it are either included in or discarded from his project. Clearing his desk before that is like tossing his ideas out before he has a chance to explore them. For Jeff, having this information at his fingertips helps him make connections and find creative solutions that he's unable to without this chaos surrounding him.

TIP

If your clutter helps you think, don't be so quick to get rid of it. But be honest with yourself: Don't pretend the clutter is helpful when you're just not able to clean it up.

Being able to tolerate and even thrive in chaos is a talent that may allow a person with ADHD to work in a situation where other people can't function at all, such as a nurse in an emergency department, a restaurant manager, or a disaster relief worker.

Accessing energy

High-energy people — if they use their energy wisely — often get a lot done. Many people with ADHD have difficulty directing their energy, but with practice, many find that they can channel it into satisfying, productive activities. Carol has always had abundant energy, and friends would often comment that she got more done before 9 a.m. than most people did in a day.

To use your energy wisely, you need to find something you're passionate about doing. Your activity of choice may be anything from running marathons (that'll wear you out!) to running your own business.

Recognizing your risk-taking nature

Risk-taking is a common trait of people with ADHD and can be a tremendous asset if you harness it. In fact, risk-taking has fueled innovation throughout history. By being able to throw caution to the wind and try an idea without hesitating — or at least without stopping yourself completely — you're able to accomplish things that other people are afraid to try. It can help you start a business, tackle tough projects, or scale a mountain — both literally and figuratively.

WARNING

Unfortunately, this risk-taking nature of some people with ADHD is a problem. It can cause injury; financial difficulties; and problems at home, school, or work or with the law. Someone who's impulsive has difficulty handling a mundane existence. If you have this trait, you must identify positive ways to channel your need for risk and stimulation. If you can't find a healthy way to express this desire, you'll likely find an unhealthy way to do it. The best thing you can do is to seek out a lifestyle that supports this need, whether that means you're a river guide, a firefighter, or an entrepreneur.

REMEMBER

The risks you take don't need to be physical; they can be mental or emotional. So before you go climb Mount Everest to get your thrills, maybe consider a less dangerous option. (Of course, if you really need to climb the mountain, go for it.) And remember that just because a risk isn't physical doesn't mean it can't be dangerous.

Supporting your desire for independence

As we discuss elsewhere in the book (such as in Chapters 15 and 17), many people with ADHD have problems with authority. They don't like being told what to do and often believe that their ideas are the best ones. What better way to honor this tendency than by working independently?

This trait is the reason many people with ADHD look for careers and other activities that give them a large dose of independence. If you have this trait, you do best when you're not tied to a single location (an office cubicle, for example) and you have the freedom to come and go when you want without someone constantly looking over your shoulder. Perhaps your ideal situation is to own your own business, or perhaps being a freelancer or a salesperson is appealing. The challenge is to find a job that allows you the freedom to do your thing but also provides you with the security you need to support yourself and your family.

Being able to stand on your own without the support and approval of "the system" or other people has certain advantages. The world always needs innovators who are breaking new ground and exploring new territories. This area is one where many ADHD people shine.

Exploring ambition

Many people with ADHD are very ambitious. Couple this ambition with the other abilities we discuss in this chapter, and you can end up with a person who has tremendous potential.

Ambition is a topic worth exploring. When you want something, that means you don't yet have it. To cross the gap between where you are and where you think you want to be, you need some kind of propulsion. You need a plan to get around or over any obstacles between you and the thing you want, and you also need a super energy pack.

The problem some people with ADHD have is that getting wrapped up in the goal without a realistic view of what it takes to get there is easy. If you're impulsive, you may look before you leap. If you have unbridled enthusiasm, you may be hoping to accomplish something that isn't even humanly possible.

For some people who have less-than-great social skills, ambition also can cause them to treat other people not so nicely while they chase their goals. If your tendency is not to consider the feelings of other people when you say or do something, you may have to work on managing your behavior to improve your social skills (see Chapter 10). Or you may need to find a goal whose pursuit isn't dependent on working with other people.

TIP

Ambition can be a good thing if you power it with extraordinary enthusiasm and temper it with realistic goals and a solid plan of action. If you have an idea for a breakthrough technology, for example, do your homework and get plenty of reinforcements before you drop everything in pursuit of this golden egg.

On the other hand, some people with ADHD have everything going for them *except* ambition. In this case, what's lacking is motivation, and we strongly encourage you to work on figuring out your personal values — the things that have the greatest importance to you.

Leaning into intuition

Earlier in the chapter we discuss distractible people who observe things that other people don't. Many people with this ability are also able to intuit things about others or their surroundings.

Most people are conscious of only a small percentage of the information available to them in the environment. If you have ADHD, you don't always focus in a linear, logical manner, so you may be more suited than others to pick up on the millions of clues that the unconscious mind uses to perceive the world. That's *intuition.* The ability really stems from not getting caught up in the accepted ways of perceiving things. If you don't have to see a spade as a spade, you may be more likely to see it as a heart with a handle. Ancient wisdom traditions have always valued this way of gathering information, but it has been mostly lost in today's technological world.

With this intuition often comes a deep well of empathy and compassion for other people. That's because you can see through the differences of conventional appearance to understand the basic similarities of everyone's situations. When someone gets to that level, ADHD shows itself to be an unusual gift, indeed. Combine this with the creative capacity, and you have a connection you didn't even imagine could happen (unless you have ADHD and were paying attention).

Examining adaptability

People with ADHD are often highly adaptable. In many cases, in fact, their adapt-ability may have prevented others from detecting their ADHD at a young age. ADHD professional circles recognize a phenomenon called the wall. *The wall* is the point when a person with ADHD can't rely on adaptability alone to get by. For some people, the wall appears during middle or high school, when the social and academic challenges force them to confront their ADHD symptoms. For other people the wall doesn't hit until even later.

The challenge these people face is learning how to transcend this ability. Being clever can cover up a host of insecurities and ineptitude, but when you hit the wall, suddenly you can't cope the way you used to. This shift gives rise to feelings of fear, frustration, confusion, and shame. When you hit the wall, you have only two choices: Give up being who you are, or give up thinking that being clever is the only answer. If you're lucky, you realize that being who you are is the most important thing you can do. There's always someone smarter, stronger, taller, or better looking than you, but there's no one exactly like you — anywhere.

Some people with ADHD don't know how to use their talents. Instead, they get wrapped up in trying to be someone different. If this scenario describes you, we encourage you to seek out the best treatments you can (check out Chapter 7) so your ADHD symptoms don't limit your abilities.

REMEMBER

One of the most widely recognized forms of adaptability is intelligence, but it isn't the only form. Intelligence is a tool, just like physical strength or the ability to carry a tune. Don't let society's value system convince you that intelligence is more important than it is.

Assessing athleticism

Couple high energy with the desire for stimulation, and you have a great mix for someone to get involved in athletics. Many people with ADHD like the way they feel when they're playing sports, so they get involved and spend a lot of time pursuing athletics. Over time, they discover that they've gotten pretty good at them, too.

One of the best things about athletics for people with ADHD is that the exercise can help reduce the impact of the ADHD symptoms (see Chapter 15). Developing skills in sports can also increase self-esteem and a sense of belonging and acceptance.

Research has shown the value of getting outside in nature. If you have access to hiking, biking, or simply walking somewhere with trees and plants, the experience can offer both exercise and an increased sense of well-being.

Finding and Nurturing the Areas Where You Excel

Maybe you have boundless energy but have never been able to harness it in a positive way. Maybe your "crazy" ideas are your innate creativity trying to get noticed. Or maybe your inability to get along with others is just a sign of your desire to work by yourself.

The first step toward developing your positive ADHD attributes is to figure out how to see them in yourself and others. Here are some ways to do that:

>> **Look for the positive.** Take a good, hard look at yourself and how you work. Watch for the areas where you have some skills (or at least innate abilities). Look for the positive in yourself, and you'll likely find it.

>> **Find a role model.** Somewhere between 3 and 6 percent of the U.S. population has ADHD. With so many people in the same boat, you shouldn't have too much trouble finding someone who can act as a role model for you. We introduce just a few in the earlier section "Seeing the Positive in Your Symptoms."

>> **Get help.** Sometimes an impartial observer, such as a therapist, can help you identify your best traits. We cover counseling and therapy in detail in Chapter 9.

After you identify a few of your abilities, you can work on developing them by doing the following:

>> **Get treatment.** Without some sort of biological, psychological, and social treatment for your symptoms, you may have a hard time developing your strengths. (Flip to Chapter 7 for more on this three-pronged approach.) Take your ADHD seriously enough to treat it properly, and you'll be more able to develop your skills.

>> **Seek out opportunity.** With your areas of ability identified, start to find ways to incorporate them into your life. If you have a ton of energy, for example, look for situations and activities where you can burn this energy in a healthy, socially appropriate way.

>> **Keep assessing.** As you uncover areas where you can excel and you work on developing your talents, you'll likely find other skills lurking under the surface. Keep on evaluating your abilities so you can see the areas that get uncovered.

REMEMBER

If you struggle to nurture your positive attributes, you may lack self-esteem. One of the best ways that you can develop your skills is to work on enhancing your self-esteem (see Chapters 15, 16, and 17). Likewise, by finding areas where you excel and discovering the benefits of these abilities, your self-esteem will begin to grow. This positive cycle can help you to slowly reach your potential and allow you to discard the feeling of failure that haunts many people with ADHD.

Chapter 15

Creating Harmony at Home

Many people with ADHD don't realize the impact their symptoms have on the people they live with. Symptoms like distractibility, impulsivity, hyperactivity, disorganization, and moodiness can create chaos and conflict in an otherwise controlled and positive living situation.

In this chapter, we get to the heart of relationships to help you create a stronger household bond and reduce conflict. We explore ways to make parenting a child with ADHD less difficult, we suggest how you and your significant other can work together to make both your lives easier, and we present important things you can do daily to keep the symptoms (and disruption) of ADHD to a minimum where you live.

Laying the Foundation for a Healthy Homelife

Regardless of whether you, your child, your partner, or your roommate has ADHD, you can take steps to encourage harmony by understanding some principles that help reduce conflict and create a more harmonious environment. Having empathy, being able to communicate effectively, expressing emotions in a healthy way, and showing appreciation are the cornerstones of strong relationships. We cover them all in detail in the following sections.

REMEMBER

The more you discover about how ADHD impacts you personally and your household as a whole, the more your perspective changes. What you now see as a difficult problem may later look like a gift. And what you now consider to be a "cute quirk" may seem like a much more serious issue down the road.

Exercising empathy

When someone has ADHD, their close contacts often suffer because the person may not be able to perform the seemingly simple task of empathizing. *Empathy* is the ability to identify with and understand what another person is feeling. It's a felt sense of the other person. Empathy is important in relationships because if you're able to put yourself in another person's place, you can see how your own actions impact that person.

By having empathy for a person with ADHD, you realize that many of their behaviors aren't intended to hurt you or anyone else. The problem isn't that they *choose* not to empathize; it's that they don't know how. (Many people without ADHD also have this problem.) Everyone in the home needs to actively learn how to have empathy toward everyone else.

To exercise empathy, you need to do the following:

>> **Recognize that everyone feels things differently.** One of the most important prerequisites for empathy is to realize that other people — even those in your own family who have similar values and beliefs — don't necessarily feel the same way about things as you do. Just because you believe in treating ADHD with medication doesn't mean that everyone else does too.

>> **Pay attention to the other person and validate their feelings.** You must actively focus on other people's reactions and the messages they communicate, both verbally and nonverbally. Practicing validation is an essential step in empathic communication (and it may take practice). If someone says they're

cold, you wouldn't say "What's wrong with you?" You'd (we hope) offer a validating comment such as "You're cold; would you like to borrow my sweater?"

>> **Understand how *you* feel and think.** For this step, the famous ADHD trait of being brutally honest is very useful; you just need to focus that honesty on yourself.

The key to empathy is to be aware of the people around you and how they're affected by your actions. People in the household who don't have ADHD must demonstrate compassion and understanding for the person with ADHD, who may really struggle with demonstrating empathy. In other words, a person without ADHD needs to have an extra dose of empathy for the person with it. And if you're the one with ADHD, you need to try to understand how your behavior affects the people in your life.

TIP

Here are some additional suggestions for developing empathy toward others:

>> Identify the struggle that the other person is going through. Listen to them, not to your own spin on their experience.

>> Try to understand the person's feelings.

>> Anticipate how what you're going to say or do is going to affect that other person.

>> Ask the other person how they feel about a situation or interaction.

Effectively expressing emotions

When you have ADHD or live with someone who does, you may believe that you need to keep a stiff upper lip in the face of the stresses and challenges. But holding in your emotions is a surefire way to end up feeling unappreciated and angry.

REMEMBER

Acknowledging your feelings and expressing them in healthy ways are vitally important. If you're the person with ADHD, you may have to put out extra effort to figure out how to express your feelings verbally instead of acting them out. The effort is worthwhile in terms of improving domestic harmony.

Following are some of the most common negative feelings that color interactions when someone in the home has ADHD, along with suggestions for how to deal with them effectively:

>> **Frustration:** If you have ADHD and get frustrated or impatient when trying to complete a task — either because you don't know how to do it or can't ever

seem to finish it — you may take out your frustration on the people around you (or on the object at hand). A healthy solution is to take a few minutes to self-regulate and then to talk about how thwarted you feel. Then you can take some steps to make success more likely. For example, you can read a tutorial or watch a video about what you're trying to do, acknowledge the amount of time the project may require, or ask (nicely) for help.

>> **Anger:** Perhaps you often feel angry at your child, partner, or roommate with ADHD for not doing what you want them to do, or maybe you get angry at yourself for letting other people down. Expressing anger is fine, as long as it's not accompanied by blame. Acknowledge your anger, but don't let the anger control you and make you do or say something that you'll regret later. Anger releases the neurotransmitter dopamine (see Chapter 2), which is something an ADHD brain seeks.

>> **Guilt:** Guilt has many shades. You may feel guilty for any number of reasons, such as for acting the way you did in a certain situation, for not finding help for your (or your family member's) ADHD sooner, or for having angry thoughts and feelings about someone you live with. A healthy way to deal with guilt is to express remorse — to recognize the pain that you and other people feel because of your actions or inaction and to put that recognition into words.

>> **Embarrassment:** Feeling embarrassment when you or your loved one with ADHD does something inappropriate is normal. Resist the temptation to criticize or blame yourself (or your loved one) for the inappropriate behavior. Instead, focus on correcting the behavior and trying to make amends, if necessary. Also, try to use a sense of humor in these situations (without making fun of a loved one's actions, of course).

Embarrassment is the close cousin of shame, which can often be the second skin of someone who has ADHD.

REMEMBER

The best way to deal with emotions such as these is to work at recognizing them and allow yourself time to reflect on them before taking action. While you're delaying acting, you can think about how to express your feelings in a way that doesn't judge or criticize yourself or others. Many times, poorly expressed (or unexpressed) emotions are the cause of further conflict in a relationship. Something you say in three seconds can take three hours, days, months, or even three years to repair. When that's the case, seeing a therapist or counselor to help you work through them (either individually or as a family) is often helpful.

Focusing on clear and effective communication

Miscommunication runs rampant in relationships that cope with ADHD. First, many people (with or without ADHD) tend to make assumptions about what others are thinking or doing. Second, many people with ADHD start talking without listening first, or they tend to speak without thinking. The result is some serious miscommunication.

To prevent these communication issues from taking over your home, the entire household needs to learn how to listen and express themselves effectively. In many instances, clearing up communication problems requires the help of a skilled counselor or therapist, but here are some ideas for getting started:

>> **Actively listen as the other person talks.** Active listening involves reiterating and validating the other person's point before responding with one of your own. For example, perhaps your partner says they're angry because you didn't clean the garage like you said you would. Before making an excuse, first acknowledge the fact that they're angry.

Validating the other person's experience doesn't mean you agree, but it does mean you "get" them.

When people don't feel heard, they say it louder and then with more anger and frustration. Most fights can be avoided or quickly deescalated with this strategy.

>> **If you're unsure what someone means, ask for clarification.** Don't just make an assumption.

>> **Don't criticize.** Removing criticism from your playbook also removes a considerable amount of conflict. People often experience criticism as an assault on their character, particularly when the criticizer tees it up with "you always" or "you never." Criticism simply props up the person giving it while belittling the person receiving it, and it's usually met with defensiveness.

>> **Offer a positive before bringing up a negative.** When you discuss how you feel and what you want to have changed in your relationship, avoid jumping right into the things you don't like. Start by mentioning the aspects you appreciate about your current relationship, and then gently move into the parts you want to see change.

The key to effective communication is listening and making sure you understand the other person. Most conflict occurs when one person misunderstands or misinterprets what another person means.

Acknowledging your appreciation

Nothing is more powerful in fostering a bond than expressing your appreciation for another person. When people feel appreciated, they're more willing to be helpful and appreciative back. Don't be shy about telling those around you when you appreciate something they've done. To get you started, here are some suggestions:

>> **Say "thank you" after your child has completed a chore.** Do this even if you had to remind them to do the chore or if you had to help them do it.

>> **Say "I love you" or "I appreciate you."** For example, don't be afraid to tell the people you love that you love them. Everyone likes to hear that they're valued, and saying it can help you break down feelings of anger and resentment.

>> **Offer a smile or a hug.** You can do this anytime, but it's often especially appreciated after a person has done something for you.

Defusing conflict

Some professionals believe that people with ADHD have an almost compulsive need to create conflict. If that's the case, most people with ADHD don't realize it (and few, if any, would acknowledge it if asked). One possibility is that conflict is stimulating for the person with ADHD, and a stimulating situation may help their symptoms subside. Certain brain chemicals can also reinforce this behavior.

The problem is that a person creating conflict obviously makes life extremely frustrating for the people around them, and that may end up being downright dangerous. Even if the theory of the stimulating effects of conflict isn't right, a lot of people practice conflict as a way of life. Conflict usually isn't the best way to get ahead.

TIP

The big question is how to deal with a (possibly unconscious) need for conflict. If stimulation is what you crave, one suggestion is to engage in positive, productive activities, such as exercise or a hobby that really holds your interest. By doing so, you may be able to cancel the unconscious trigger to stir up tensions.

When conflict does happen, one of the most effective strategies for defusing it is to take a time-out/time-in. Stop the conversation or activity that's causing the conflict and come back to it later. Use your breather to regroup and take a time-in to center yourself; when you're calmer, think and talk about feelings and beliefs that may be contributing to your need to stir up trouble.

Healing the past

Your past influences your present, and many people harbor resentments over the past. These feelings of resentment often come up at the worst possible times — during arguments and stressful situations — and can cause considerable problems in the home. The part of your brain that holds these feelings can be easily triggered and you can become reactive rather than responsive. Before you can effectively live in the present and hope for the future, you need to let go of past hurts and resentment. Doing so can be very difficult and almost always involves seeing a therapist who can help you work through your feelings.

You may have lived a long time before finding out that you or your loved one has ADHD. The legacies of your life before the diagnosis include many disappointments, failures, stresses, and frustrations. Your challenge now is to realize that you have an explanation to help make sense out of a lot of things that were probably mysterious sources of bad feelings and experiences in the past. You have enough work to do to make your present and future as positive as possible; be compassionate toward yourself and others for the pain and failures of the past.

REMEMBER

You can't embrace the future if you're still holding on to the past. Take whatever steps necessary to let go of your resentment and self-blame so you can move forward with your life.

Being realistic

When you undertake a new ADHD treatment plan, be practical about the changes you'll see and be leery of treatments that claim to offer quick-fix "cures" for your symptoms. You don't want to set yourself up for disappointment and further feelings of failure.

Being unrealistic about the degree and rate of improvement to expect from ADHD treatments is a common source of home conflict. The only way past this problem is to rein in unrealistic expectations. Recognize that progress is often slow, and it doesn't necessarily take a straight path. You'll have many gains and setbacks along the way. And in some areas, you may not see any change whatsoever.

Improving Your Homelife When You Have ADHD

As we stress many times in this book, having ADHD presents a lot of challenges, especially when you interact with people who don't have the condition. In this section, we tackle some of the more important issues that people with ADHD have when they live with people who don't have it.

Managing moods

One of the main characteristics of ADHD for most people is extreme, frequent changes in mood. One minute you may feel happy and hopeful, and a minute later you feel angry and frustrated without anything outside of you causing the change. This phenomenon is a product of several different factors, the most important of which are these:

>> **A biological disposition to react more strongly than other people to the ups and downs of life:** The biological treatments we discuss in Chapter 8 usually help this tendency to some degree. Other biological causes, such as depression, anxiety, or bipolar disorder, can also contribute.

>> **Past experiences:** Most people with ADHD have come up short on meeting their (and others') expectations, so they tend to have an internal dialogue that's demeaning and negative.

>> **Others' words:** That tendency to have a low self-esteem we cover in the preceding bullet can be formed, worsened, or reinforced by what other people say. How many times can a person hear "I'm disappointed in you" or "You could do so much better if only you tried harder" before turning that criticism inward (and often making it even stronger)? We submit, very few. Most people with ADHD bear deep scars from criticism directed at them over and over again, which is why shame is their second skin.

>> **A tendency to jump to conclusions:** As we say in the earlier section "Focusing on clear and effective communication," people with ADHD have a talent for jumping to conclusions ahead of the evidence. (This talent can also be called "being intuitive.") After you've jumped to a conclusion, an attitude isn't far behind. If you have an attitude about every conclusion you jump to, you're probably going to come across as moody.

>> **A medication that's wearing off:** If you take medication for your ADHD, as it wears off you may experience changes in mood. If you notice a mood pattern that seems to coincide with your medication schedule, talk to your physician about adjusting your medication, dosage, or schedule.

Here are some suggestions to deal with negative thoughts that can lead to negative moods:

>> **Stop the thought and ask yourself whether it's based on what's happening at the moment.** Most of the time, negative thoughts are simply popping up without relating to your life at the moment.

>> **Breathe through it.** When you have negative thoughts, your body tenses up, and your breath becomes shallower. Take a few deep breaths, and you'll begin to relax.

>> **Cancel that thought.** After you acknowledge that the thought isn't based on what's happening and you've had a chance to take a breath, you can let it go.

>> **Reframe that thought.** Even if you think a negative thought *is* based on what's really happening, you don't have to let it lead you to a negative feeling. Try to reframe negative perceptions, thoughts, or words into positive ones. If you can see the humor or the benefit in a difficult situation, you can probably feel better about it.

>> **Don't take other people's negativity personally.** When someone directs a negative comment or action your way, it may not necessarily be about you; they may be taking out their issues on you. People who have ADHD are more sensitive to rejection, but if you can realize that everyone has internal pressures, reasons, or ideas that make them do the things they do, you may not feel the need to have such a strong reaction. Work on understanding the causes and consequences of your own and other people's actions and reactions.

WARNING

Extreme moodiness may be a sign of depression or bipolar disorder, both of which we cover in Chapter 6. Because these conditions are common among people with ADHD, have a professional screen you for them (see Chapter 4).

Taking responsibility

As we say elsewhere in the book, ADHD is an explanation, not an excuse. If you hurt someone, create a problem, or make situations more difficult — even unintentionally — you must take responsibility for your actions regardless of the fact that ADHD has a biological cause.

If your behavior is causing problems in your life, you need to seek the best possible help in getting it under control. You and everyone else will benefit if you can focus on understanding how your actions caused the hurt or contributed to the problem. If you can find a way to express that understanding to the other people involved — and make repairs — all the better. They can then realize that you haven't ignored their feelings and experiences. The most important thing you can do is to learn from situations in which your ADHD plays a part in creating hurt feelings or less-than-optimal outcomes. That way, you can take responsibility and continue on the road to self-improvement.

Being Single and Dating with ADHD

Being single and dating can provide a lot of stimulation, excitement, and novelty, all of which are fodder for the ADHD brain. Being romanced by someone who has ADHD is a heady experience because they center all their hyperfocus on their new relationship. However, some of the same aspects of ADHD that can cause difficulty at work or at home — such as being impulsive, missing social cues, being sensitive to rejection, or zoning out — can make your date wonder who's with them. They may be confused because on one hand you can hyperfocus on the relationship and on the other you can be out with them and become distracted by the noise or people.

When you're attracted to someone, your brain releases many neurochemicals, including high levels of dopamine and norepinephrine, which are music to an ADHD brain. You also experience a drop in serotonin. Of course, the novelty and stimulation of a new sexual partner is exciting and in its own way intoxicating.

TIP

A healthy long-term relationship doesn't sacrifice eroticism or interest in one another. It allows for stability and a foundation where partners can be fully themselves.

Handling issues with hyperfocusing and novelty

With ADHD, falling hard and fast for a new love interest isn't uncommon. Your chosen special person of the moment gets all your hyperfixation.

REMEMBER

ADHD "love-bombs" of excessive compliments, attention, and gifts can be overwhelming and overbearing; wonderful; or both. This is usually not the type of love-bombing that can be the hallmark of a controlling abusing partner.

However, after the high of the experience starts to wane, boredom can set in, and you and your ADHD are off to the impulsive next swipe on a dating app.

TIP

A question that gets asked a lot is "Should I tell someone I'm dating that I have ADHD and, if so, when?" Revealing intimate information about yourself is your choice, but beware of a tendency toward impulsive sharing before you know whether the person you're with can process this information in a nonjudgmental way. Lots of people have ideas about ADHD, many of which are untrue. A better bet is to get to know someone and assess whether they're trustworthy before impulsively revealing too much too soon.

Sticking with it long term

The best way to have a successful relationship long term is to treat your ADHD and understand the ways it shows up in a relationship. For example, when you feel restless or bored in your relationship, what do you do? Do you think about having an affair, or do you talk to your partner about feeling restless and the need to spice up your connection?

Everyone wants to experience the enthralling high of a new relationship's honeymoon period and grieves when it starts to naturally shift. This is especially true for someone with ADHD because of the dopamine release. When this high wears off, many question whether they've fallen out of love instead of understanding that they've just been high on the love drug.

Treating your ADHD makes you less likely to make an impulsive decision that you may later regret. Having split attention or not giving your partner your full attention can make them feel like you aren't interested in them or their feelings. Make certain you have time together when your phones are off and that you are not doing a project when they are trying to talk with you. Let them know what you need to be full present with them.

Choose a partner wisely, not impulsively. Do you have common values and worldviews? Are you sexually compatible? Keep in mind that not everyone you have a lot of chemistry with is someone you can create a life with. No one person can be everything to you.

That's why finding interest and stimulation in many areas of your life is important. Asking your partner to be the one and only is a recipe for unrealistic expectations that can't be fulfilled. In a long- term relationship, getting bored and not always liking everything about your partner is normal. Keep your impulsivity in check at these times and find non-threatening ways to get the stimulation you need.

Parenting a Child with ADHD

We could easily write an entire book on the best ways to parent a child with ADHD.

In this section, we discuss the most pressing concerns parents have about improving life at home with a child with ADHD. We focus on ways you can prevent problem behaviors from happening, work with those behaviors when they do show up, and perform the balancing act that comes with parenting both children with and children without ADHD in the same home.

If you have a child with ADHD, the chances are pretty high that you or your child's other parent may have it, too (see Chapter 2). If you do have ADHD, treating your own symptoms can go a long way toward making parenting easier for both you and your child.

Preventing problems

The best way to improve life at home with a child with ADHD is to minimize the possibility of behavior problems rather than deal with them after the fact. This section offers some ideas for reducing behavioral problems by using treatment effectively, establishing a clear set of rules and expectations, creating an environment that leaves little room for misbehavior, and focusing on positive behaviors rather than negative ones.

REMEMBER

Unlike some other children, those with ADHD rarely learn best by being told how to do something. They're much more likely than others to do what you do and not what you say. You and your child are going to be a lot happier if you practice the principle of setting a good example as the first rule of teaching positive behavior.

REMEMBER

Most learning from birth onward comes in the form of thousands of little, subtle messages from the people around you every moment of every day. A smile or laugh, a frown, and a little comment like "Good children don't . . ." are all ways that children learn how to behave and how not to behave. So do others' acts of responding (or not responding). These methods teach kids (everyone, really) how to think about themselves, so they have a direct impact on self-image and self-esteem. Keeping these truths in mind, along with remembering to set a good example, helps when you're trying to figure out the finer points of managing your child's (and your) emotions and behavior.

Treating your child's ADHD effectively

Years of experience and research by many clinicians and parents has shown that coping with a child's ADHD is much easier when you start out by addressing both biological and psychological issues:

>> Because undesirable behaviors are based on problematic functioning, the most important place to start is to choose one or more of the biological treatment options that we describe in Chapters 8, 11, 12, and 13. You need to allow enough time for them to start working.

>> You can address psychological factors by implementing some of the approaches we discuss in Chapters 9 and 10, such as various forms of psychotherapy and behavior modification. Doing so can help you avoid dealing with the obstacles of ongoing conflicts while you're trying to develop better living strategies.

Taking these two steps will likely lead to a significant reduction in the symptoms and behavioral problems in your child. Then you'll be better able to assess what behaviors you need to address using the tips and techniques we describe in this chapter and in Chapter 16. Also, your child will have a much easier time cooperating with your efforts and using the skills you want to help them learn.

Understanding characteristics of ADHD behavior

Many behavioral characteristics, such as those in the following list, accompany ADHD. Understanding these characteristics can help you better address the behaviors that cause problems in your life.

>> **Having difficulty following rules:** Your child with ADHD needs to learn how to comply with rules that are necessary for their safety and for the smooth operation of the household, school, and society.

>> **Looking for loopholes:** People with ADHD often have a talent for finding the loopholes in any system or set of rules.

>> **Questioning authority:** Most likely you've already discovered that your child has a knack for questioning authority and for questioning any rules they're asked to follow.

>> **Creating distractions:** Because kids with ADHD are subject to distractibility, they're also often masters of distracting other people, especially if the distraction helps them avoid being disciplined or controlled.

>> **Demanding fairness:** Being treated fairly is a major issue for many people with ADHD, even if the person doesn't make any effort to treat other people with fairness or respect.

>> **Sticking up for a cause:** People with ADHD are more likely than others to take the side of the underdog. As a result, they sometimes fight for a cause with all their might when you think they're just trying to cause trouble. It also often means that your child is more involved in other people's business than their own.

>> **Picking up skills at a slower pace:** Children with ADHD often take longer than others to learn new skills, especially if the new skill involves changing things they already do some other way. As we discuss in Chapter 16, they also often learn in slightly different ways than other people.

>> **Struggling with repetitive tasks:** ADHD children have more difficulty learning and doing repetitive and tedious tasks, such as memorizing multiplication tables, doing chores every week, or even brushing their teeth every day.

>> **Bending the truth:** Many parents find that their children with ADHD are flexible with the truth. This flexibility can take the form of telling tall tales more or less for entertainment, or it can be outright lying. Kids with ADHD (like other children) may lie for a variety of reasons, but they're often better at it than others. In many cases, they're so good at it that they believe their own lies. That's why we say they're flexible with the truth.

>> **Struggling to connect cause and effect:** Children with ADHD often have trouble connecting cause and effect if the cause is too far removed in time from the effect. That means your ADHD child needs immediate feedback: discussion, rewards, and consequences close to the time of the behaviors (see Chapter 10).

>> **Having difficulty with tasks that require planning:** Kids with ADHD may have difficulty learning how to work on — and finish — tasks that require planning and meeting intermediate goals. This place is a good one to practice spending some quality time with your child, helping them learn these skills.

>> **Having trouble getting started:** People with ADHD often have a hard time getting started on a project or switching from one activity to another. You may have to work with your child to get them over the hurdle of getting started by breaking down the task into manageable chunks and maybe even assisting in the first step.

How you deal with these characteristics depends on the age of your child. For young ADHD children (under 8 or 10), behavioral modification techniques usually work better than explanations and discussion. As your child gets older, you can enjoy the wonders of rational discussion and intellectual fencing. At all ages, you need a blend of love, patience, skill, cleverness, and luck to manage the challenges of ADHD parenting.

Setting rules and expectations

Children with ADHD have a great need for structure and clarity. Without establishing clear guidelines for proper behavior, you can't expect your child to conform.

Therefore, one of your first steps in getting the types of behaviors you want is to create a clear set of expectations based on a realistic assessment of your child's abilities. With these expectations in mind, establish a set of rules and specify clear, appropriate consequences for disobeying them. Following is a breakdown of this process:

1. **Make assessments.**

Wait until your child's ADHD treatment is well underway so you'll be able to see what areas still pose a problem and what areas don't.

2. **Set expectations and rules.**

When you know what areas you need to work on, you can create a set of rules and expectations. Here are some commonly used rules to get you started:

- Treat each family member with respect by not hitting, teasing, or arguing.
- Follow instructions without complaining.
- Finish your homework before playing video games or watching TV.
- Tell the truth.
- Clean up after yourself. Put your toys and clothes away when you're finished with them.

TIP

The best rules are both clear and positive. Instead of saying "Don't take your brother's things," say "Respect your brother by asking first (and getting his okay) before you take something that belongs to him."

3. **Explain the rules clearly.**

Before you put the rules into effect or enforce any consequences, make sure everyone in the family understands them and the rewards and consequences associated with each of them. Ask your child to repeat back what you said, using their own words. Or ask them to look you in the eye when you speak so you can feel certain they're paying attention. Neither technique is foolproof, but both should help.

4. **Reward positive behaviors and provide appropriate consequences.**

When your child does something right, reward them. This act can take the form of simply acknowledging the good deed (saying "thanks" and giving a hug), or it can be more formal, such as offering special treats or trips to someplace your child wants to go or letting them stay up a little later than usual.

The consequences for breaking the rules need to be appropriate for the situation. They also need to be enacted without emotion; don't take these actions when you're angry. Providing consequences is a complex subject that we cover in detail in the later section "Dealing with discipline."

TIP

Write your rules down. If your child is too young to read, you can make a pictograph that explains the rules. If they aren't written down, you or your child can easily forget them. Post the rules someplace prominent in the house so that your child is reminded of them throughout the day.

Creating a structured environment

Kids, especially kids with ADHD, do best in a structured environment. By providing a structured place to live, you minimize the possibilities for misbehavior and improve the opportunities for success.

REMEMBER

Structure isn't about hovering over your kid and correcting them after they make mistakes; structure is about creating an environment that makes doing the right things easy. Here are some suggestions for creating a positive structure for your child:

>> **Chart it out.** Create charts for chores and your child's daily schedule and put them somewhere your child can easily see them. Many people with ADHD relate better to pictures than words, so having a colorful graphic display of what you expect and how the day is structured can help your child better understand and follow it. Have a place in this chart for notes and stickers that show that a chore was completed.

>> **Prevent boredom.** How many parents have heard their kids chanting the mantra "I'm bored?" All kids experience boredom, but for children with ADHD who need stimulation to function, boredom is often a major problem. You can prevent boredom several ways:

- **Introduce the link between boredom and the need for stimulation.** Think about and discuss with your child the idea that people perceive boredom in situations where they're craving external stimulation that's lacking or is available in a form they can't appreciate. One good way not to get bored is to develop personal resourcefulness.

- **Keep a busy schedule.** Set up your child's day so they have little time to get bored (and into trouble). Doing so can also help keep negative behaviors at bay. However, don't make your schedule so hectic that you and your child don't have any spare time just to relax and enjoy life.

- **Have an activities board in your house with a list of fun things your child can do.** This resource will help them find ways to combat boredom.

- **Keep plenty of art supplies and other hands-on activities available and accessible.** The key here is to make these supplies accessible so that your child can dig in whenever they want.

- **Create a safe outdoor space with plenty of things to do.** Physical activity — especially outdoors — can dramatically improve ADHD symptoms. If possible, set up a play area outside, such as a fenced backyard, where your child can go safely even if you aren't available to join them.

>> **Provide supervision.** By closely supervising your child, you can keep them from making decisions without thinking — one of the hallmarks of children with impulsive-type ADHD. One difficulty that some parents have is making the transition from constant, one-on-one supervision to the child's being responsible for their own actions. This process usually takes 18 years or so to complete, but with ADHD children it can take even longer. Start early and keep at the development of self-awareness, self-discipline, and responsibility.

Perpetuating positive behavior

The best way to increase positive behaviors is to acknowledge them when you see them and accentuate them over the negative behaviors. Here are some ideas for reinforcing positive behaviors in your child:

>> **Don't dwell on the negative.** Many parents spend most of their time looking for their child to make a mistake, only to pounce on them when they do. One of the best pieces of advice Jeff was ever given about parenting was "Try not to notice so much." This concept is also called *selective ignoring*. If the behavior doesn't pose a threat to anyone's health and safety or inflict emotional stress on someone, ignore it. You have plenty of other things to focus on.

>> **Point out the positive.** Want to know the best way to encourage positive behavior? Point it out when you see it. Everyone likes praise, especially children who feel as though they can't do anything right. Praise releases dopamine in the brain, but that jolt doesn't last long. Make it your goal to point out positive behaviors ten times more often than you point out negative behaviors.

>> **Offer support.** When your child tries to do something, offer your help and support. Sometimes just knowing that someone is there to help can give them the confidence to try a little harder and actually do it. Just make sure you don't come down hard on your child if they don't get it right.

REMEMBER

Also, don't be too quick to do the job for your child — a common mistake many parents make. Your child needs to figure out how to do tasks themselves, and they also need to feel the accomplishment that comes with completing a project. Your job in offering support is to help them get over the hurdles while helping them learn. Then you and your child can both take pride in your accomplishments.

>> **Provide incentives.** Many people do better when they have some extra incentive beyond the intrinsic satisfaction of a job well done. For example, you probably prefer getting paid for your work to simply having the satisfaction of knowing you did it. Likewise, your child with ADHD will likely take more interest in doing what they need to do if they have some incentives.

Here are some examples:

- Pay your child an allowance for accomplishing their weekly tasks.

- On the chart that lists your child's chores (which we discuss in the preceding section), place a sticker next to each chore when they finish it.

- Say "thanks" and give a hug for a job well done (or even just attempted).

- For big accomplishments, like finishing a project for school, offer a special treat, such as a trip to the movies or a meal at their favorite restaurant.

- If your child finishes their homework early, give them a little more screen time than usual.

>> **Spend time together.** Nothing provides a better opportunity to shape your children's behavior than spending time with them. Get to know your kids. Talk to them about what they like and dislike, what they think and feel. Doing so helps you develop a bond so you not only gain a better understanding of what makes your children tick but also let them feel as though you care about them and understand who they are. This is especially important with teenagers.

Dealing with discipline

The purpose of discipline isn't to punish your child for misbehaving; it's to teach them how to act responsibly. We believe the best way to understand this idea is to think of the concept of *self-discipline*, which we see as the ability to act responsibly through the choices you make. Your task as a parent is to help your child learn self-discipline by the time they grow up. In this section, we offer some suggestions for disciplining your child with this goal in mind.

Use discipline to teach your child appropriate behavior, not to punish them for acting inappropriately. Maintain love and empathy for your child as you discipline them.

Doling out discipline

One of your jobs as a parent is to provide the environment in which your child can safely learn the principles and techniques that create self-discipline. This means you have to be aware of the necessary steps and watch out for the potential pitfalls. In effect, you start out providing the direction and controls for your child's behavior and then gradually — through a process of creative partnership over a number of years — hand over the reins.

The big question that many parents have when working with a child with ADHD is how to discipline them when they make mistakes or act out. First, you need to keep in mind some basic principles:

WARNING

>> **Safety is very important.** You should consider whether your child's actions endanger them or someone else. Basically, the principle behind this is that if someone is dead or seriously injured, it's hard for them to have a lot of fun ever again. A related idea is that if you're the cause of someone not being able to have fun, you can't really have fun either.

The best way to head off dangerous situations is by anticipating the possibility and making arrangements to avoid negative outcomes. Violations of safety may require immediate, physical restraint. If that does become necessary, you probably want to discuss the situation with your child after the dust settles.

>> **Image isn't everything.** Just because your child does something unusual or out of the ordinary doesn't mean the attention they attract deserves punishment. Stop and think about whether your child did something wrong or whether you're just embarrassed by what they did.

>> **Life is a process of gradual progress toward the goal.** Nothing is ever perfect, especially people's behavior. You aren't going to make your life or your child's life better by trying to create a rule for everything that may enter their little mind to try out. If you can teach them the values of a good life and give them a chance to try, stumble, and try again, they'll gradually get closer and closer to what you're striving for.

REMEMBER

>> **Steer, don't direct.** You're probably never going to be able to ram your ideas of what your child ought to be doing down their throat, especially if they have ADHD. Besides, you're trying to teach your child how to choose wisely, not how to follow directions. Offer guidance instead of directing your child's every move: You'll be happier, and your child will be more responsive to your desires.

If, after considering the points in the preceding list, you think you need to put the brakes on your child's behavior, here are five simple steps to follow:

1. **While making eye contact with your child, calmly but firmly explain — in simple terms — that their behavior isn't acceptable.**

2. **State what you expect from them.**

   Again, maintain eye contact and speak clearly and firmly.

3. **Ask them to repeat your expectations back to you.**

   You don't need them to quote you verbatim. In fact, if they use their own words, they're more likely to understand and remember what you said.

TIP

   Repeating expectations is very helpful for a younger child but may cause resentment with an older child. You don't want to risk causing further problems, so determine how necessary this step is based on who your child is.

4. **Explain the consequences for not obeying you.**

   Make the consequences logical to the situation, and make sure your child understands them. (See the following section for a detailed discussion of consequences.)

5. **If you're sure your child understood your instructions and didn't follow them, employ the consequences.**

   Do so without getting angry or belittling your child.

TIP

Keep the following suggestions in mind as you follow this five-step plan:

>> **Don't act out of anger.** Doing so just creates anger and resentment on your child's end and guilt and remorse on your end. Always wait to enforce discipline until you have your own emotions under control. Tell your child that you're angry at them for their behavior and that you'll deal with the consequences of their action after you've had a chance to cool off. Self-regulation is key to your success. Everyone loses their cool sometimes, but your job is to figure out how to remain in control.

>> **Use few words.** Avoid nagging or rambling on about how what your child did was wrong. Talking too much is the surest way to get them to tune you out. Explain yourself in a few carefully chosen words.

>> **Stay calm and speak softly but firmly.** Yelling only escalates the feelings of frustration and anger for both of you; speaking calmly is much more likely to get your child's attention.

>> **Don't withhold love or affection.** Withholding love or affection as punishment only creates more problems, such as lowered self-esteem and increased anger and resentment.

Considering consequences

As much as possible, consequences for your child's misbehavior need to be logical and natural. That is, they need to fit with what would generally happen anyway. For example:

>> If your child doesn't do their homework, they go to school without it.

>> If they don't want to wear mittens or a jacket waiting for the bus, they're cold and uncomfortable at the bus stop.

>> If they hit their brother or sister, have them apologize and perform a helpful task or an assigned chore for the person they hit.

This list could go on and on, but we're sure you get the idea.

For behaviors that don't have natural consequences, or whose natural consequences aren't desirable (such as getting hit by a car for riding a bicycle on a busy street), you need to set some specific consequences that your child knows about ahead of time.

REMEMBER

The purpose of consequences is to discourage or stop undesirable behavior. Enforcing consequences for behaving undesirably or not behaving desirably is a lot more work for everyone than arranging for the appropriate choices and actions to be taken in the first place, as we explain in the earlier section "Preventing problems."

Dealing with defiance

Children with ADHD are often perceived to be defiant. However, we believe that in many cases the defiance parents and other people in authority experience is really a failure to communicate. In many cases, a child with ADHD either doesn't appreciate that their style of communication is offensive, or they don't understand that the person talking to them has certain expectations about how they'll respond to that communication.

In other words, children with ADHD don't quite get the concept that they need authority figures for their safety and well-being. Lots of times, the child with ADHD is just going on their own self-directed way, not differentiating between people of different ages or ranks they meet, and the authority figure stumbles into their path. When this happens, the child with ADHD is likely to say something like what they've heard all their life — something they'd say to any of their friends — such as, "Hey, stupid, watch where you're going. Get out of my way."

Of course, at times children with ADHD are intentionally insolent and defiant. Our guess is that many children learn that sort of behavior from watching how others in their lives cope with conflict. Heading this sort of behavior off is easier than stopping it after it's started (see the earlier section "Preventing problems").

Defiant behavior may also be a way for children with ADHD to get their daily dose of stimulation (see the "Defusing conflict" section earlier in the chapter). If that seems to be the issue, work with your child to find alternative forms of stimulation, including physical exercise.

REMEMBER

If your child's antisocial behaviors affect people outside the family, you may need the aid of a mediator. You don't necessarily need a formal sort of mediation, but having an objective, nonpartisan participant involved in the discussion of how to deal with a conflict may help. Mostly, you want to avoid involving the police and the legal system. Occasionally, parents of a child with ADHD find they need to involve juvenile justice or a psychiatric hospital to take control of a very bad situation.

REMEMBER

As we explain in Chapter 6, many people with ADHD also have oppositional defiant disorder (ODD), the main symptom of which is breaking rules. This defiance can range from breaking family rules to perpetrating violence and getting in trouble with the law. If ODD is the reason for your child's defiance, your approach needs to be firm, and you likely need to wait until your child calms down before taking any steps to discipline them. If you experience these levels of defiance, you most likely need the skills of a professional counselor to help you deal with the behaviors. (You also need to use biological treatments for the disorder, such as medication. In this case talk to your prescribing physician.)

Raising more than one child

The more children in your household, the more complicated raising them becomes. When you add one or more children with ADHD to the mix, you get a very complex, stressful situation. You find yourself frequently needing to deal with how your kids interact. In this section, we explore some of the most common areas of concern for families with more than one child.

Creating cooperation

Most people misunderstand competition and think that it's the way to get ahead in the world. That may be true in sports, but it doesn't always work in the rest of the world, especially in interpersonal relationships (one-on-one interactions). Any parent with more than one child will tell you that cooperation is much more pleasant than competition.

TIP

Here are some ideas for fostering cooperation among your children:

>> **Play cooperative games rather than competitive ones.** Lots of games allow you and your children (you may as well play with them) to work toward a common goal instead of being pitted against each other. An Internet search for "cooperative game for kids" will provide you with a lot of great options.

>> **Set up the household chores so that they're a team effort.** For example, if toys need to be picked up in the family room, have everyone work together to get it done instead of assigning one person to do it. Or when doing dishes, have one person empty the dishwasher while the other one fills it. (Or, if you do dishes by hand, have one wash and the other dry.) When cleaning the floor, have one person sweep and the other mop. Be creative with having fun while doing chores, such as singing or telling jokes.

>> **Create a family project that involves everyone.** Plant a garden, for example. Select a project that allows people of different abilities to work together. In the case of planting a garden, the younger kids can help plant the plants or pull the weeds, and the bigger kids can dig the holes.

If you use your imagination, you can identify many ways to create cooperation among your children (and the entire family) and remove competition from your life.

Settling sibling rivalry

If you have more than one child and not all of them have ADHD, you have a challenging situation. We're sure you've already discovered that you can't possibly treat your children exactly the same way; a child with ADHD needs more supervision and attention than a child without the condition.

The result is often jealousy and anger on the part of the child who doesn't have ADHD; they may feel like they have to compete for your attention. Also, as they see their sibling being treated differently and seemingly being allowed to get away with things they can't, they may get resentful and feel as though they're being treated unfairly.

TIP

Although no one has yet found a cure for sibling rivalry, here are some ideas for defusing a tense situation:

>> **Treat each child according to their abilities.** Concern yourself with being fair to each child. If your non-ADHD child is better at following the rules and acting appropriately, give them more responsibility and more freedom to do things that your less responsible child isn't allowed to do.

>> **Provide each child with the same opportunities.** As you offer more freedom to the more responsible child, let the less responsible one know that they can earn the same freedoms as they show more responsibility.

>> **Talk openly about your situation.** Tell your non-ADHD child that you have higher expectations for her because you believe that she can meet them. And let her know that the extra attention and "freedom" that your child with ADHD receives is a result of his misbehavior and his difficulties rather than a reward. This attention and perceived freedoms come at a cost that your non-ADHD child doesn't have to pay.

>> **Arrange for special time with each child alone.** Plan dates to play with each of your children one-on-one. Spending time together playing and talking create a bond that isn't broken by having to parent each child according to their abilities. The non-ADHD child gets the attention they want without having to resort to misbehavior, and the child with ADHD is reassured that you love them in spite of the difficulties you go through together. You benefit by being able to know your kids better.

Encouraging play and fun

Life can get hectic (how's that for an understatement?), and placing fun way down on your to-do list is easy. But we strongly suggest that you move it up the list a bit. Try to set aside at least part of one day a week to do something fun like go to the park, a museum, or a movie. Putting an emphasis on fun makes you less stressed.

Enhancing self-esteem

Self-esteem is fragile for a person with ADHD. The symptoms that accompany ADHD — inattention, distractibility, impulsivity, and hyperactivity — often make the person feel like a failure because they can't control certain behaviors. We see very young kids — even as young as 5 — suffer from eroding self-esteem and stop trying because of fear of failure.

REMEMBER

The single most important thing you can do for your child with ADHD is to help them improve their self-esteem. With strong self-esteem, all the challenges that come up when dealing with the symptoms of ADHD are much easier to handle. Here are some suggestions that we've found to help children, especially those with ADHD, enhance their self-esteem:

>> **Offer encouragement.** Be a cheerleader for your child's cause. Spur them on with encouraging words when they're trying to do something challenging.

>> **Have faith.** Your child needs to sense that you have faith in their abilities. Faith goes beyond offering encouragement when they're doing something — it means believing in them and letting them know that you do even when they aren't involved in any particular task. Seeing your child as whole is a great gift to them and to you.

>> **Point out positives.** Acknowledge the things they do right.

>> **Offer assistance.** Helping your child with tough tasks is a tricky venture. You want to offer assistance, but you don't want to do too much. Be available to your child and make it clear that you'll help when they ask, but only after they've honestly tried to do it themselves.

>> **Acknowledge improvement.** Just as you point out the positive things your child does, also be sure to acknowledge the progress they're making. *Remember:* Don't be afraid to praise your child. You won't spoil them, and you won't make them not want to keep improving (both common misconceptions about praise). Instead, you'll give them the confidence and desire to keep striving to do better.

>> **Minimize mistakes.** This doesn't mean that you don't let your child make mistakes; it means that you help put mistakes they make into perspective. Let them know that making and learning from mistakes is a natural part of life. Keep in mind that children with ADHD often make the same mistake over and over; you need to be patient in dealing with the same mistake more than once.

>> **Focus on the process rather than the product.** Don't be overly concerned with how well something is done. Instead, revel in that fact that it was done at all.

>> **Empathize.** We cover this subject in the earlier section "Exercising empathy," but it bears repeating. Empathize with the difficulty your child is having. Let them know you realize things are difficult for them.

>> **Identify your child's strengths.** Help your child find something they're really good at, and encourage them to practice that activity to get even better. Such *islands of competence* are very important, especially to people who have a hard time getting approval for many of the things they try to do.

Parenting as a team

As parents of a child with ADHD, you'll often have disagreements about how to best deal with your child's behaviors. Add to this the fact that many children with ADHD are masters at manipulating by pitting each parent against the other, and you end up with a situation where chaos can easily reign. Furthermore, divorce is common in families with a child with ADHD, so you often have to contend with the stresses of having two separate households as well as up to four different parents.

The most effective strategy for parenting a child with ADHD is to practice what's called *co-parenting*. This means that both (or all) parents work together on every aspect of raising their child(ren). Obviously, this is an ideal to strive for, and it may not work for everyone, but here are some basic tenets of co-parenting:

>> Agree to discipline only according to a pre-established list of consequences or by conferring before issuing a consequence for improper behavior.

>> Make all household decisions together, especially the ones regarding raising your child.

>> Let your child know that all decisions require both/all parents' consent, not just one.

By eliminating your child's ability to act as a wedge between you, you're able to address your child's behavior more effectively.

Living with a Partner Who Has ADHD

Having an adult with ADHD in the house has its own issues. If your partner has ADHD, the following sections offer suggestions to help both of you improve your relationship.

REMEMBER

Your best strategy for learning to live with an ADHD adult is to find out everything you can about ADHD. Understand its symptoms and causes. Keep up-to-date on the various treatment options available. Find coping strategies to help you deal with the behaviors that come with ADHD. Obviously, you've already started this process by picking up this book — good for you! Chapter 20 offers suggestions for other resources that offer even more information on ADHD.

The more you know about ADHD, the better you'll be able to understand and respond to the challenges that this condition creates in an adult relationship.

Working together

Healthy relationships involve give and take. Determine each of your strengths and weaknesses, and try to work them into your relationship. If you're the organized one, for example, support your loved one by taking the lead in this area and helping them build their skills at it.

WARNING

Be careful not to fall into the trap of *overfunctioning* (taking on the responsibilities, emotions, and well-being of others). If your partner has ADHD, don't do everything for them, and don't allow them to treat you or anyone else poorly or to rely too much on you to do things for them. Allowing this type of behavior is called *enabling*. This issue is particularly important in relationships where more than one adult has ADHD. In this case, take everything we say and square it, then multiply by four.

Working together means just that: working *together*. Be supportive without enabling. Be a partner, not a servant. Demand responsibility, but be available to help out in areas where your partner with ADHD has difficulties.

Staying close

One of the healthiest things you can do for your relationship is to schedule time for dates. These events aren't a time to talk about your differences; they're a time to nourish your relationship and connect with your partner. Some couples go out to the movies or dinner, while others simply carve out a couple of hours at least once a week to check in with each other. Do what you can to schedule time each week to just hang out, have some fun, or have sex or some type of physical connection.

Taking time for yourself

In addition to scheduling weekly dates with your partner (see the preceding section), make sure you regularly set aside time for yourself to just be alone doing something you enjoy. Read a book, take a bath, go to the gym, take a walk. Living 24/7 with anyone — regardless of whether ADHD is a factor — takes its toll on your ability to know yourself, and knowing yourself is key to being able to have a successful relationship with another person.

Adopting Good Habits

You can do several things to make the day-to-day struggles of your ADHD fewer and help reduce the level or impact of your ADHD symptoms. Our suggestions include getting organized, doing aerobic exercise, limiting TV and video games, ensuring that you get enough sleep, and having some fun.

Getting organized

Disorganization is a hallmark of people with ADHD. Distractibility leads to scattered thinking, which leads to a disorganized environment. One of the best things you can do to improve life at home is to get organized. We offer a bunch of organizational strategies in Chapter 18, but here are the basics:

>> **Keep track of your schedule.** Use whatever technology you need (smartphone, computer, calendar) to keep track of where you need to be, when, and (if necessary) why you need to be there. Put all your appointments in this tool, and use it. Doing so means you don't need to keep all this information in your head.

>> **Plan your projects ahead of time, and follow the plan.** With a plan in hand, you're more likely to get through your project because you won't forget what it involves and what else you still need to do.

>> **Get rid of the clutter in your house.** Create a place for everything in your house, and use color-coding (see Chapter 18) to make finding what you need easy.

REMEMBER

Disorganization doesn't need to be a problem if you understand where you tend to have trouble and develop strategies to overcome these tendencies. For example, if you often get lost, use map apps on your phone. If you tend to lose your keys, wallet, or purse, designate one place in your house to store these items, and make a habit of always putting them there. (This approach is something we have to do. If we don't put our wallets, car keys, or sunglasses in their designated places, it takes us hours to find them.)

Exercising regularly

As we say many times throughout this book, the best way to reduce your ADHD symptoms is to get adequate physical activity. For kids, that can mean simply playing outside with other kids; for adults, it means getting some form of aerobic exercise.

Exercise offers many benefits, including the following:

>> Lifting your mood

>> Developing coordination

>> Improving self-esteem

>> Releasing pent-up energy

Many people report being able to focus better and/or have an easier time sitting still after intense exercise, including us. When Jeff was younger, he relied heavily on exercise to cope with his symptoms. In fact, he had a boss once tell him that unless he exercised before going to work, he shouldn't even bother to show up at all. Without the exercise, Jeff was irritable, edgy, and unfocused, but with it he was calm and able to concentrate and get his job done. Similarly, Carol was unable to literally sit through a day seeing clients unless she went to the gym for an hour before work.

As far as the best exercise for people with ADHD, here are some suggestions:

>> **Make it last.** It takes time for exercise to trigger a release of endorphins, and you really want this release to happen, so plan on at least 30 minutes of intense exercise to get the most benefit. We know of many people who regularly exercise for an hour at a time to have the most reduction in their symptoms.

>> **Make it intense.** You need aerobic exercise to get the blood flowing. Intense exercise also increases levels of endorphins and other chemicals in the brain, which seems to help with the symptoms of ADHD. This creates a feeling of euphoria and can reduce the feelings of depression that many (most) people with ADHD experience. If you go for a walk, make it a fast walk. If you do yoga, make it ashtanga or kundalini yoga rather than one of the more passive types.

>> **Keep it interesting.** Running on a treadmill or mounting a stair-climber machine can be agonizing for people with ADHD because these activities are so boring. Listen to music or mix up which machines you use. If you want to run, run outside. The scenery will help keep you from getting bored.

>> **Make it flexible.** Choose an activity that allows you to keep control of both the intensity and the time that you do it. This increases the chances that you'll enjoy what you're doing and allows you the flexibility to follow your desires for the day. That's why some people with ADHD don't enjoy team sports — they can't march to the beat of their own drums. (Plus, the social interactions can be challenging.)

>> **Make it convenient.** If you have to drive across town or go through some elaborate ritual in order to get your exercise, we guarantee that you won't keep it up for very long. Finding an exercise program that's easy to get to and get started with increases the chances that you'll keep it up.

>> **Keep it simple.** Avoid exercise that takes too much mental energy to figure out or that can be frustrating if done incorrectly. Choose activities that allow room for error so you can focus on getting your heart rate up rather than having to focus on making sure you do everything right. For adults, this means staying away from golf (just kidding!). For children, this means choosing exercises that match their level of ability. For example, if you enroll your child into a martial arts program, make sure it isn't too advanced for them.

Limiting media

The rise of smartphones and tablets has put digital media at everyone's fingertips. Most people have ready access to a smartphone, with about half spending the majority of their waking hours texting, checking social media, watching videos, or otherwise engaged online.

Social media, video games, and TV provide ample opportunity for distraction, promote solitary activity and passivity, and can influence your nervous system. The Internet, social media in particular, is an endlessly distracting potential time-sink for the ADHD brain. The attractions of the Internet and social media are especially difficult for people with ADHD to resist, thanks in large part to traits like time blindness, impulsivity, and hyperfocus.

REMEMBER

We aren't saying media consumption causes ADHD, but it can exacerbate the symptoms. Limiting your media consumption, difficult as it may be, can go a long way to minimizing your ADHD symptoms.

Ensuring the best sleep possible

One very difficult aspect of ADHD is that your sleep is generally disturbed. And if you're the partner or parent of someone with ADHD, chances are their sleep problems sometimes keep you awake.

TIP

The key to getting a good night's sleep is following what's called good *sleep hygiene*. Here are some suggestions for improving your own sleep hygiene:

>> **Use sugar and caffeine wisely.** For many people, avoiding sugar and caffeine for at least two hours before bedtime can help them wind down to go to sleep. But this isn't always the case. Some people with ADHD find that caffeine can actually help them go to sleep. And if you happen to drink a glass of warm milk to help you go to sleep, putting some sugar or honey in it will actually help the *tryptophan* (an amino acid) get absorbed into the brain, where it can promote sleep.

>> **Get enough exercise during the day.** We know of no better way to ensure good sleep than to be physically tired. However, be aware that exercising late in the day may cause sleeplessness. For more on the benefits of physical activity for ADHD, head to the earlier section "Exercising regularly."

>> **Eat a protein-rich snack before bed.** Nighttime hunger is one of the more common reasons a person can't get to sleep. This can be more of a problem if you experience a loss of appetite due to the medication you're taking for your ADHD. Eating a protein-rich snack can fill you up and calm you down.

>> **Make your room a quiet and dark sanctuary.** Eliminating light and noise can do wonders for your sleep. (Of course, exceptions do exist — you may be the sort of person who can't sleep without a radio or TV on.) For younger children who need a light on, try using a nightlight or a slightly opened door to create a subdued light.

» **Set a consistent bedtime.** Most people function best with a consistent routine, and bedtime is no exception. Set a bedtime and try to stick to it. You'll find that your body gets into the groove, and the transition becomes easier. This is especially important for kids, who thrive on consistency and need their sleep.

» **Create a bedtime transition ritual.** This practice can involve reading a book, taking a bath, or doing any low-key activity that helps you transition from the bustle of the day and allows you to calm down.

» **Listen to calming music.** Find some music that calms you down, or use music specifically designed to help calm your nervous system. (Shameless plug time: Check out Jeff's website, www.stronginstitute.com, for some options.)

» **Turn off technology before bed.** The blue light from devices interferes with your body's production of *melatonin,* the hormone that helps you get to sleep and wake in the morning. Ideally, you want to shut tech down as early as two to three hours before bed, but that may not be an option if, say, someone is doing homework on their computer. At the very least, turn it off 30 minutes before bedtime. (And check out your device's display settings; many now offer an option that helps filter blue light.)

IN THIS CHAPTER

» Charting school challenges

» Understanding your legal rights

» Taking steps to get your child help at school

» Helping your child's teachers

» Considering other types of schooling

» Offering academic support at home

Chapter **16**

Creating Success at School

For a child with ADHD, school can seem like an endless source of confusion and frustration. In fact, failure in school is often the first indication of ADHD.

Helping your child succeed in school requires you to understand the challenges that kids of different ages experience, know your legal rights and how to assert them, work with your child's teachers, and help your child study at home. In this chapter, we discuss each of these topics, plus a few more, so you can be prepared to help your child get the most out of their educational opportunities.

REMEMBER

As a parent, you can do only so much for your child's education. You also need the help of teachers and other school professionals. We encourage you to share this chapter with your child's teachers and work with them to implement some of the ideas we suggest.

Overcoming Challenges at Any Age

Students with ADHD face several challenges that get in the way of being able to learn in a traditional school environment. We don't mean that all people with ADHD have learning disabilities, although many do. What we mean is that the symptoms of inattention, distractibility, impulsivity, and hyperactivity result in specific difficulties in a classroom. The following sections explore how these difficulties manifest at different ages, as well as how to overcome them.

Addressing elementary school issues

Elementary-age children face a host of challenges that can make learning difficult. These challenges include the following:

>> **Understanding instructions:** Misunderstanding is a common problem for people with ADHD. Some people struggle mostly with written instructions, while for others verbal instructions are more difficult. To minimize misunderstandings, you (or your child's teacher) can provide instructions in both verbal and written forms. Also, you can break down instructions into single steps instead of expecting your child to remember a sequence of steps. For younger children who can't yet read, use simple language or pictographs, and ask your child to repeat back what you want them to do.

>> **Reading:** ADHD and reading problems are closely related. Many people with ADHD also have specific reading problems, such as dyslexia. If your child has trouble reading, we suggest you have an evaluation done to determine whether a reading disorder exists. This evaluation usually isn't performed until second grade because many 7-year-olds have some delay in reading that corrects itself naturally.

Other problems that may be related are difficulties with spelling and arithmetic. By identifying these problems early, you can minimize the damage and work with your child's school to develop strategies for coping with them.

>> **Handwriting:** Try as they may, many people with ADHD have difficulty with handwriting. The mechanics of writing — especially in cursive — take a tremendous amount of effort. Some ADHD adults still print because they can't read their own cursive handwriting.

>> **Maintaining attention:** Obviously, inattention is one of the central aspects of ADHD. For children with ADHD, maintaining attention in school is the most difficult task they face. The best way to get and keep an ADHD child's attention is to create a stimulating environment. If you make something interesting, most people with ADHD can focus very well. Of course, this task is easier said

than done in a classroom with 20+ students, because they don't all find the same things interesting.

>> **Sitting still:** This one almost goes without saying, but sitting still is next to impossible for children with the hyperactive/impulsive type of ADHD. The best ways around this issue are to make sure that whatever biological treatments you're using (such as medications or supplements) are working as well as possible and to try to ensure your child has the freedom to move in the classroom occasionally. This movement may mean taking periodic breaks, providing flexible seating options such as exercise balls, or having tools to fidget with. (Check out the sidebar "A few tips for teachers" in this chapter for more details.)

>> **Following rules:** Many youngsters with ADHD don't remember rules. Encourage your child's teacher to post the classroom rules at the front of the class and to frequently repeat them.

>> **Understanding boundaries:** Young students with ADHD often invade other children's space, take their things, and just generally annoy them. If this description fits your child, you need to work hard to help them realize the impact they have on the people (and the environment) around them. You can use repeated reminders or behavioral interventions, such as those we discuss in Chapter 10.

>> **Getting started:** Getting a young student with ADHD started on an activity can be difficult. Two strategies seem particularly helpful: Provide a specific motivation for doing the activity, and show the child how to get past the obstacles that prevent them from starting.

>> **Changing activities:** After you manage to get your child started on a project, you may have a hard time getting them to change to something else. The most effective way to deal with this situation is to prepare them for the change by telling them what's coming up next and reminding them of the change until it happens. Then when the time comes, redirect them to the new activity.

>> **Being organized:** One of the earliest and most persistent problems that a person with ADHD has is getting and staying organized. The sooner you start teaching your child methods for organization, and the more you practice them, the better off you all will be. Your child will probably struggle to keep track of their personal possessions, to remember school papers and assignments, and to maintain order in their work and play spaces. We cover organization in more detail later in this chapter and in Chapter 18.

Managing middle school difficulties

Middle school (junior high) has its own challenges that arise out of both the age of the student and the vastly different structure of upper-level schools compared to elementary schools. The schools themselves have less structure, more transitions throughout the day (often a child goes from having just one teacher all day to having five or six), and more social pressure. Here are some common challenges that the middle school student with ADHD encounters:

>> **Being organized:** Stop us if you've heard this one, but disorganization really is a constant issue. As a student with ADHD reaches middle school, the problems of disorganization expand. Because of this fact, we cover this important subject in detail in the later section "Helping your child stay organized" and offer ways that you can help your child become (and stay) more organized.

>> **Managing conflict:** The combination of a more chaotic atmosphere, less supervision, and added importance on peer relationships means that many middle school students with ADHD have problems getting along with other students. Couple this fact with the tendency of people with ADHD to have less-than-ideal judgment, and the result may be fights and other adverse social interaction, including ridicule and bullying. For tips on reducing opportunities for conflict to arise, see the section "Dealing with Difficult Times in School" later in the chapter.

>> **Completing homework:** Moving from elementary school to middle school usually results in an increase in the amount of homework assigned each day. Your child may struggle with forgetting assignments, getting distracted while doing the work, misunderstanding assignments, procrastinating, and (perhaps most frustrating) doing assignments and not turning them in! Homework is such an important issue that we cover ways to improve performance in detail in the section "Helping with homework" later in the chapter.

>> **Relating to peers:** Many people with ADHD have troubles in peer relationships, and these relationships become more important in adolescence. Several problems may be at work:

- A person with ADHD can be very self-involved, thus not really paying attention to other people's needs.

- Many children with ADHD feel that they must go out of their way to please other people (a result of low self-esteem).

- Some children with ADHD just don't have very good social skills in terms of meeting and getting along with others.

We hasten to add that some children and adolescents with ADHD have better-than-average social skills. We cover this topic more in the section "Opportunities for socialization" later in this chapter and in Chapters 15 and 19.

>> **Composing essays or research papers:** Many people with ADHD struggle to understand the structure of what they're trying to write. Perhaps they can't see the main ideas and how to link them, or they have too many ideas, or they don't have a clear grasp of the mechanics of composition. Having a good teacher who can analyze the particular difficulties a child is having and devise methods for overcoming them can help tremendously.

Another common problem with composition is that many students with ADHD struggle to put their thoughts onto paper. Many times the person's mind goes completely blank as they try to write. Using a computer to write can sometimes help. In addition, software programs are available that can change speech into written text.

>> **Remembering:** Forgetfulness is a big problem for people with ADHD. Your child can deal with this problem in many ways. For example, many phone apps offer tools for timers, note-taking, and organization. You can also use a homework traveler (an item we discuss in the later section "Helping with homework") to record all school-related information. This subject is another big one, so we cover ways to keep from forgetting in the section "Working with Your Child at Home" later in the chapter.

Aside from these added challenges, middle school students also struggle with many of the same challenges that elementary students face (see the preceding section). However, these challenges manifest slightly differently due to the environment and age differences. For example, the lack of ability to honor personal boundaries in elementary-age children can result in a verbal fight over a toy, whereas in middle school it can turn into a major brawl.

Handling high school challenges

Most of the challenges that exist among younger children also exist for teenagers with ADHD. Again, these challenges change over time. For example, a child who had a tough time sitting still (or at all) in elementary school may be able to do so in high school, but they now need to fidget and feel restless while they're sitting. Additional issues that high school students face include these:

>> **Taking notes:** A student with ADHD may struggle to separate important facts from unimportant ones, which makes taking notes tricky. You may find that your child records unimportant information or fails to make important connections. The other problem with note-taking relates to the following

bullet: Many people with ADHD have difficulty listening and writing at the same time. Talk with your child's teachers about allowing them to use a voice recorder in the classroom to alleviate this struggle.

>> **Following lectures:** Listening to a lecture requires the ability to stay focused on the speaker and the content of the speech. People with ADHD struggle with wandering attention, so they miss pieces of information in this situation. In many cases, neither they nor the teacher is aware that information has been missed. Again, requesting the teacher's permission to use a recorder during the lecture may be the solution.

Even if a student can muster the attention to focus and follow what's said, they may have an auditory processing problem, which is common among people with ADHD (see Chapter 6). The result is that they can't discern the meaning. This problem can happen because extraneous sounds mask the important stimulus, or because the student can't decode what they actually hear (this condition is called a *central auditory processing disorder*). Using visual aids and limiting background noises can help reduce this issue.

>> **Getting lost academically:** Because of the added number of kids in the school and the added demands placed on them, many high school students with ADHD get lost and aren't helped or, in some cases, even identified. This situation can lead to all sorts of problems, including poor academic performance, dropping out, violence, and drug use. Being an active participant in your child's education and being their advocate when dealing with school staff and teachers are the best defenses against this downward spiral.

>> **Using drugs:** Drug use among high school kids rises sharply as students get older, and research shows that untreated teens with ADHD are especially prone to this problem. You must keep a close eye on any possible drug use and shut it down before it becomes a problem. Fortunately, several studies show that adolescents with ADHD who are treated for their condition are less likely than their peers to abuse illicit drugs.

>> **Facing an increased workload:** The added workload high school students face often pushes the person with ADHD farther behind. This distance can lead to feeling overwhelmed, failing, or even dropping out. You must closely supervise your child's performance, help them stay on top of their homework, and help them overcome issues of time management. You may find that providing a private tutor is necessary to help them get through the tough areas.

>> **Lacking motivation:** Lack of motivation is common throughout the life of a person with ADHD, and keeping a high school student with ADHD on track requires ingenuity. In high school, conflicts between academic and social demands on the student's time and energy increase substantially. One of the best ways to ensure academic performance is to tie it to something your child is already motivated to do. For example, most schools have a minimum grade

point necessary to play sports, and many children with ADHD like sports. Perhaps this tie is the carrot you need to motivate your child to pay attention to academics.

Cluing into college challenges

By the time a student with ADHD hits college, they've likely developed a variety of strategies to compensate for their condition. However, they still face some challenges. Many of the high school issues we discuss in the preceding section are still relevant in college, and some — such as getting lost academically — become more serious with the additional level of responsibility and academic stress that can accompany college life.

Additional challenges that are specific to the adult education years include the following:

>> **Managing time:** Without parents looking over their shoulders and the structure of high school to keep them in line, many students have difficulty managing their time efficiently and effectively. For example, they may sleep through their alarm in the morning or stay up all night talking or partying.

>> **Maintaining self-discipline:** Many college students start a semester with great enthusiasm only to drop classes by midterm because they don't keep track of their class assignments and they fall behind.

>> **Getting lost academically:** Often college students with ADHD don't recognize when they're having academic difficulties and don't seek out help in time to avoid catastrophe.

TIP

One of the best ways to avoid these potential problems is to enlist the services of an ADHD coach (see Chapter 9) to help you develop some systems for managing your time and set (and follow through on) realistic goals. A coach also checks in with you to make sure you're not getting lost academically and to keep you on track toward your goals. If hiring a coach isn't possible, be sure you meet regularly with your academic advisor at school and work closely with your professors to keep tabs on your progress in your classes.

REMEMBER

Because the legal age of adulthood is 18 in most states (it can be as old as age 21), your child will likely become a legal adult before or during college. At that point your child has the right and responsibility to manage their own life. As a parent, you will not have a voice at your child's school.

Getting to Know Your Legal Rights

Three laws, which apply to people with a variety of conditions, may support your efforts to get the best education you can for your child:

>> The Individuals with Disabilities Education Act (IDEA)

>> Section 504 of the 1973 Rehabilitation Act

>> The Americans with Disabilities Act (ADA)

IDEA and Section 504 are the most used of the three acts for people with ADHD (and any conditions that may occur with ADHD). Although the ADA may come into play for some children, it's not the first place to look for help for your child, so we don't cover it in this chapter. However, Chapter 16 has more information on the role of the ADA for people with ADHD.

This section gives you a glimpse into the often-misunderstood IDEA and Section 504 laws and offers some suggestions for using them to help your child.

TIP

For more detailed information about IDEA and Section 504, check out the website www.wrightslaw.com. This attorney-owned site contains comprehensive information about the legal aspects of special education and childhood disabilities.

Having realistic expectations

We don't want to sugarcoat the situation: Figuring out whether your child is eligible for services under one of these laws is tough. Although many schools try hard to follow the law, getting your child's school to provide these services may require some effort.

REMEMBER

To receive any special services from your child's school, your child must be evaluated. Schools require that the evaluation be conducted by the school district's educational diagnostician (see Chapter 4), but some school districts also accept a diagnosis from a private psychiatrist or psychologist for inclusion in this process. Be sure to talk with your school to find out what criteria exist within your district.

Also, just because your child is officially diagnosed with ADHD — and the school district acknowledges they have it — doesn't mean they're eligible for accommodations or special services. As of this writing, the current interpretation of these laws tends to be that in order to receive accommodations for a disability, the person must be shown both to have a potentially disabling condition and to be suffering from this condition to a degree that it significantly impacts their abilities.

Regardless of your child's legal status, your goal is to help them get the best education they can. The best way to do so is to develop a positive relationship with your child's school and not an antagonistic one. (We discuss this topic in the section "Working with your child's teacher" later in this chapter.) Work on communicating well with the staff, guidance counselors, and teachers at your child's school, and avoid trying to strong-arm them with the law (unless doing so becomes necessary).

Examining IDEA

The *Individuals with Disabilities Education Act* (IDEA) is designed to make sure children with disabilities receive "free appropriate public education." This education is determined through an Individual Education Plan (IEP), which we discuss in the "Addressing Your Child's Needs: Developing an Educational Plan" section later in this chapter.

IDEA is a great idea, but figuring out whether the law applies to your child isn't easy. Some children with ADHD qualify for services under this law, while others don't. Qualification is largely based on a school district's interpretation of the IDEA statutes — not on your child's diagnosis or level of symptoms.

TIP

Because the criteria for qualification under IDEA are up to the school's interpretation, we recommend that you read the IDEA statutes yourself. This way, you can understand how the school is interpreting the law and challenge that interpretation if necessary.

If your child's school performance suggests a problem with their ability to learn, your child's school is obligated to evaluate them to determine whether they're eligible for services under IDEA. Unfortunately, just having a diagnosis of ADHD doesn't ensure that your child is evaluated; the school must decide whether to do so.

REMEMBER

If your child's school refuses to evaluate your child for protection under IDEA, it must give you notice of your due-process rights to contest this decision. Likewise, if the school does evaluate and decides that your child doesn't qualify for IDEA, you have an opportunity to appeal that decision.

If your child does qualify for services under IDEA, you can expect to be involved in an IEP process where your child is given services to try to deal with their impairments. These services can (but may not) include the following:

>> Special education classes

>> One-on-one tutoring

- » A classroom aide
- » Speech/language therapy
- » Occupational therapy
- » Other services offered under Section 504, which we discuss in the following section

Many times, a school refuses services under IDEA and allows accommodations under Section 504 instead. This trade-off may sound fine, but (as we explain in the following section) under Section 504 your school isn't obligated to offer the same level of services for your child.

REMEMBER

Securing IDEA status for your child doesn't guarantee that their education will improve. It means only that your child receives special education services. Your job is to make sure these services are right for them and that they result in a better education. We cover this topic in the "Addressing Your Child's Needs: Developing an Educational Plan" section later in this chapter.

Utilizing Section 504

Section 504 is a more general law that ensures children with disabilities have access to the same education as children without disabilities. Many people refer to Section 504 as a consolation prize for children who are disabled but don't fit the more stringent criteria for special education services under IDEA (see the preceding section).

To qualify for Section 504, your child must have "an impairment that substantially limits a major life activity," such as learning. Compare this wording to the diagnostic criteria for ADHD in Chapter 3, and you can see a pattern emerging.

Yep. It's not a black-and-white issue. The subjective nature of both the ADHD diagnosis and the Section 504 protections leaves a lot of room for interpretation (just like with IDEA). Guess who does the interpreting? Right again: your child's school. That's why, as with the IDEA statutes, we suggest that you educate yourself about Section 504 and be prepared to fight for your rights if you need to.

REMEMBER

If your child has ADHD and demonstrates difficulties with learning, your child's school must evaluate for qualification under Section 504 after you've put the formal request in writing. If the school doesn't recommend an evaluation, you're notified of due process and able to contest this decision. Likewise, if the school does evaluate and decides that your child doesn't qualify for Section 504 designation, you can appeal that decision.

If the school determines that your child is eligible for services under Section 504, you have access to certain accommodations in their regular classroom. These may (or may not) include

>> A more structured learning environment

>> Modified tests and/or homework assignments

>> Additional learning aids, such as audiovisual equipment or computer-assisted lessons

>> The ability to use a voice recorder for lectures and instructions

>> Simplified or repeated instructions

>> Visual study aids

>> Modified class schedules and increased time on tests

Your child may also be able to attend special education classes, but this option isn't common under Section 504.

Some schools create an educational plan for your child to determine what accommodations they need, while other schools just offer certain adjustments as a matter of course. Both IDEA and Section 504 require that a student be placed in the "least restrictive environment" consistent with their educational needs.

Addressing Your Child's Needs: Developing an Educational Plan

If your child qualifies for services under IDEA or, in some instances, Section 504, the school creates an educational plan designed to address their unique needs. (We cover these statutes in the earlier section "Getting to Know Your Legal Rights.")

REMEMBER

A word about our conventions: Section 504 calls it an Educational Plan. IDEA calls it an Individual Education Plan [IEP]. If we use the term *educational plan*, that means we're referring to both.

The process of developing an educational plan involves evaluating your child's educational needs and laying out strategies to meet them. To get the best education for your child, you need to be a key player, along with the teachers, in both the development and implementation of this plan. In this section, we offer advice for getting the right plan created and for making sure that it's followed up on properly.

Understanding what an educational plan is

An educational plan is simply a method for educators to determine the best way to teach your child and to help them with them difficult areas. Although each plan is slightly different, they all cover the same basic issues:

>> Your child's present skill/knowledge level

>> The ways the student learns best

>> Goals and objectives

>> The means to accomplish these goals and objectives

>> A way to determine progress (or lack thereof)

We cover each of these issues in detail in the later section "Developing an accurate plan."

Your child's educational plan should spell out exactly where your child is lagging behind and provide detailed strategies for getting them up to speed. Of course, this is an ideal scenario. You must work with the school to make sure that the areas addressed in the plan are indeed the areas your child struggles with and that the plan provides clear objectives and steps for implementation.

Getting involved

If your child qualifies for services under IDEA, your school schedules an IEP meeting, which you're invited to attend. If your child receives services under Section 504, they may or may not get an educational plan — talk with the school staff to find out.

TIP

Make sure you attend the meeting(s) scheduled to set up your child's educational plan. You can play a big role in the process and serve as your child's advocate. Some schools may say that you don't need to attend, or they may even discourage you from coming. We strongly recommend that you don't bow to that pressure — insist on being there, and be ready to fight for your child's rights if you need to.

Developing an accurate plan

When you go to the educational plan meeting, one of the most important things you can do is to make sure the meeting covers the areas of concern for your child and that these areas are adequately addressed.

We certainly hope that your experience with developing an educational plan is positive, but we want you to prepare yourself for the possibility that it won't be. Educate yourself on IDEA and Section 504 before you go into the meeting. Also, bring all the records you've kept for your child (see the "Documenting Your School Experiences" section later in this chapter).

Following are the areas you and the school representatives address as you develop the educational plan:

>> **Your child's present skill/knowledge level:** To know where you're going, you must first know where you are. Therefore, you must first assess where your child is lacking — the areas in which they lag behind other kids their age. The school should use objective measures, such as tests, along with observations to determine your child's skill level. The plan should contain scores from those tests.

>> **Goals and objectives:** A good educational plan has clear, realistic goals for improving your child's performance in problem areas. The goals and objectives should be specific, and they should relate to each of your child's problem areas.

>> **The means to accomplish these goals and objectives:** Goals are useless without a plan for accomplishing them. Your child's plan should list clear, detailed steps for meeting each goal. For example, if one of the goals is to improve reading skills by one grade level, make sure the plan indicates specific reading programs.

>> **A way to determine progress (or lack thereof):** During the meeting you should ask, "How will you determine whether my child is making progress?" The plan should include specific steps for measuring its success, including tests and other objective evaluations as well as homework and in-class exams.

TIP

While you're at the educational plan meeting, make sure you understand who's accountable for implementing your child's plan. Get that person's contact information so you can follow up over the course of the plan.

Keeping tabs on the progress

Call or meet with your child's teacher(s) regularly, and ask for progress reports. Make sure these reports use objective measures to determine whether your child is making progress.

If your child isn't making progress using the educational plan, you have the right to request that the plan be revised. IDEA requires that each student who has an IEP be reevaluated every three years. Overworked school staff may miss that deadline, so you need to keep track of when the reevaluation is due.

Getting the Most from Your Child's Teachers

The teacher your child learns from each day has a huge impact on whether they succeed. (As if teachers weren't under enough pressure.) Finding a good teacher — if you have options — and working with them to develop the best learning environment for your child is in your best interest and your child's. We discuss both topics in this section.

Looking for the right teacher

If you have the luxury of choosing your child's teacher (and not everyone does), here are some characteristics to look for in a teacher who can handle the challenges of a student with ADHD:

>> **Acknowledges that ADHD is real:** A few teachers and other education professionals still don't believe ADHD is real. A teacher who takes this stand in the face of evidence to the contrary shouldn't be teaching your child. If your child's teacher falls into this small category, do whatever is in your power to get them a new teacher.

>> **Is educated or is willing to be educated about ADHD:** With the level of press ADHD has received, your child's teacher most likely knows quite a bit about ADHD or at least has a pretty good idea of where to find more information.

>> **Is patient:** Teaching is a tough job, and the best teachers are very patient people. Look for a teacher with deep reserves of this attribute — students with ADHD need patient people around them.

>> **Employs multisensory learning strategies:** Find a teacher who creates a lively classroom and uses teaching aids that encompass more than simply lecturing in front of the class.

>> **Understands how much effort students with ADHD exert:** As you probably know, your child with ADHD has to work very hard to do things that are fairly easy for people without ADHD. Unless a teacher has worked with a

student with ADHD, they may not know this simple fact. If they don't, let them know. If they accept this fact, they're a good candidate for teaching your child.

>> **Adapts assignments as needed:** Teachers who have experience working with students with ADHD almost always make minor adjustments to assignments to accommodate them. These accommodations can be as simple as letting the student print rather than write in cursive or giving them a little more time to finish an assignment.

>> **Supports your treatment efforts:** Many treatment approaches need to be adhered to while your child is in school, and everyone seems to have strong opinions about different approaches. Your child's teacher needs to be able to honor your wishes as a parent as well as assert their professional point of view.

REMEMBER

This list could go on, but the most important thing to look for in a teacher is someone who's able to treat your child as a unique person and who's willing to work with you to ensure your child gets the best education they can.

Working with your child's teacher

One way to improve your child's success in school is to develop a positive relationship with their teacher(s). Your child is in the presence of their teacher all day long, so you need to have an open line of communication with this person.

TIP

Here are some suggestions for developing a positive relationship with your child's teacher:

>> **Meet with the teacher.** Use this opportunity to explain your child's specific situation.

>> **Offer insight and education.** Provide insights into your child's specific challenges as well as strategies you've developed to deal with them. If the teacher isn't well versed in ADHD, offer to help them learn about it. (For example, lend them this book.)

>> **Develop a plan together.** Help the teacher develop a plan to work with your child. Because you understand your child better than anyone, you can offer valuable ideas and feedback. You can do so when your child's educational plan is developed, but even if your child doesn't have one, you can still work with the teacher to figure out a less formal plan. Most teachers welcome the input and involvement from a concerned parent. (You can find info on educational plans in the earlier section "Addressing Your Child's Needs: Developing an Educational Plan.")

>> **Keep in contact.** Talk to your child's teacher on a regular basis to keep in touch about progress and areas that are causing problems in the classroom.

>> **Respond to concerns.** If the teacher presents a concern to you, take it seriously and work with them to try to address it. This show of goodwill can go a long way to developing trust between the two of you.

>> **Offer support.** Let the teacher know they have an ally when working with your child. The suggestions in this list are good starting points, and you can also consider volunteering in the classroom or helping with difficult times in school, such as transitions. (See the section "Dealing with Difficult Times in School" later in this chapter.)

Trusting relationships between parents and teachers diffuse many of the problems students (and their parents) have in school. If, for some reason, your child's teacher isn't interested in working together, you may need to talk to the school administrators and arrange a meeting with the teacher to work out problems. Or you may need to lobby the school for a different teacher for your child.

A FEW TIPS FOR TEACHERS

Following are a few tips for teaching children with ADHD:

- **Involve as many senses as possible.** Use visual aids, such as charts and diagrams. Employ as many interactive teaching tools as possible, such as lab work, role-playing, group discussions, and multimedia presentations. Use your imagination to get as many senses involved in the learning process as possible.

- **Be clear about your expectations.** When you ask the student to do something, be clear about what you want. You may have to get in the habit of checking to make sure the student hears and understands you. (For example, ask them for immediate feedback.)

- **Help develop study skills.** Pacing and planning — the heart of good study skills — are harder for people with ADHD to develop. By helping students with ADHD develop these skills, you provide them solid abilities that carry over to many other aspects of their lives. Supervise and direct your students in being able to plan for the long term and to create (and implement) intermediate goals. Chapter 17 discusses planning and creating goals as they relate to adults and careers; the same principles apply to students.

- **Create structure.** People with ADHD usually work better when they have an external structure to follow. This structure doesn't need to be rigid, but it does need to be clear (see Chapter 15).

- **Encourage organization.** Help your student with ADHD organize their work and time so they can complete an assignment or project. Lay out a schedule or a list of steps for them to follow, and check to see that they're following it. Use frequent communication and reinforcement to keep motivation high.

- **Make it interesting.** People with ADHD need stimulus to focus. By making lessons interesting (as we're sure you always do!), you provide a stimulus that encourages a person with ADHD to be able to maintain their attention.

- **Avoid the phrase "if you'd only try harder."** Anyone who knows a person with ADHD understands that a lack of desire or effort isn't causing the academic problems associated with ADHD. In fact, by trying harder, they may actually make the biological mechanism responsible for ADHD worse (see Chapter 2).

- **Encourage self-esteem.** Or at least try to preserve it. One way to do so is to avoid singling out the child with ADHD or putting them down in front of the class. Try to find and emphasize areas where the student shines.

- **Eliminate distractions.** Most students with ADHD benefit from sitting in the front of the class and away from the windows. However, sometimes a student needs different accommodations for their distractibility. For instance, some people are more distracted by noise behind them than by things going on in front of them; they'd benefit from not having any other students sitting behind them. Use your observations and judgment and work with your student to find the best place for them in the classroom.

- **Give instructions slowly and clearly.** Also be prepared to repeat instructions if necessary. This task takes patience. It helps if you can remember that the student isn't willfully misunderstanding; they may be trying as hard as you are. Providing input in both a verbal and a written format is helpful.

  Also, many students with ADHD benefit from receiving instructions in the same format and at the same time each day. This consistency helps the student develop the ability to pay attention and comply reliably without having to be monitored constantly.

- **Respect parents' wishes.** A student with ADHD may be engaged in a treatment program that requires adherence to a schedule (such as taking medications or herbal remedies) or certain restrictions (such as being on a special diet). Be as consistent as possible. Whenever you have information that indicates the treatments are ineffective or need adjustment, let the parents know so they can do something about it.

- **Allow breaks.** If you can, allow students a few minutes to move around once in a while. This activity can stimulate the student with ADHD and help them stay on task longer.

(continued)

(continued)

- **Encourage participation.** The more you get the student involved in the learning process, the better they'll be able to understand and retain the information. (This point goes for all students but is especially key for students with ADHD.) Design your lesson plans around participation, even if it's as simple as asking questions. If you do ask questions to encourage participation, let the class know you're going to do so. Otherwise, the ADHD student may freeze up when you call on them.

These suggestions are just a few of the ways you can help your students with ADHD. Many resources are available to help teachers deal with the ADHD student's problems, such as these:

- *Teaching Teens with ADD, ADHD & Executive Function Deficits: A Quick Reference Guide for Teachers and Parents* by Chris A. Zeigler Dendy (Woodbine House)

- *How to Reach and Teach ADD/ADHD Children: Practical Techniques, Strategies, and Interventions for Helping Children with Attention Problems and Hyperactivity* by Sandra F. Rief (Wiley)

Teaching a student with ADHD uses the same basic skills as teaching any other student, but it definitely takes more time, energy, and patience than teaching the average child. If you approach this work as a challenge and get to know the student, the experience will be rewarding for both of you.

Documenting Your School Experiences

We're willing to bet that you're going to have quite a bit of interaction with your child's school over the course of their education. We're also willing to bet that not all of this interaction is going to go smoothly. So to ensure that your child gets the most appropriate education possible and that you have the information you need to make this happen, we strongly recommend that you keep detailed records of your child's school experiences. Doing so can help you keep your child's education on track. These records should include the following:

- » **Report cards:** These records offer a big-picture view of your child's progress.

- » **Educational evaluations:** In particular, make sure you get (and file) copies of any evaluations the school or other professionals that you hired privately have conducted.

- » **Schoolwork samples:** A sampling of schoolwork, including tests, reports, and papers, can provide an overview of your child's progress.

- » **Correspondence between you and the school:** Keep all letters, memos, and original text, email, and voicemail messages that you receive from the school, along with your responses to them.

- » **Notes from meetings and telephone conversations:** Try to take notes as you interact with anyone from the school. This tactic may help you ensure accountability later if you need to.

- » **Medical records:** These records should include not only a health history but also documentation of all the ADHD medications you've tried for your child, what dosages you've used, and their results.

- » **Treatments and results:** List all the treatments you've tried for your child, when they took place, how long they lasted, and how effective they were.

- » **School personnel contact information:** This list should include all your child's teachers and counselors, as well as the nurse, the principal, and any other administrators you've talked to or dealt with.

- » **Healthcare professional contact information:** All the professionals you work with should be on this list, along with their physical and email addresses and phone numbers.

- » **Diagnostic records:** These records include results of any neuropsychological, medical, and psychiatric exams, along with any other information you gathered when trying to determine a diagnosis.

- » **IDEA and Section 504 statutes:** You can find these statutes at www. wrightslaw.com. We also provide information about them in the earlier section "Getting to Know Your Legal Rights."

- » **Educational plan data:** This information should include notes from the meetings, the educational plan itself, and any data regarding the outcome of the plan. Flip to the earlier section "Addressing Your Child's Needs: Developing an Educational Plan" for more on these plans.

REMEMBER

The purpose of these records is to track and evaluate your child's progress in school, or lack thereof. This monitoring is very helpful for making future decisions regarding their education. These records are especially important if you're seeking (or have already received) accommodations for your child under either IDEA or Section 504.

Dealing with Difficult Times in School

Certain times of the day, and certain situations, cause more problems than others for a student with ADHD. The culprits are often the less structured times of the day, such as lunchtime and recess. Other problem situations include transitioning from one activity to another, interacting with fellow students or teachers, and dealing with people who don't understand ADHD.

Lunchtime and recess

Even though lunchtime and recess can allow great opportunities for your child to burn off some energy, they're also two of the most difficult time periods for students with ADHD for several reasons:

>> **The noise and chaos can be overwhelming.** Overstimulation in a noisy or busy environment can cause behaviors that are difficult to control, such as tantrums (for younger kids), frustration, and aggression. Try to keep the student out of the main thrust of activity, and offer a calm, quiet place for them to retreat to.

>> **Other kids can pick on them.** Without the structure of a classroom and the close oversight of the teacher, lunchtime and recess often provide an opportunity for other kids to pick on a student who's "different."

>> **They can get into trouble.** Again, because of the lower level of supervision during lunchtime and recess, many students with the hyperactive/impulsive type of ADHD can get into trouble. They may impulsively do things they shouldn't or act out in inappropriate ways.

>> **Getting back to work is tough.** Going from the high-stimulation lunchroom or playground to the (supposed) quiet of a classroom takes time for someone with ADHD. Building this time into the student's day is important for them to get any work done after lunch.

TIP

Because lunchtime can be overwhelming for students with ADHD, offering younger students a quiet place to eat may be beneficial so they don't become over-stimulated and difficult to calm down when it's time to get back to work. Another option is to schedule their mealtime at a different time of the day. Naturally, this type of accommodation needs to be weighed against students' need for socialization and the need to avoid being stigmatized. If separating a student from their peers doesn't seem like the best option, the suggestions in the next two sections can help mitigate the problems that lunchtime can pose.

Transitions

Changing activities (moving from one class, assignment, or activity to the next), environments (such as coming inside after recess), and schools are all hard on children with ADHD. These transitions can cause frustration, depression, tantrums, and other reactions. Many children with ADHD tend to get stuck and not want to change activities.

The best way to deal with transitions is to prepare the student for them. You can do so by trying these ideas:

>> **Tell them what's coming next.** Repeatedly let the student know what activity or change is coming and what you expect from them during the transition. By knowing what's ahead, many people with ADHD can more easily break from one thing and move on to another.

>> **Make the change gradual.** You can soften some transitions by creating a gradual change, such as by adding an interim activity that allows for a change in mindset and makes a ritual event out of the transition itself.

>> **Create a set routine.** When you do things in a routine way, everyone involved gets in the groove, and you all know automatically what comes next and when. This kind of routine is self-reinforcing, too.

Opportunities for socialization

Many children with ADHD have problems socially. These issues can stem from the person with ADHD struggling to understand boundaries, recognize how other people feel (empathy, which we discuss in Chapter 15), and regulate their own emotions or attention. Sometimes problems arise from a simple lack of training in the necessary skills.

Some of the most common social problems ADHD children have are these:

>> **Being self-centered:** Sometimes children (and adults) with ADHD don't seem to understand that other people have their own interests and needs. This trait may come from a lack of self-awareness or from the child's difficulty understanding themselves in the context of the groups they belong to. It often causes problems with peers, parents, and teachers.

>> **Taking over:** Many children with ADHD dominate their peers through bullying or being bossy. This tendency can cause them to have trouble making and keeping friends, especially in their own age group.

>> **Being a poor sport:** Some children with ADHD have a serious problem with losing. They may cheat to win at games or may throw tantrums if they lose.

>> **Commanding all the attention:** In a classroom, a student with ADHD may try to take all the teacher's attention. (Often the class clown is a person with ADHD; making their peers laugh may give their self-esteem a needed boost.) Sometimes the child has difficulty modulating the intensity of their communications, so they speak too loudly, talk too much, or intrude physically into

ongoing activities. At other times, the child may simply require a lot of the teacher's attention to stay on task and behave appropriately.

>> **Invading another person's space:** Children (and adults) with ADHD often have a hard time recognizing other people's personal space. They may also have a poor concept of their own presence in space. As a result, they often invade the space of others.

>> **Butting into conversations:** ADHD makes it difficult for children to keep a thought in mind for long, especially if they have to wait for someone else to finish speaking. Because of this issue, and because of the difficulty people with ADHD have picking up on subtle body language, they often miss the rhythm of a conversation and choose the wrong time to add to it.

>> **Being unable to follow a conversation:** Many times, children with ADHD misunderstand what's being said in a conversation. As a result, they may say something that doesn't relate to what's been said.

>> **Taking over a conversation:** Again, because someone with ADHD may not pick up on cues relating to other people's needs, they may command the conversation and not let other people have their say.

>> **Not understanding why others get upset at them:** Because people with ADHD often miss social cues and have difficulty understanding another person's viewpoint, your child may not understand why someone is upset with them.

>> **Misinterpreting what others say or do:** This point causes a lot of conflict in the lives of people with ADHD. Because they often misinterpret what others say or do, they tend to get upset for what may appear to be no reason — or the wrong reason.

Improving social skills is crucial to improving the educational success of a child with ADHD. The best way for them to learn better social skills is in a group context. Some schools offer social skills classes given by a teacher, school guidance counselor, psychologist, or social worker. Church groups that focus on social interactions are another possibility. And modeling is the best teacher, so be sure you schedule family practice and discussion times.

TIP

One of the best ways you can improve your child's ability to get along with other people — and to understand social cues — is to get them involved in a mediation training program (if your school has one). *Mediation training* involves learning about interpersonal social interactions, learning to see another person's view, and understanding the nature of conflict and how to defuse it.

Interactions with some teachers and administrators

Unfortunately, some teachers and administrators don't yet understand ADHD. Even though ADHD gets a good deal of media attention these days, and professional training on the condition is available, your child is bound to encounter a teacher or school administrator who's uneducated about ADHD.

Most likely, your child will encounter a well-meaning educator who thinks they know about ADHD but holds false impressions or personal biases about the condition and its treatments. Some teachers and administrators still apply methods of teaching or behavior management that are counterproductive for the ADHD student.

WARNING

Obviously, you don't want to tolerate actions such as a teacher humiliating your child in front of peers to attempt behavior control. Nor should you tolerate a principal refusing to provide accommodations on the grounds that they aren't necessary for "troublemakers."

Sometimes you'll deal with educators who have strong opinions about your choice of ADHD treatment(s). Usually the central issue is whether you choose to give your child medication. You may be lucky enough to have a rational discussion with the educator in question, or you may find yourself in a power struggle with the school.

In this type of situation, you may have to defend your actions and beliefs to your child's teacher or the school administration. The best way to do so is to remain unemotional (easier said than done, we know) and arm yourself with as much scientific data regarding the validity of your position as you can find. Obviously, you benefit from having close contact with professional resources, such as your child's doctor, so you can get outside support.

Exploring Schooling Alternatives

Even with an effective treatment plan and solid life strategies, some children with ADHD just don't fit very well into the modern-day school system because of their different learning styles (see the sidebar "How does your child learn?"). A standard classroom with a teacher lecturing most of the day is often the worst possible environment for acquiring information and knowledge.

Your child may not have to be stuck in this type of classroom. Other types of school environments offer a variety of teaching styles that may be more effective for your child with ADHD. Depending on where you live and your lifestyle, you may have alternative options for schooling your child. These options include the following:

- >> **Charter/magnet schools:** Most school districts have at least one school that uses alternative methods of teaching or that focuses its curriculum on a specific area of study. These schools are called *charter* or *magnet schools*. Check with your district to see whether a charter school exists and whether any that do have a program that relies less on classroom lectures and more on interactive or hands-on approaches.

- >> **Private schools:** Most large towns and cities have a variety of private schools, and some offer a more varied learning environment than the traditional public school. Even if the teaching style is traditional, private schools often offer smaller classes, so each child is more likely to get individual attention. If a private school is a possibility for you financially (you may find a school that offers scholarships or other financial aid), you may find a program that meets your child's needs.

  Residential private (boarding) schools also exist, some of which offer help for specific learning problems. Your child may be a long way from home, but they may also get a super education.

- >> **Homeschooling:** Homeschooling is a viable option for families that have a parent at home during the day. Once relegated to the lunatic fringe (we mean this in the nicest way possible — your coauthor Jeff raised a homeschooled child), homeschooling has become a legitimate form of education and can offer much more flexibility for a child who has difficulty in a traditional schoolroom setting.

  Homeschooling takes many forms, from *unschooling* (unstructured, natural learning) to curriculum-based programs, and each state has different requirements for monitoring homeschool education. If you're interested in exploring this approach, do an Internet search for "homeschooling resources."

REMEMBER

If your child's school isn't cutting it for you (or them), don't be afraid to look into alternatives. You may end up finding (or creating) a better schooling situation for your child — one where they can learn the way they learn best.

HOW DOES YOUR CHILD LEARN?

People learn in different ways. For example, many people with ADHD don't do well in traditional classrooms because they have a difficult time learning through verbal instruction.

Understanding how your child learns can help you make sure they get the best possible education. Learners fall into at least one of these learning categories:

- **Auditory:** *Auditory learners* absorb information best through verbal instruction. They may have problems with reading or writing and often miss subtle body language cues. Some students with ADHD, though not most, fall into this category.

- **Visual:** *Visual learners* learn best through visual teaching methods, such as images, color, graphs, diagrams, and charts. These people may have a hard time with verbal instructions and need to have assignments written down for them. More people with ADHD seem to be visual learners than auditory learners.

- **Kinesthetic:** *Kinesthetic learners* do best when they can get their hands and bodies involved in the process, such as by doing lab work, building models, or role-playing. Kinesthetic learners often struggle in traditional classrooms because of the lack of movement; they may have a hard time sitting still. The majority of people without the inattentive type of ADHD seem to learn best this way.

If your child is a kinesthetic learner, a regular classroom setting is probably difficult for them (even without the ADHD symptoms interfering with learning) because the modern public school relies for the most part on auditory and visual approaches. If you have the option, look for a school environment that employs teaching methods that incorporate multisensory activities, interactive computer learning, and hands-on projects.

Working with Your Child at Home

To help your child succeed at school, you need to deal with many aspects of their education at home.

REMEMBER

Children with ADHD take longer than others to learn self-discipline, and they need a much more structured environment (though not a *rigid* one) in which to learn this skill. Helping your child develop self-discipline is necessary so that they can take care of themselves. This job often means letting them experience the consequences of bad choices (not doing their homework, for example) or inappropriate behaviors.

Helping with homework

You'll almost certainly need to offer more help with homework to your child with ADHD than you would to a child without ADHD. Here are some suggestions for helping your child with their homework:

>> **Provide a quiet, distraction-free place to study.** The fewer distractions — such as other people or TV — the better the chance your child will be able to concentrate. Help your child find a quiet place to work, or help them screen out noise by providing aids such as earplugs, a white noise generator, or their favorite music (as long as the music actually helps them focus).

>> **Encourage breaks.** Allowing for a break every 20 minutes or so can help tremendously. Many families use a timer and set it for 20 to 25 minutes. When it dings, your child takes a 5-minute break, which should include some physical activity.

>> **Have them work in small chunks.** Set a time limit on a particular piece of homework. During one 20-minute work period, for example, have your child work on one thing. Then, even if that project isn't complete, switch to another activity during the next work period, and come back to the first project later. By varying the activity, your child has a better chance of getting something done rather than staring at the same thing over and over again.

>> **When it's beneficial, let your child work for as long as they're on track.** The previous two bullets are true for many students with ADHD; but if your child has difficulty getting started on a project, letting them work undisturbed after they get going may be best.

>> **Set a schedule.** Having a set time of the day to do homework can help your child remember to do it and be more prepared to focus on it.

>> **Establish a way to keep track of assignments.** One of the main problems that students with ADHD face is not remembering the homework assignment or forgetting to bring the proper materials (such as books) home to do it. Develop a system to keep track of homework.

TIP

One common solution is what's called a *homework tracker* or *traveler*. This journal goes back and forth between school and home and documents whether homework assignments are received, completed, and turned in. Having a homework tracker makes keeping track of schoolwork much easier and helps you understand where the breakdown in follow-through occurs. Talk to your child's teacher about setting one up.

>> **Help get the homework back to the teacher.** A good method is to have one folder where finished homework goes as soon as it's complete. Nothing but ungraded, finished homework goes in the folder, and the folder is permanently bonded to your child's skin so they can't forget it (just kidding).

Develop the habit of making sure the folder is in your child's possession (in their backpack or notebook) as they leave for school.

>> **Empower your child's time management.** Most students with ADHD have no idea how to manage their time. They may look at an assignment and not know how long to expect it to take, or they may doodle on something for hours, not getting anything done. Help your child manage their time by looking over their assignments and helping them devise a schedule to follow when doing the work. This point is especially important with long-term projects that are easily pushed off until the last minute. Teach your child to pace themselves so they can get a bit of work done on a long-term assignment every day. A big, monthly calendar with enough space to write out assignments and work plans can be very helpful.

REMEMBER

You walk a fine line between helping your child do their homework and doing it for them. Resist the temptation to help too much. You want to help keep them on task and help them over any hurdles that stop them while they work. But make sure you don't fall into the trap of having to ride your child in order for any work to get done. This pattern is called *negative reinforcement*, and it's a hard one for everyone to break. (We cover this important point in more detail in Chapter 10.)

Arranging for a private tutor

In spite of your best efforts, and the school's, you may not be able to get your child to learn what they need to know. In this case, you may find that a private tutor can help break ground that you or the school can't on your own. With a private tutor, your child gets one-on-one instruction from someone who (we hope) is an expert at helping kids with learning difficulties.

TIP

Sometimes a child just needs some tips and motivation from someone who has done the work before. In that case, an older student who did well in the subject may be the ticket. The tutoring doesn't cost you as much, and finding a willing student may be easier than finding a professional tutor.

If you decide to seek a professional tutor for your child, here are some things to look for:

>> **Experience with children with ADHD:** Look for a tutor who has worked with children with ADHD before and understands the special needs they have. For example, most experienced tutors know a student with ADHD can't sit for long periods of time and learns best when they're actively engaged in the learning process. Look for a tutor who uses a lot of multisensory teaching aids.

>> **An evaluation that identifies problem areas:** Many tutors look at school-work samples and report cards, and they talk with parents at length about the areas that need addressing.

>> **A clear, specific plan for your child:** After an evaluation, most tutors develop a clear plan — much like a school's educational plan — to show you what they're going to work on with your child.

>> **Communication and follow-up:** Because the tutor works only for you, you can expect direct communication and follow-up regarding your child's progress.

Private tutors can do wonders for helping your child get over some learning hurdles. You can generally find good ones in your area by asking your child's teachers or by asking your ADHD professional.

Supporting self-esteem

REMEMBER

The biggest hit to self-esteem that a child with ADHD takes is from school. Between peers, teachers, and failed schoolwork, a student with ADHD struggles to keep a positive view of themselves. Add to this perception the fact that many people with ADHD are barraged by negative thought patterns, and you end up with a recipe for low self-esteem.

According to psychologist Robert Brooks, the most important keys to self-esteem are the approval and attention of a respected elder and the development of *islands of competence* — areas of activity that the child is good at already and encouraged to develop further.

Check out Chapter 15 for ways to keep school from eroding self-esteem as well as ideas to help build it back up again.

Helping your child stay organized

Organization and planning are two of the most difficult areas for people of any age with ADHD to handle, but for children these areas can be exceptionally problematic. We offer suggestions for getting organized in Chapter 18. But this issue is such an important one that we want to provide some specific suggestions for things that you can do with your child to help them be organized:

>> **Document your child's schedule.** Write your child's daily schedule on the calendar and post it where they and you can easily see it.

>> **Get your child a wristwatch.** By having your child wear a wristwatch or smartwatch you reinforce the idea that time means something. Smartwatches can also be programmed to include alarms and alerts (see the next bullet), increasing their chances of keeping on schedule throughout the day.

>> **Use alarms and alerts.** Many people with ADHD find alarms and alerts helpful because they can be reminded of important events. Most alarm and alert cellphone or smartwatch apps vibrate quietly instead of making noise, which prevents the notification from distracting others.

REMEMBER

Devices that provide alarms and alerts may not be welcome in some classrooms, but may be allowed as part of an individual education plan (see the "Addressing Your Child's Needs: Developing an Educational Plan" section earlier in this chapter).

>> **Use a smartphone.** As we discuss in Chapter 18, a smartphone is a great tool for a person with ADHD. You can find apps for almost any need someone with ADHD may have. The most relevant apps for children tend to be those that aid in organization or keeping a schedule (see the earlier alarm and alerts bullet).

>> **Color code.** Using visual reinforcement for the placement of your child's things can go a long way to helping them keep their stuff organized — especially schoolwork. Chapter 18 has more on color-coding.

>> **Use organizing systems.** Develop simple systems that improve organization. For example, keep a series of well-marked notebooks to assist with homework assignments or list upcoming long-term project deadlines on a bulletin board or white board.

TECHNICAL STUFF

>> **Set aside time to keep organized.** Okay, this one isn't really school-specific, but it's a great organizational strategy. Have a set time each day to go over what's happened and what needs to happen and to help return order to spaces that have gotten out of control. This period can also serve as family time; you don't want to do all the work yourself, and your child probably won't want to do it without some congenial company to help them keep on task.

Chapter **17**

Winning at Work

The symptoms of ADHD obviously affect your ability to perform a job. For example, distractibility often makes keeping on task and doing the job at hand difficult. Inattention often leads to misunderstanding what other people say and can cause problems with work relationships or assignments. Impulsivity in the form of saying the wrong thing without thinking first can result in problems with coworkers or your boss. Hyperactivity or restlessness makes sitting at a desk for long periods of time uncomfortable, if not impossible.

In this chapter, we explore many of the challenges that people with ADHD face in the workplace. We let you know what your legal rights are and discuss whether you should let your boss or coworkers know about your condition. We also explore ways that you can more effectively manage yourself and your symptoms, as well as ways to improve work relationships. The chapter ends with ideas to help you be successful both on a daily basis and in creating a career that's rewarding and enjoyable long term.

TIP

Many of the challenges that present themselves at work are the same as those you have to deal with at home or your child confronts at school. Check out Chapters 15 and 16 for ideas about daily life skills that may help you in your professional life as well.

Getting an Overview of ADHD Challenges at Work

For people with ADHD, work presents a variety of challenges. Many of these challenges mirror difficulties that exist in any other relationships, but some are unique to a job or career. This section offers a glimpse into some of the struggles that may be present in your daily work environment, which we discuss in more detail throughout the chapter. These include the following:

» **Creating balance:** People with ADHD have a real tendency to go to extremes. You may tend to either avoid work or be totally absorbed in it (a workaholic). As a person with ADHD, you need to work harder than other people at the job of creating and maintaining balance in your life.

» **Getting along with others:** Relationships are often tough for people with ADHD, and the various relationships at work present specific challenges. Depending on your position, you need to ensure that your relationships with coworkers, your boss, and/or your employees (if you're the boss) are as strong as possible.

» **Maintaining perspective:** Seeing the big picture while also dealing with the day-to-day aspects of a job can be especially tricky for someone with ADHD. You can easily get lost in the project at hand and forget that other work needs to be done as well. On the flip side, you may have trouble focusing on the task at hand because you're so fascinated with the grand scheme of things.

» **Being organized:** Organization (as we say many times in this book) is a major life challenge for people with ADHD. Being organized at work isn't as impossible as you may imagine, though. The tips we offer in this chapter can make it fairly painless.

» **Managing yourself:** To be an effective employee or boss, you must be able to control your emotions, take responsibility for your actions, and just generally have a handle on yourself.

» **Planning ahead:** One of the areas where people with ADHD struggle is in being able to make a plan to achieve a specific end, whether that end is related to a single task or your entire career. The ability to plan, execute, and completely follow through takes some skill, which we help you develop in this chapter.

» **Sticking with it:** Being able to stay on task — both on small and big projects — is difficult for many people with ADHD. You need to be able to follow through on a project, and you need to not quit your job impulsively.

To Tell or Not to Tell: Sharing Your Diagnosis with Coworkers

Should you inform your coworkers and boss about your ADHD? The answer isn't clear-cut. In this section, we explore some legal and practical aspects of making this decision.

Legally speaking: Understanding your rights

If you have ADHD, the Americans with Disabilities Act (ADA) may offer you some legal protection at your job. The ADA was designed to protect workers against discrimination based on their disabilities and to allow for some accommodations on the job or in the work environment.

REMEMBER

Just because you're officially diagnosed with ADHD doesn't mean that you're eligible for accommodations under the ADA. (As we explain in Chapter 4, an *official* diagnosis is one made by a professional who's legally entitled to give one.) The current interpretation of the law is that to receive accommodations for a disability, you must demonstrate both that you have a disabling condition and that you're disabled by the condition to a significant degree. The way eligibility is determined varies depending on where you work, such as if you have a government job or work in private industry, and whether you work for a big or small business. You need to check with your human resources office to find out what the procedures are for determining your eligibility.

For people with ADHD, the ADA may offer accommodations such as the following:

>> **Altering your work environment:** This step may include such things as letting you use a white noise generator or music to block out the sounds around you or allowing you to work in a private office rather than in a large room with other people.

>> **Trading for a different job:** Sometimes a person covered under the ADA can trade jobs with another employee and end up in a more suitable position.

>> **Moving to a vacant position:** If another job exists that you can do better than the one you're in, and that position is vacant, you may be able to change jobs.

REMEMBER

The ADA isn't designed to help you find or keep a job. It's intended only to protect you from discrimination due to your disability. What this distinction means in the real world is that you still need to be qualified for the job and able to perform the job offered to you.

Even if you do receive accommodations at work, you're still required to perform your job according to the job description at the level required by your employer. Accommodations under the ADA don't entitle you to slack off or protect you from being let go if you don't meet your employer's expectations.

The ADA offers some protection, but an employer can fire you — or not hire you in the first place — for many reasons. For this reason, suing an employer and winning on the grounds of discrimination under the ADA is extremely difficult. For more information about the ADA, check out www.ada.gov.

Practically speaking: Making your decision

After you know a little something about the limitations of the ADA (see the preceding section), you may still be asking, "Should I disclose my ADHD at work or not?" Well, in some cases you must disclose your ADHD. These instances include the following:

>> **If you're on medication and your employer uses drug tests to enforce a zero-tolerance policy:** The ADHD medication you take may cause you to test positive for amphetamines. You must let your employer know ahead of time that you're taking medication for your ADHD so you avoid being fired as a result of a positive test.

>> **If your employer requires that you disclose your health as a condition for employment:** You may face this requirement if you need a security clearance, for instance. Not telling your employer about something like having ADHD may be grounds for not hiring you or for dismissal.

>> **If your employer requires a medical history for health insurance coverage:** When you apply for the job, you may not be required to tell your employer that you have ADHD. Or you may have to declare your past medical history for coverage under your employer's health insurance. If you have a formal ADHD diagnosis that is in your medical records, you may have to disclose your ADHD or else risk having your insurance canceled when the company discovers that you didn't report your condition.

If these scenarios don't apply to you, and if your symptoms don't deter you from doing your job, you may not need to let your employer know about your ADHD. Only you can make the final decision, based on figuring out who your employer is and how they treat people who require some accommodations.

REMEMBER

Even if you decide not to disclose your ADHD at first, you may need to rethink your decision later, so keep your options open by not misleading the boss or your supervisor. Being private isn't dishonest, but some people with ADHD can't resist embellishing the truth. If you tell a tall tale about yourself to cover up the fact that you have ADHD, don't be surprised when the boss gets upset about finding out the truth.

Managing Yourself

No matter how you slice it, *you* are the person responsible for conducting yourself in a professional manner at work. Some of the issues you may need to work on include these:

>> **Improving your self-esteem:** People with ADHD often have fragile self-esteem, if they have any at all. Low self-esteem in the workplace can manifest in a variety of ways, but a key thing to beware of is relying too much on other people's perceptions of you and your abilities. If you put too much weight on what other people think, you risk feeling defensive or trying too hard to please them. As a result, you may feel angry and underappreciated.

>> **Coping with emotions:** The biggest emotional struggles people with ADHD have are not acknowledging their emotions and/or externalizing them. If you don't acknowledge your emotions, you may react strongly (externalize) without knowing why. Acting out your feelings can result in various difficulties with your coworkers. You must work on recognizing what you really feel. When you know what your feelings are, you can more easily communicate them to other people and get what you need.

>> **Getting to know yourself:** ADHD can inhibit self-awareness; as a result, you may not even know where your strengths and weaknesses lie. Such knowledge is crucial for success both on the job and in personal relationships. Knowing how you think and react can help you develop skills for handling situations better. In Chapter 9, we discuss many forms of counseling and therapy that can help increase your self-knowledge.

REMEMBER

Part of knowing yourself is understanding your values. Being honest and consistent is easier when you know what's important to you. Developing an awareness of your value system helps improve your self-esteem, too.

>> **Taking responsibility:** To be successful in any aspect of life, you must be able to own up to your responsibilities and understand your role in the situation you're in. But many people with ADHD aren't able to see the role their own actions play in their lives. For example, perhaps you struggle to understand that pointing out where your boss is wrong may not be a good career move.

If you get fired for being insubordinate, you may think your boss is at fault, not you.

>> **Sticking with it:** If you're impulsive and easily distracted, you're going to have to work hard at sticking with projects, jobs, relationships — anything that requires long-term commitment. For example, you may need to pay close attention to your periodic desire to bail from your job. See the sections "Doing Day-to-Day Tasks" and "Creating Overall Success for Yourself" later in the chapter for tips on developing skills to help you stay focused for the long haul.

Working on Work Relationships

Success at work depends on being able to get along with other people, which isn't always easy regardless of whether you have ADHD. When ADHD is part of the mix, you may struggle to understand subtle nonverbal cues that make up a good portion of everyday communication.

Also, distractibility impedes communication. For example, you may be talking to someone but not paying close attention to what you're saying, or you may not be listening because you're thinking of what to say next. Or you may jump from one topic to another. We discuss communication in Chapter 15, and we delve into work-specific topics in the following sections.

Paying attention to office dynamics

To be in tune with what's happening at your workplace, you must develop skills for understanding subtle nonverbal messages, which play a large role in interpersonal relationships. Here are some suggestions:

>> **Ask for clarification.** If you tend to misunderstand what other people say, take this as a cue to ask for clarification. Sometimes the real intent of what someone says isn't very clear, so even if you clearly understand the explicit message, you may miss the point.

>> **Find allies.** Talking to your coworkers and getting their take on what's happening can be helpful. It's always nice to make friends where you work anyway.

>> **Study.** Even though people with ADHD don't come by the skill of interpreting nonverbal messages naturally, you can learn how to do it with practice. For example, try watching TV with the sound off or going to a public place and watching people communicate without being able to hear what they say.

TIP

You can also find books on body language, some of which have a greater scientific basis than others.

Another aspect of politics in the office is understanding how the workplace works. In other words, you need to know where everyone fits in, especially you! You'll be much happier if you know whose toes you can step on without getting chewed out and who you need to keep your toes away from. Getting things done is usually easier if you know how your job fits with everyone else's, too.

REMEMBER

An organization usually has an *official* structure and an *unofficial* one. Finding the official structure should be easy; it's usually published as an organizational chart or written down as a description of the relationships between various job titles (the *organizational hierarchy*). Finding the unofficial structure requires some sleuthing or experience. This task involves watching carefully or talking to old-timers in the workplace to see how things get done.

Dealing with authority

That many people with ADHD have a problem with authority is no secret. Some feel that they can do a better job than their bosses or that their bosses lack vision. Others just don't want anyone to tell them what to do or how to do it. If either description fits you, you need to work on dealing with your feelings about authority without getting fired.

Perhaps you've already developed mechanisms for controlling the impulse to tell your boss exactly what you think every time you think it. If you haven't, we're willing to bet that you've been fired at least once for saying a little too much. You may be asking, "What can I do about my propensity to want to tell my boss off?" We're glad you asked. Here are some suggestions:

>> **Consider the possibility that you're wrong.** Most people tend to believe they're right most of the time, and ADHD can inflate this belief. If you stop to consider that maybe, just maybe, you're wrong and your boss is right, you can often stop yourself from saying something that wouldn't be good for your career.

>> **Consider that being right isn't really the point.** As hard as this idea may be to accept, in the workplace the important issue isn't always who's right but rather who's in charge. You may have the greatest idea in the world or be absolutely correct about something, but if your boss doesn't agree, you're outta luck. This scenario is Office Politics 101 and a hard thing for many people with ADHD to accept.

But before you open your mouth, you must take a moment to decide whether being right is the best thing for your career. If you can resist the impulse to be right and wait for a better time to offer your insight, you may get to keep your job and get a positive response to your ideas.

>> **Take a breath.** By taking a deep breath before you blurt out what you want to say, you give the impulse a chance to abate a bit. Taking a deep breath can also help diffuse the feelings of anger or frustration you may feel, which contribute to your impulse to speak.

>> **Bite your tongue.** The idea here is to develop a personal cue that helps you stop from saying anything that you may regret later (or that may be bad for your career). Choose a discreet physical cue that gets your attention. It can take many forms, from actually biting your tongue (you thought we were kidding, didn't you?) to squeezing your wrist with your opposite hand.

>> **Tell your boss.** If your boss knows about your ADHD, letting them know that one of your symptoms is to say things without thinking them through may be helpful. Doing so may buy you some leeway and get you out of trouble when your mouth runs off on you.

Getting along with coworkers

To be fair, we can't make a blanket statement about how all people with ADHD relate to their coworkers, but we're going to try. People with ADHD generally fall into one of two broad categories: those who are socially adept and those who aren't. (Of course, some people are socially competent in some situations and incompetent in others.)

Many people with ADHD are very social, gregarious, and fun-loving. They're great to have around, at least until everyone (specifically the boss) realizes that no work is getting done. If you're this type of person, your main challenge is to resist the temptation to drop your work and talk to your coworkers.

Other people with ADHD may be very uncomfortable in social situations and often come across as being unfriendly or odd. These impressions may arise because these people often misunderstand or misinterpret what others say. Or the problem may be distractibility, an inability to pick up on nonverbal cues, or the tendency to misread the emotions of other people. These people may also struggle to communicate how they feel.

If you fall into this general category, you may need to improve your social skills with the help of a counselor or therapist. Or, if you're confident that you can't or don't want to develop your social skills, you may need to find a job that requires minimal social contact so you're not forced to interact with others.

Working remotely

Flexible work arrangements have become important in both attracting and retaining talented workers. This shift to remote work or a *hybrid* model which consists of both in-person and remote work, has advantages and disadvantages for workers with ADHD. The areas of maintaining focus, avoiding distractibility, managing time, and setting priorities can create the most challenges. For example, it may be hard to focus at home where you can see that laundry needs to be washed or the animals want your attention. Ideally, it's best to have a separate room in the house with a door that can close. Better yet close the door and put a do-not-disturb sign on it. Don't work in your bedroom or in front of the TV.

Without the structure and external accountability of having to sign in at a specific time or having the routines and rituals of daily office life, some people with ADHD flounder. One solution is to get a work buddy and plan your day. This is someone who can be supportive and help you stay on task. In addition, some people work better when they're able to bounce ideas off their colleagues. They also can exercise their "empathy muscle" by hearing about their colleague's daily struggles during a coffee break. Hybrid models offer some direct in-person contact which many workers prefer.

The flip side of not being distracted is to become hyperfocused on work. You can easily forget to take breaks, eat lunch, or exercise, which are all important for your brain to function well. It's important to stick to routines both before and after work. Remember, work can bleed into family time as it is often hard to put a period at the end of your day. Connection with others, play, meditation, exercise, and socializing, eating well, and sleeping will make you much more effective at your job.

Carol has a client who needs to fidget to focus. She loves that no one can see her tap her feet or do yoga stretches while on a webinar or phone call. She is also sensitive to overhead lighting and other people's noises, which interfere with her focus more so in an office environment. She reports far more productivity without these distractions. She uses many of the strategies listed in this chapter whether she's working in the office or remotely from home.

Being the boss

Being the boss has many advantages for a person with ADHD. One of the biggest is the ability to have other people do the work that you're not so good at doing, such as tending to the little details of a project. Unfortunately, this advantage also opens a can of worms because in order to have someone else do something, you need to communicate what you expect. This management task isn't always simple.

As the boss, you have several challenges when working with your employees. Here are some of the most common challenges and ways to overcome them, or at least minimize their impact:

>> **Speaking too quickly:** People with ADHD tend to talk rapidly. If you speak too quickly when handing out assignments or running a meeting, both you and your employees may become frustrated, and you may need to repeat yourself frequently. Make a conscious effort to slow your speech down. Sure, getting your point across takes longer, but you ultimately spend less time explaining yourself or dealing with misunderstandings.

>> **Not completing your thoughts:** Scattered thinking — a common symptom of ADHD — often manifests outwardly as incomplete thoughts when talking to other people. If you tend to lose track of what you're saying, you may need to use an outline when you're talking with employees, or consult a list of points you want to make. This approach requires preparation, but it's time well spent.

>> **Being unclear:** Because of scattered or fast thinking, many people with ADHD aren't able to express themselves clearly. If this area is one of your challenges, make a conscious effort to be clear when communicating with your employees. Often, providing written as well as verbal instructions and checking to make sure people understand you is helpful.

>> **Not following through:** If you agree to do something for an employee, write it down and follow through on it.

>> **Being impatient:** People with ADHD are notoriously impatient. If you have this tendency, work on developing patience skills. Taking deep breaths in times of stress can help, but your situation may be severe enough to warrant a trip to a therapist (see Chapter 9).

>> **Expecting too much:** Along with the tendency to expect too much of themselves, many people with ADHD also expect too much from others. Be realistic about what your employees can accomplish, and don't pile so much work on them that they burn out.

When you're the boss, you can tailor your work environment to accentuate your strengths and minimize your weaknesses. Unfortunately, many people with ADHD don't stick around their jobs long enough to get a chance to move up the ladder into a leadership position. We talk about this problem in more detail in the "Creating Overall Success for Yourself" section later in the chapter.

Doing Day-to-Day Tasks

In the following sections, we offer tips for getting your work done as efficiently and painlessly as possible.

Getting organized

In Chapters 15, 16, and 18, we devote a lot of attention to organization — obviously, this area is a real problem for someone with ADHD. Following are ideas for creating an organized workspace:

>> **Use a calendar.** Write down every aspect of your schedule on a calendar, and use it! If you're electronically adept, use your computer or smartphone to accomplish the same thing. Or purchase an organizer that has a calendar, pages to create to-do lists, and a planning section.

>> **Color code.** Using visual reinforcement for the placement of your things can go a long way to helping you keep your stuff organized. See Chapter 18 for specifics about using this system.

>> **Use systems.** Develop simple systems, such as file cabinets, In and Out boxes, white boards, or other things that can help you keep track of both your time and things. For example, keep an In box and an Out box on your desk and set aside time each day — even if it's only five minutes — to review what's in each.

>> **Make time to organize.** Schedule a few minutes during the day to get organized. But be careful: A ten-minute "put stuff away" period can easily turn into a day-long "gut it and start over" affair. Limit yourself to a set amount of time. *Warning:* As logical as setting aside a few minutes at the end of the day to straighten your desk may seem, this time of day is often the worst for organizing. By the end of the day, you may be so far behind schedule that performing this seemingly simple task keeps you at work all night. You're better off starting your day with some organizing time. Set the alarms and reminders on your phone to keep you on task throughout the day. When the alarm goes off, go on to the next project.

TIP

If being organized is especially difficult for you, you can hire a professional organizer to help develop a system that works for you. You can find a professional by checking with the National Association of Professional Organizers (NAPO).

Managing your time

When you have ADHD, you can easily spend an entire workday doing inconsequential things (that seem important at the time), such as watering plants and making copies. The day may come and go without your getting any significant work done.

To avoid this problem, create structure for yourself and stick with it. (We talk more about the importance of structure in Chapter 16.) Here are some suggestions for structuring your day:

>> **Plan your time.** Set a schedule for yourself. Many people with ADHD find day calendars or computer appointment programs indispensable.

>> **Make priorities.** If you have a list of things to do that don't have to occur at a certain time, such as researching facts for a report, organize your list in order of importance. For example, cleaning off your desk is a lower priority task than returning phone calls from yesterday (unless your desk hasn't been cleared off for three months, and you know it has some papers on it that need your attention).

REMEMBER

Prioritizing takes practice, because when you have ADHD, cleaning your desk and watering the plants may seem as important as writing a report. In fact, your thinking may go like this: I can't write a report on a messy desk, and I can't focus properly if I'm worried about my plants withering up! We hear ya, and we understand that perception may be a problem. But as you make prioritized lists (perhaps with the help of your boss or a coworker at first), and as you see the results of following them, you discover which tasks are more important than others.

Of course, the same activity may be important to one person in your office and unimportant to another. You won't always please everyone, but with practice the task of prioritizing gets easier.

>> **Set manageable goals.** People with ADHD tend to think they can do more than is humanly possible in a day. Don't put so much on your list for a given day that you set yourself up to fail. Choose a few important things to focus on, and leave others for tomorrow. If you get to the end of your list and have time left in the day, you can always start working on tomorrow's tasks. This area is another where a professional, such as an ADHD coach (see Chapter 9), can help you get started.

>> **Stay on task.** When you have your list set, follow it. Resist the temptation to veer from the list, even if you notice how desperately your file cabinet needs to be reorganized.

>> **Avoid missing appointments.** If your job requires that you meet with people, and you tend to get distracted, develop a method of keeping your

appointments. For example, consider using your smartphone alarm to set alerts that remind you before the meeting begins. Whatever method you use, allow yourself ample time to travel to the meeting site and get yourself focused before the meeting begins.

>> **Ask for help.** If you're lucky enough to have an assistant or someone else you work with to manage your schedule, this person can help provide the structure you need. (College students are often great assistants.) Take advantage of the assistance by asking this person to remind you about returning important phone calls, attending meetings, following up on details of a project, and so on.

Handling larger projects

Compared with tasks that can be completed in a single workday, long-term projects are exponentially more difficult. In Chapter 18, we offer ideas for successfully handling any type of project. If you combine that information with the tips we offer here, you can tackle every project that lands on your desk:

>> **Create an overview.** Start by looking at the big picture. Write down the goal of the project and its major components, such as who is involved, what interim deadlines need to be met, and what resources (financial and human) are required to get it done.

>> **Break it down and set a schedule.** Create manageable steps to follow and determine when they need to occur. Depending on the size of the project, this task may mean creating a daily schedule for yourself or establishing milestones that you must meet each week or month. Build some flexibility into the schedule because becoming accurate at gauging how long certain tasks take needs practice.

>> **Take it one step at a time.** With a solid plan in hand, your job is simple: Follow the steps and the schedule you've created. (Sounds easy, right?) Don't forget to give yourself some reinforcement for getting steps done. If you have opportunities in staff meetings to report on your progress, do so. And consider giving yourself incentives for reaching significant milestones, such as "If I complete the database on Thursday, like I've planned, then on Friday I'll go out to lunch instead of eating at my desk."

>> **Reassess when you get stuck.** Until you have lots of practice breaking down and scheduling a project, you may find yourself getting stuck either because you didn't allow enough time for a step or because you missed an important part of the process. As you work on your project, take time occasionally to reassess whether you're on the right track. Adjust as you need to. This reassessment helps you avoid the pitfall of just giving up when you hit a snag.

REMEMBER

Whatever you do, don't wait until the last minute to start a big project. Procrastination is a common problem for people with ADHD. Some people may need to have the stress of a deadline to motivate them; others may not know where to start on a project; still others may simply forget to keep working because of other things taking up all their time. Regardless of the reason, you must do a little bit each day to move your project forward instead of waiting until the last minute to get started.

If you're the boss and you have other people to help with your project, you also need to learn how to delegate. Yes, we said *de-le-gate*. If you don't know what this term means or have a physical aversion to the concept (which many people with ADHD have), we're talking about letting someone else do some of the work. For tips on working successfully with employees, see the "Being the boss" section earlier in this chapter.

Staying focused

With all the distractions inherent in the workplace — coworkers talking, phones ringing — staying focused and getting work done can be hard for anyone, let alone someone with ADHD. Try employing these strategies to help you stay focused:

>> **Don't forget treatment.** If you're on medication or doing other treatments to improve your attention, follow your treatment plan.

>> **Manage distractions.** Learn to recognize things that easily distract you, and develop techniques for getting back on task. For example, if you have a window in your office, you may need to keep the blinds down or curtains closed whenever you need to concentrate. If pictures on the walls or your desk frequently attract your attention, get rid of them. If the ding of notifications brings you running every time, use the do-not-disturb function on your devices. *Remember:* However, some people find concentrating easier when they're surrounded by chaos; figure out what works best for you before putting yourself in solitary confinement.

>> **Take breaks.** Taking a break every half-hour or so to walk around or stretch can help you focus. Though a little physical activity is ideal, you can also just take an occasional daydream break. After all, you're the most creative person in the office *because* you daydream, right? Just beware of falling into the social media sinkhole during your break, because it can turn into a distraction.

>> **Use music and sound wisely.** Some people find that certain music or background noise can help mask the sound of other people talking. Depending on your work environment, you may need to ask your boss for permission to play music or sound, or you may need to use headphones.

Dealing with details

Everyone, even the boss, has to deal with some details on the job — minor tasks such as returning phone calls. Unfortunately, many people with ADHD aren't good at taking care of details. Here are some things you can do to make sure that you get even the uninteresting parts of your job done:

>> **Write each job down.** Write down even the little tasks so you'll remember them.

>> **Put the list where you can see it.** If your desk is a complete mess, don't put your list on it — you'll never find it. Post it on a wall or door or wherever you're sure to see it frequently.

>> **Consult your list regularly.** Having a list does no good unless you use it.

>> **Set a schedule.** Determine which tasks you're going to accomplish in a given day. But be careful: Many people with ADHD have an unrealistic view of what they can accomplish. Every task takes time, and with practice on the job you'll get better at figuring out how much.

>> **Check the steps off when you're done.** Doing so reminds you that you finished the task and gives you a sense of accomplishment.

REMEMBER

Use technology to help you keep track of the details of your job. For example, computer calendars with alarms can be very useful, especially if your job requires you to be at a computer during the day.

Creating Overall Success for Yourself

With all the challenges that ADHD creates in the workplace, you may be wondering whether having a successful career is even possible. This section assures you that it is. We can't guarantee that you'll earn millions (although that'd be nice), but we can help you figure out how to be happy and satisfied with your life on the job.

Finding the right field for you

If you have ADHD, identifying a career or job that suits you is even more important than it is if you don't have ADHD. Your symptoms may make certain types of jobs (or certain duties at many jobs) impossible, or at least very difficult, to accomplish.

To find the best career or job, you must have a clear picture of your strengths and weaknesses. Chances are that you have a pretty solid idea of where you tend to struggle, and you've probably learned some skills and techniques for minimizing these areas. Finding your strengths may be more difficult. If you don't know where to start, check out Chapter 14. You may also find that therapy can help you discover your strengths (see Chapter 9).

After you identify your strengths and weaknesses, you can then start looking for a job that fits them. This process may involve seeing a career counselor. You can locate a career counselor on the Internet, through colleges' and universities' career counseling offices, and perhaps government agencies such as the Division of Vocational Rehabilitation. (Check your state's website to find the department responsible in your area.)

A wide variety of resources deal with the issue of finding a career. You can find a lot of information by doing an Internet search for "best jobs/careers for people with ADHD."

Pondering long-term plans

How do you want your career to progress? Where do you want to be five years from now? How can you get there? These are all questions that many people with ADHD don't know how to answer (or perhaps even recognize to ask). Even if they do know how to answer them, the answers may be vastly different from one day to the next. But to have a career that advances, you need to know where you want to go and how to get there.

As we note in the previous section, some great resources, such as career counselors, are available to help you manage your career, and we suggest that you take advantage of them. When you have a plan, follow it consistently and reassess it periodically to ensure that you're going where you want to go.

REMEMBER

You'll spend a *lot* of time working in your life. You should absolutely strive to do something that you enjoy and that's rewarding. Having a plan can help you make this happen.

Making your current job work for you

Job-hopping is a common problem for people with ADHD. For some people, it results from being impulsive; they quit because something doesn't go their way. Others take the wrong job in the first place and become disillusioned. Still others struggle with repeatedly making mistakes and being fired for not performing the job properly.

REMEMBER

One of the problems with job-hopping, regardless of the reason, is that it makes finding another job more difficult; employers want employees who are going to stay around for a while. If you're constantly starting over, your chances of moving up the ladder at work are slim as well. If you want a career that has forward momentum, you need to learn how to stick with a job long enough to move up from an entry-level position.

If you're currently in the wrong job, make sure you stay with it long enough to find a job better suited for you so you can keep a roof over your head and food on your table. Resist the temptation to quit without having another job to move into.

TIP

Sometimes "the wrong job" may really be the wrong way of thinking about what you're doing. If you suspect this mindset is the case, have a friendly chat with yourself and make sure your mental mirror didn't come from a funhouse.

Sticking it out when you're in an unpleasant situation can be hard. Here are some ideas to help cope with the situation:

>> **Talk to yourself positively.** Remind yourself why you're working at this job and the reasons you need to stick with it.

>> **Take breaks.** When the stress starts getting to you, take a break if you can. Go to the restroom, step outside, or take a walk if that's an option. Most jobs allow you some ability to take a short break.

>> **Make a plan and follow it.** Create a plan for finding a job that fits you better and follow it. Having a goal can help keep you motivated enough not to do something impulsive like quitting before you can afford to.

Understanding your value in the workplace

Every employee needs to recognize their economic and practical value to other people. As a person with ADHD, you must work on developing a realistic understanding of your value in the workplace (which relates to your skills and education level) and how it relates to the current job market. (For example, jobs that pay you what you think you're worth may not be available.)

People with ADHD often have an unrealistic view of their value in the workforce. Some people, often because of low self-esteem, undervalue themselves and end up in jobs that don't pay enough or don't tap into their skills and abilities. This situation can lead to many problems, including the person quitting even if it isn't in their best interest to do so.

Other people with ADHD have the opposite problem: They overvalue themselves and have an unrealistic view of their worth. They may believe they're indispensable and end up wondering why they were fired or passed over for a promotion.

Sometimes, too, people take jobs they're totally unsuited for out of perceived necessity. Before long, they're forced to recognize that they hate the job or can't do it properly. They quit the job, only to be forced to repeat the cycle. Understanding your economic value, as well as your personal values, can help avoid this frustration.

Striking a healthy work-life balance

Workaholism is rampant among the ADHD population. People with ADHD who find work that suits them generally do very well and get a feeling of success from it. And because many people with ADHD tend to be hyperfocused and have trouble changing activities, everything but work may get pushed aside.

If this description fits you, you must make a conscious effort to create and maintain a healthy balance in your life. Consider these steps:

>> **Honestly evaluate your schedule.** Take a hard look at what you spend your time doing. If your days are filled with work and you don't spend time with your family or pursuing other interests, your life isn't balanced.

>> **Adjust.** After you've evaluated how you spend your time and energy, adjust to create more balance. Talk with your boss or (if you're the boss) your employees about the fact that you need to reduce your work schedule.

>> **Schedule family or other activities.** Initially, you may feel like you're forcing yourself to spend time with your family or to do other activities. With practice, the effort of doing so decreases, and your enjoyment increases. The time away from work may also enhance your abilities at work, and it will certainly make you a more well-rounded person.

Going It Alone: Being Self-Employed

Many people with ADHD dream of being self-employed. Self-employment means not having to answer to a boss who doesn't have a clue, being able to work the way you want to, and being able to take your great ideas all the way to the top. Sounds good, right?

Yeah, but — and it's a big *but* — self-employment also means having to be self-motivated (through large doses of self-discipline), having to plan projects and follow through on them, and having to figure out what your clients want and delivering it to them in a timely manner. Do you see a pattern emerging?

Yep, the skills you need to be successful running your own business are precisely the skills many ADHD people struggle with. Does that mean you can't or shouldn't work for yourself? Absolutely not. It just means you need to understand what you're getting into and figure out how to overcome your weaknesses.

Here are some suggestions for succeeding at self-employment:

>> **Know your strengths and weaknesses.** This advice is the same we offer earlier in the chapter for finding the right career. By knowing where you excel and where you have difficulty, you can create a situation that emphasizes your strengths and find ways to compensate for your weaknesses.

For example, your creativity is probably one of your best strengths. You can use it to help you find a place for yourself in the work world, and you can use it to help you find a way to make the world work for you, too. See Chapter 14 if you need help identifying other strengths.

>> **Get organized.** The earlier section "Doing Day-to-Day Tasks" has a variety of suggestions on this topic, and we suggest you also check out Chapter 18.

>> **Be realistic.** Grandiose thinking is common among people with ADHD. Couple this tendency with wanting to start a business, and you may end up with an unrealistic expectation of your ability to succeed. On the other hand, your boundless enthusiasm (if you happen to be blessed with that) can give your business a tremendous leg up.

>> **Get help.** Being self-employed doesn't have to mean working alone. You can get the help you need in many ways:

- **Hire an employee.** If you can afford it, hire someone to help you in areas that you don't have the time or the skills to deal with yourself.

- **Subcontract.** If you don't want to (or can't afford to) hire someone to work for you consistently, hire out aspects of your business on a per-project basis.

- **Hire a professional.** If you're not a detail-oriented person, you can hire a variety of professionals to help you with some annoying tasks. For example, a bookkeeper or accountant can help you keep your finances straight and pay your taxes on time, an attorney can review contracts, and a secretarial service can provide key support when stacks of unanswered requests are piling up.

TIP

If you want to go the self-employment route, read about starting and running a business, attend business seminars, meet with people who've been successful doing what you want to do, create a business plan, and save enough money for start-up costs before you quit your day job. In other words, look before you leap.

The Small Business Administration (SBA) can be a big help with all these steps. You can reach this organization at www.sba.gov or 1-800-827-5722. The SBA has local chapters, and its website offers tons of information.

5
The Part of Tens

Get organized (and stay there).

Improve your relationships with family members, friends, coworkers, and classmates.

Locate resources for further information about ADHD.

Chapter **18**

Ten (Plus) Tips to Organize Your Life

D isorganization is one of the hallmark problems of ADHD and affects every aspect of life. Someone with ADHD struggles with scattered thoughts, poor time management, cluttered spaces, and unfinished projects, to name a few examples.

In this chapter, we explore ways you can improve the organization of your thoughts, your time, your physical space, and the projects you undertake. At their core, many of these steps are similar, because the key is to develop a system to help minimize the scattered thinking most people with ADHD experience. In some instances, this system may employ high-tech toys, such as smartphone apps. Other situations are decidedly low-tech, such as sorting the mail as soon as you get it rather than waiting until you've got a few feet of paper stacked on your kitchen table.

Writing Down Ideas and Appointments

People with ADHD battle with scattered thinking, forgetfulness, an inability to think things through sequentially, and other symptoms that emerge from an unfocused mind. This section offers some ideas to help you win the battle.

One of the best ways to start organizing your life and your thoughts is to use your smartphone to make notes of things you want to remember. Get a voice note or voice recorder app and dictate into it the things you need to remember. At the end of the day (or when you think you may have forgotten something), review what you've recorded and write it down. (See the next section for tips.)

TIP

The only real drawback to recording is that you may have a hard time quickly locating the information you need. However, some apps can categorize pieces of information, which makes finding a specific section much easier.

If you don't want to use a voice recorder, you can always use a notepad app or go the low-tech route and write the important things down. Even if you use your cellphone to record audio, you may need to periodically write down what you've recorded so you don't have to search through hours of messages later listening for a specific piece of information.

Many people with ADHD write notes on personal calendars, and others simply scrawl their ideas and appointments onto small notepads. If you prefer having a hard copy record, you're better off keeping everything in one notebook rather than scribbling on a lot of loose papers. The main thing to remember is that your writing must be legible and organized if these notes are going to be useful.

Setting Reminders

Another way to use your smartphone is to set reminders for appointments, projects, and other things you need to do (or even to stop doing).

Reminders work best if they contain specific, actionable tasks rather than general events. For example, "Call Steve about the remodel project at 3 p.m." works better than simply saying, "Call the contractor."

Organizing Your Time

Most people with ADHD aren't good time managers. Some may be chronically late, while others are chronically early. ADHD seems to create a disconnect between the reality of how long doing something takes and the perception of how long it takes. In the sections that follow, we offer some solutions for better organizing your time.

Employing Technology

Technology alone can't make sure that you show up on time (see the "Planning Ahead" section later in this chapter). However, cellphone apps can certainly make remembering appointments and deadlines easier.

REMEMBER

With all this help, you just have to make sure you don't lose the device, faithfully enter all important appointment times and deadlines into it, keep it charged, and back up your data regularly.

You may need some time to get the hang of using these aids, but after you get into the groove you can rely on them to keep you on track throughout your day.

Charting Your Schedule

Many people with ADHD have a tough time retaining verbal information and keeping track of things in their minds. For this reason, having a visual layout of your schedule may be helpful.

Day planners and other calendars can help you keep track of appointments and things that need to be done, but you still need to be able to first lay out your day's events in the proper order. This task is easy for things like meetings or school schedules, but for activities that have no set start and end time, the challenge is much greater.

Here are some steps that can help:

1. **Enter all your timed events for the day on your cellphone, day planner, or calendar.**

   Be certain to leave ample time to get to and from each one.

2. **Identify periods of time available for untimed events, and assign an event to each time slot.**

   For example, if you have 30 minutes available after lunch before your next appointment starts, give yourself 20 minutes or so to work on one part of a project you need to do.

3. **Avoid the tendency to try to fit too much in a limited amount of open time.**

   Overscheduling your day can be frustrating and actually defeat the purpose of trying to get things done; you'll develop an aversion to doing tasks if you repeatedly fail at getting anything done.

Planning Ahead

Many people with ADHD have trouble showing up on time for appointments and meetings and gauging how long activities take. To improve your time management skills, you need to work at realistically reviewing your schedule and determining whether you can fit everything into the time you've allotted.

REMEMBER

If you find yourself often (or always) running out of time, let that serve as a red flag: You must adjust your thinking about how long activities take and start adding in buffers to minimize your chances of lateness. Many adults with ADHD do this, and the result is that they're chronically early for appointments. This situation is much better than being chronically late; just make sure you bring some reading material or a portable project with you so you don't become antsy while you wait.

Here are a couple of ideas for gauging the amount of time required for certain activities and arriving to appointments on time:

» **Time your everyday activities.** If you know you need 10 minutes to shower or 30 minutes to drive from home to work, you can look at the clock and decide whether you have time for that activity before you have to move on to the next event in your day.

» **Plan your routes ahead of time.** When you need to travel to a new place, use a travel app or a website and print out a map for yourself. This map not only shows the best route to take but also tells you how long the drive is under normal conditions.

REMEMBER

This can be a tough lesson for some people with ADHD: Just because you have five minutes before you have to leave for your next appointment, you probably don't have time to rearrange the patio furniture or wash the walls in the kids' bedrooms. Don't start a project unless you're confident you have time to complete it, or unless you're aware that you'll need to leave it unfinished and are willing to complete it at a later time.

TIP

Here's another hint: If you always have trouble locating your car keys when you head out the door, start looking for them early enough to find them and still get where you're going on time. Even better, make it a habit to put things in the same place every time. (Then again, that would probably take all the fun out of your day!)

Completing Your Projects

Despite the best of intentions, many people with ADHD can't seem to finish (or sometimes even start) projects such as reports for school or work. Often, the person with ADHD isn't procrastinating because they don't want to do something or needs to feel the pressure of a deadline before getting into gear. Rather, they can't make sense of a project and turn it into manageable pieces.

As you get used to breaking your projects down into small steps, prioritizing these steps, and implementing them (as we explain in the following sections), you'll find yourself creating better breakdowns that will, in turn, make following through that much easier.

REMEMBER

Don't expect miracles the first time you break a project down into small chunks and create a plan to complete each step. Developing plans that work takes experience through trial and error. As you get used to using this process, your project planning skills will improve, and eventually you may be able to tackle projects this way without having to think so deliberately about it.

Breaking things down

Before you try to begin working on a project, take some time to break it down into its core elements. For example, say you have a book report to write. Assuming that you've already read the book, create an outline that lists the main ideas of what you want to cover in the report. Then think in terms of writing each piece of the report separately so you have manageable chunks of work to do each day rather than an entire report to start and finish in one sitting.

Or say you want to clean out the garage, which is on the verge of chaos. Before you start cleaning, take an inventory of the contents of the garage — in general categories such as sporting goods, automotive, junk, household, and so on. Next, make a sketch that indicates where each category of items should be stored. By doing so, you reduce the chances of feeling overwhelmed, and you improve your odds of starting — and completing — the project.

Making a plan

When you have the basic steps of a project laid out (see the preceding section), you can start to develop a plan of attack. Look at your list of things to do and prioritize the order of steps. For example, before you can organize the sporting equipment in your garage, you need to first remove everything and clean the space itself. Only then can you put things back into place. In the case of a book report, before you can write you need to do some research (by reading the book, for example).

TIP

Your plan should address all the steps in the breakdown you create for your project and have these steps in the order that makes the most sense to you. Consider writing down each of the steps on a separate index card and shuffling the cards around until they make sense.

Taking one step at a time

With your plan in hand, tackle the first step on the list before moving on to the second. (If you haven't created a plan, check out the preceding section.) Try not to overthink your plan; just follow it. If you find that your plan isn't working, step back and reassess your approach to the project. Feel free to make adjustments, but only if doing so is necessary to completing the project; don't spend so much time reworking your plan that you neglect to act on it.

Cutting Clutter Off at the Source

You can often get a glimpse into the chaotic minds of people with ADHD by looking at how they live. Many people with ADHD (and many without it) live in clutter. This clutter can make keeping track of things hard for anyone. People with ADHD often lose their car keys, homework, wallets, and cellphones. The best way to deal with this problem is to eliminate the clutter.

The U.S. Post Office is responsible for a lot of the clutter in people's homes. Junk mail, catalogs, magazines, and newspapers add up quickly. Here are some ideas for reducing clutter at its source:

>> **Remove your name from mailing lists and phone books.** You can do this in a couple of ways:

- Call the individual companies that send you unwanted mail and ask to be removed from their lists.

- To get rid of offers for insurance or credit, use the OptOut service by going to www.optoutprescreen.com or calling 1-888-5-OPT-OUT (1-888-567-8688).

- Go to www.usphonebook.com, choose the "do not sell my personal information" option, and follow the prompts.

>> **Cancel subscriptions you no longer read.** Most people have subscriptions to magazines, newsletters, and newspapers that they don't have time to read. Take a good, hard look at all the subscriptions you have, including online subscriptions, and determine which ones you actually read. If you haven't looked at a certain magazine or online newsletter for the past several months, cancel the subscription, unsubscribe, or at least request receiving fewer emails.

>> **Handle the mail only twice.** The first time you handle it, dump all the nonessentials (such as unrequested catalogs or solicitations), file the things that need to be filed, read what needs to be read, and put the bills in a designated place so you can easily find them when it's time to pay them.

TIP

If paper clutter is your nemesis, arrange to pay all your bills online. This approach not only reduces your postal mail load but also is much easier because you can set up most of your bills to pay automatically.

If you truly prefer to pay bills by hand, you should store your bills somewhere prominent, such as on the wall in your kitchen, so you see them every day and are less likely to forget to pay them. On the outside of the bill's envelope, write in large numbers the date you need to mail the payment. Arrange the bills in order of their payment dates, with the earliest due date in front.

Putting Things in Their Places

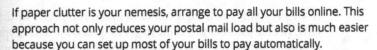

Commit to memory the old saying "a place for everything and everything in its place." If you create a place for all your things and make a habit of returning those things to their places when you're done using them, you've just taken care of one of the worst producers of clutter in your life.

Of course, this process is easier said than done; it requires that you actually find a place for everything. The best way to do so is to follow the steps we outline in the "Completing Your Projects" section earlier in this chapter. And after you've done a large-scale organization of your household, be diligent about finding spaces for new items you bring home.

TIP

One problem that many people with ADHD have is the "out of sight, out of mind" principle: If you put things away, you may forget where they are. You must be clever in this case so you can balance the need for workable space with the need to see your stuff. Here are some of the many ways to accomplish this balance:

>> Take pictures of your possessions and write on each picture the location of that item.

>> Store items in clear plastic boxes so you can see where things are even when they're put away.

>> Color code, as we discuss in the following section.

Creating a Color-Coding System

One of the best ways to remember where you've put your stuff is to develop a color-coding system that lets you know at a glance what's in a particular space.

In this system, you assign colors to broad categories of things, such as blue for bills, red for projects you want to get to, green for letters you need to answer, and yellow for things that may be interesting if you find time for them. Another example is red for screwdrivers, blue for wrenches, green for nails, and so forth.

TIP

You can color code just about anything in your home; just use colored labels, pens, envelopes, or storage containers, and be sure you keep a list of the color key for each area of the house where you apply this system.

Deciding What's Really Important to You

A key step to getting organized is deciding what's important to you. Many people live unfulfilled lives because they think they can do a lot more than is humanly possible; they start hundreds of projects, and they can't possibly finish half of them. People with that tendency (which includes a lot of people with ADHD) must realize that sometimes letting a good idea go, or writing it down on a list of things to do on that hypothetical rainy day, is okay.

REMEMBER

If you can figure out what's important to you and concentrate on that, you'll likely get rid of a lot of confusion and clutter. The good news is that many people with ADHD have a superior ability to be brutally frank. If you focus that ability on yourself, you can probably drum up the honesty it takes to decide what you really want.

realize that sometimes letting a good idea go, or writing it down on a list of things to do on that hypothetical rainy day, is okay.

If you can figure out what's important to you and concentrate on that, you'll likely get rid of a lot of confusion and clutter. The good news is that many people with ADHD have a superior ability to be brutally frank. If you focus that ability on yourself, you can probably drum up the honesty it takes to decide what you really want.

Chapter 19

Ten (or So) Ways to Improve Your Family Relationships

ADHD is hard on relationships. The symptoms of inattention, impulsivity, hyperactivity, distractibility, and forgetfulness, among others, often cause conflict and stress within a family. Because of these challenges we dedicate an entire chapter to ways you can reduce the stress and conflict in your family and improve your relationships.

In this chapter, we offer suggestions for creating and keeping relationship harmony. We suggest ways to help reduce conflict, support personal growth, encourage individual responsibility, and make sure everyone in the family gets what they need.

Taking Responsibility

Some people try to use their diagnosis of ADHD as a "get out of jail free" card and think they can act irresponsibly. After all, they can't control their behaviors because those behaviors are hard-wired in the brain, right? Wrong. ADHD is not an excuse; it's merely an explanation. You'd expect someone with a visible disability to continue treating themselves and other people with respect, and the same goes for people with ADHD.

TIP

Don't let yourself fall into the trap of thinking that you can do nothing about your symptoms or your behavior. Take responsibility not only for your actions but also for your ADHD treatment. When you hurt someone's feelings, acknowledge it and apologize. If you forget to take your medication, develop a better system so you remember the next time. Regardless of the cause of ADHD, you're still responsible for managing your own behavior.

Likewise, if your loved one has ADHD and keeps interrupting, being late, piling papers, and exhibiting other behaviors that are challenging, require them to take responsibility for their behavior while doing your best to understand them and not shame them for their struggles. (In other words, have empathy.)

Focusing on the Positive

Many people are so focused on keeping themselves (or their child or spouse with ADHD) in line that they focus almost exclusively on trying to stop and prevent undesirable behaviors. They fail to acknowledge — or even notice — the types of behaviors they want to encourage.

REMEMBER

People respond better to praise than to criticism. One of the best ways to increase the frequency of desirable behavior is to acknowledge it. If you're the one with ADHD, make a concerted effort to dwell on the positive things you do while putting less stress on the negative. If your loved one has ADHD, help them correct negative behaviors without focusing on blame instead of criticizing those behaviors. Chapter 14 explores the many positive aspects people with ADHD often have.

Releasing Anger and Resentment

One of the most common problems in families that have a member with ADHD is the anger and resentment that can build up before ADHD is discovered or while trying to cope with the challenges it creates.

Here are some suggestions for helping you release anger and resentment:

>> **Don't take it personally.** When a loved one has ADHD, interpreting their behavior as a personal affront to you is easy.

>> **Try to distinguish between the person and the behavior.** ADHD is a brain difference, and the behaviors that result are only partly based on choice.

>> **Find professional help.** Sometimes just being able to talk to someone else can help you recognize when and why you get angry and help you develop ways to diffuse that anger.

Getting Rid of Guilt

Regardless of whether you're the one with ADHD or your child or spouse has it, chances are that you have frequent feelings of *guilt* (feeling that you deserve blame) or *remorse* (feeling distress because of that guilt).

As the parent of a child with ADHD, you may feel guilty about not discovering the ADHD sooner, about the parenting choices you've made, or about the feelings of anger you may have toward your child. As the spouse of a person with ADHD, you may feel guilty about being so hard on your spouse or about not demanding that they seek help sooner. You may also feel guilt or shame because you have feelings of anger and resentment toward your spouse for the way they've treated you. If you have ADHD, you likely feel remorse about all the times you've made mistakes or let people down.

For many people, just knowing they have a biological explanation for their (or their loved one's) difficulties is enough to release the guilt. But if your guilt doesn't go away quite so easily, don't beat yourself up any further. Chances are your guilt has been part of your life for years; you may need time and the help of a therapist to work through these feelings.

REMEMBER

Don't be afraid to seek professional help for dealing with your feelings. The feelings have a long arc, and working through them takes willingness and courage.

Talking It Out

One of the best ways to maintain family harmony is to talk about your feelings before they turn into anger and resentment. Keeping an open channel of dialogue can help everyone feel like their voices are heard. And by creating an environment where everyone feels safe to express their feelings, you prevent resentments from building up over time. Following are a few things you can do to foster healthy communication in your family:

>> **Avoid blame.** Blaming or criticizing someone is a surefire way to put the other person on the defensive. You simply won't get your point across to someone who's feeling blamed.

>> **Don't react emotionally.** After years of misunderstanding and being misunderstood, people can easily jump to conclusions and feel like they're being picked on. Take a breath and ask your partner or child to explain what they mean before you jump to the wrong conclusion.

>> **Get professional help.** If you find that you're not able to communicate without someone getting angry or hurt, find a therapist to help you and your family.

Working Together

Everyone has strengths and weaknesses, and people with ADHD are no exception. Be willing to work with a family member who has ADHD to cultivate their strengths and improve their weak areas.

For example, if you or your spouse has trouble being on time to appointments, work together to get organized ahead of time and develop a system so the less-than-punctual person can leave the house early enough to be on time. In some instances, this approach may even mean yourself or your spouse tricking yourselves into leaving early by having alarms or reminders in your calendar that go off prior to the target departure time.

If your child has difficulty getting homework done, work with them to stay on task, or break down the task into small pieces for them. That doesn't mean doing the homework for them; as we've heard many a parent say, "I already passed the fourth grade once."

Having Regular Family Meetings

Regular family meetings are a way for everyone to get together and have their voices heard. The meetings should be highly organized and follow set guidelines. Here are some suggestions for running a family meeting:

TIP

>> **Establish a set meeting time each week or every other week.** For example, you may choose to meet Tuesdays immediately after dinner or every other Thursday. Having a set time allows you to develop some consistency and offers the best chance that everyone shows up.

Don't have family meetings during mealtime; enjoy that time together as a family talking about non-stressful topics.

>> **Don't force participation.** If you have a teen who shuns authority, forcing them to attend will likely cause conflict and resentment. Make your meetings voluntary, but offer an incentive for being there — for example, an activity that's fun or good food before or after the meeting. People who want to attend get more from the meeting than people who don't.

>> **Focus on the positive.** Avoid making the family meeting a time for complaining. Instead, focus on the positive things that have been going on since the last meeting. When you do address uncomfortable situations — such as undesirable behaviors — do so with tact and avoid blame and shame.

>> **Schedule family activities.** One of the main reasons for having a family meeting should be to talk about the fun activities you want to do together. Doing so improves the morale during the meeting and gives everyone something to look forward to, even during tough times.

>> **Encourage togetherness.** The whole point of a family meeting is to bring the group closer together. Assuming you treat each other with love and kindness, having these meetings can build harmony and help you weather the tough times better.

Being Realistic

After you set up a treatment plan for your or your loved one's ADHD, you're on the road to making positive changes. (See Part 3 of this book for discussions of various treatment options.) The only problem is that you can easily have unrealistic expectations of the changes you'll see. No matter how good your ADHD professional or treatment programs are, you can't expect overnight changes (although some people do experience such rapid progress).

TIP

Set goals for yourself and employ coping strategies so you can make steady progress to getting your symptoms under control. For some people, controlling symptoms takes very little time, but not everyone is so lucky. Show yourself (or your loved one) some compassion, and avoid getting frustrated if you don't see immediate progress.

Having Fun Together

Nothing breaks tension better than having fun and laughing. Schedule some time to do fun activities as a family. Go to a park, take a hike, go to the beach, or play a game. Try to pick an activity that everyone wants to do. Choose something that doesn't create more stress, such as going to a fancy restaurant or to a movie with a child who has a hard time sitting still.

TIP

The best family adventures involve being outside and active. As we say many times in this book, one of the best ways to reduce the symptoms of ADHD is to be more physically active. So whenever possible, choose family outings that get everybody moving.

Walking Away before Blowing Up

If you feel stress building up and tempers starting to flare, take a time-out. Walk away from an argument or stressful situation for a few minutes to cool down. Avoid saying anything in anger that you may regret later.

TIP

Just walking away doesn't mean that you actually calm down, though. We suggest that you take a time-in, which means that you reach into your bag of coping tricks and find the responsive, not reactive, solution. Don't go back and try to resolve anything until you are calmer and more reasonable.

REMEMBER

Heeding this advice can be especially difficult if you're dealing with an impulsive-type person with ADHD because they may say things that make you angry or hurt you (Chapter 3 has more info about the various types of ADHD). You may need to develop your own self-regulation skills and practice walking away before you react.

WARNING

You may want to discuss the walking-away tactic with your family before you use it. Otherwise, loved ones may feel resentment or assume they aren't being heard if they see you simply walking away.

Prioritizing Time to Destress

If your child or spouse has ADHD, dealing with the daily struggles of trying to keep your child on track or coping with your spouse's symptoms is draining. You need to make sure you don't add to the problems by burning out. The best way to avoid getting burned out is to take some time for yourself. Try working at least one of these stress relievers into your life:

- » Taking a bath
- » Reading a book in a quiet place, uninterrupted
- » Journaling.
- » Meditating
- » Taking a yoga class
- » Going for a walk alone
- » Working out at a gym
- » Getting a massage

Really, you can relieve stress by doing anything that gives you some space and helps you tune in to your own feelings and desires. Giving yourself a break helps you feel refreshed and more prepared to handle the challenges that ADHD creates.

Chapter **20**

Ten Resources for More Information and Ongoing Support

As much as we try to cover everything about ADHD in this book, we couldn't possibly squeeze in every bit of information. Even if we could somehow cover everything, new information about ADHD would be discovered tomorrow. In light of this fact, we've created this chapter to help you discover other sources of information and further support.

In this chapter, we present several online resources — from discussion groups to information clearinghouses to sources for support groups. We also recommend ways of finding people in your area to learn from or commiserate with.

REMEMBER
When you get information on any health topic from online communities, social media, or blogs, keep in mind that they represent the personal viewpoints of people who live with ADHD, which come from their unique experience and not necessarily factual. Also ask yourself these questions:

» Who created and runs the site? Are they selling either products or services?

>> Does it make claims that are too good to be true?

>> Is the information current, based on scientific research, and professionally reviewed?

Internet Forums

Internet *forums* (sites for user-generated discussion and questions) are a great way to communicate with other people without having to actually go out and meet them. For people who live in rural areas or don't have a lot of resources for ADHD in their towns, these forums can be extremely useful.

Countless forums are available on the Internet. You can find them by typing the keywords "ADD forums" or "ADHD forums" into your favorite search engine. Look for forums that are active and where people are kind.

Websites

The Internet is a great place to find information on just about anything. You just have to go to a search engine, type in your keywords, and sift through the results. The only problem with this approach is that you sometimes have to weed through a bunch of junk in order to find quality information. And if you're not sure what information is quality and what isn't, you can find yourself going down some dead-end roads.

To prevent you from wasting your time searching for credible sites, we've created a short list here:

>> **add.org:** This site is the home of the Attention Deficit Disorder Association (ADDA). ADDA is a membership organization that conducts an annual conference, publishes a quarterly newsletter, and offers general ADHD information through its website and webinars.

>> **www.chadd.org:** This site is home of one of the oldest resource and educational organizations of ADHD. There you can link to CHADD's National Resource Center on ADHD (NRC), the national *clearinghouse* (centralized distribution channel) for the latest evidence-based information on ADHD.

>> **www.additudemag.com:** This site is the home of ADDitude Magazine and offers lots of articles, information, and resources on ADHD.

These sites are just a few of many hundreds of Internet sites on ADHD. If you want to research a specific area of ADHD, you can narrow the list down very easily. For example, if you want more info about using homeopathics to help with the symptoms of ADHD, do a search with the keywords "ADHD homeopathic." You'll get a lot of hits, and you'll likely need to weed through the ads from homeopathic manufacturers first, but you'll undoubtedly find one or two good sites with reasonably unbiased information.

Support Groups

Support groups can be invaluable, and many different types of ADHD support groups exist throughout the country and online. Here are some ways to go about it:

>> Check the websites for CHADD and ADDA (which we cover in the preceding section) for support groups listed there. CHADD in particular sponsors support groups throughout the country. They may also have options for attending meetings remotely online if there aren't any groups in your area.

>> Ask your local ADHD professional about local groups. (See the later section "Your ADHD Professional".)

>> Call your local college or university mental health program. (Check out the "Local Colleges and Universities" section later in this chapter for details on who to contact at a college or university.)

>> If your child is the one with ADHD, talk to their teacher.

REMEMBER

If all else fails, you can create your own support group by finding other people with ADHD in your area. Talk to your ADHD professional or your child's teachers, put an ad in your local paper, or post flyers in public places such as local markets.

As for finding a space to hold group meetings in, most churches will let you use their facilities for a group of this sort. Call your local churches and ask whether you can use a room for your meetings.

Your Child's School

Teachers, school counselors, and schools' educational diagnosticians (see Chapter 4) are generally well connected within the community. They often know about many of the ADHD professionals and resources in your area and can be a great resource whether you or your child is the one with ADHD.

Local Colleges and Universities

If your local college or university has a department for any of the following professions (which we cover in Chapter 4), it can generally steer you toward resources in your area. Call your local college or university and ask to be connected to one of the following departments:

>> Psychology/counseling

>> Psychiatry

>> Neurology

>> General medical education

>> Special education

>> Occupational therapy

>> Speech–language pathology

Most colleges and universities offer at least one of these disciplines, and people in these departments are generally knowledgeable about who works with ADHD in your area and whether support groups exist.

Your ADHD Professional

For most people, the first place to look for information and resources on ADHD is your healthcare professional. Depending on the professional you see, they may be connected to a larger group of professionals that they can refer you to while still overseeing your care.

We cover details about how to work with several professionals at once in Chapter 7.

Books on Specific Aspects of ADHD

Chances are that when you found this book you also discovered a bunch of other books on ADHD that caught your eye. If you want to read more books about this subject, we've found the following to be especially helpful:

>> *Delivered from Distraction: Getting the Most out of Life with Attention Deficit Disorder* **by Drs. Edward M. Hallowell and John J. Ratey (Ballantine Books):** *Delivered from Distraction* is the sequel to their original book *Driven to Distraction* and focuses on the full spectrum of living with ADHD.

>> *ADHD 2.0* **by Drs. Edward M. Hallowell and John J. Ratey (Random House Publishing Group):** In this book, the authors conceptualize minimizing the downsides and maximizing the benefits of ADHD. They draw on the latest scientific advances and their own depth of experience.

>> *Women with Attention Deficit Disorder,* **2nd Edition, by Sari Solden (Introspect Press):** This title is a very gender-specific book looking at the special needs and differences of how ADHD expresses in women.

>> *A Hunter in a Farmer's World,* **3rd Edition, by Thom Hartmann (Healing Arts Press):** Thom Hartmann looks at people with ADHD as "hunters in a farmer's world," and his perspective is heartening for those who have ADHD. This title focuses on the positive attributes of people with ADHD and offers great insight into this condition (as do all his books).

Dozens of ADHD books are on the market, with more coming out every year. A good place to keep up-to-date on the best books — or at least the best-selling books — is online booksellers like Amazon. Do a search using "ADD" or "ADHD" as the keyword, and feast your eyes on the results. (Just be mindful of which results are actually sponsored.)

TIP

One helpful thing about online booksellers is the customer reviews. They can save you time and money by letting you know ahead of time whether the book is any good. Reviews also give you insight into the author's perspective to help you determine if its content may be something that you can relate to.

The Library

Your local library, aside from offering some books on ADHD, may have resources such as a copy of the DSM-V (the American Psychiatric Association's diagnostic manual), specialized magazines or reports, or other ADHD reference materials. Most libraries also have bulletin boards, where you may find information about an ADHD support group.

Libraries are also interconnected, and through the interlibrary loan program you can borrow books that your local library doesn't have on the shelf.

TIP

Many libraries also offer a broad range of programming. Ask a librarian or check your library's website for upcoming programs related to ADHD.

Family and Friends

Because so many people have ADHD (at least 3 percent of the U.S. population), you likely already know someone who has been down the road you're traveling. Ask your family and friends whether they have any ADHD resources and what professionals they may recommend — chances are you'll find someone who can share some valuable information.

Talk Therapy

Group therapy is not only a great place to talk with other people who are confronting the same issues as you but also a place where you can share resources with one another. Ask your ADHD professional about group therapy in your area, or call someone listed under "counseling" or "psychologist" in an online directory. We cover several group therapy options in Chapter 9.

Caregivers and family members often get burned out and have difficulty getting the care they need. Individual talk therapy can be an invaluable tool to give you a chance to talk about your feelings and get support in taking care of your well-being. Many of the approaches we present in Chapter 9 can be beneficial for the non-ADHD family members as well. These options include insight-oriented therapy, supportive therapy, and cognitive-behavioral therapy. You can also ask your ADHD professional to recommend someone who works specifically with family members and the types of issues they face.

Appendix

Treatment Tracking Forms

As we discuss in Part 3 of this book, treating ADHD effectively often involves juggling more than one treatment at a time, and adjustments need to be made on a regular basis. For this reason, you must have a way to keep track of your progress and any side effects from the treatments. (This point is especially important if you include medication in your treatment strategy.)

This appendix contains some suggestions to help you keep on top of your treatment's effectiveness as well as some tracking forms to help you monitor your progress. (Access online versions of these forms at www.dummies.com\ADHD.)

REMEMBER

If you try more than one treatment at a time, you may have a hard time seeing exactly what effect each individual treatment is having. That's especially true if you use more than one biological treatment at a time. To see what each approach is doing, you may want to limit how many you do at the same time. For example, if you undertake only one other biological treatment with medication, such as a neuromodulation therapy (see Chapter 12), distinguishing the results of the two approaches is fairly easy because the effects of medication often follow your ingestion schedule.

TIP

Some treatments, such as the neuromodulation and rebalancing therapies (see Chapters 12 and 13, respectively), include intake and exit assessments to determine the level of success you have on the program. In this case, your treatment professional helps keep track of your progress.

Keeping Daily Tabs on Your Treatment

The main treatments you need to track from day to day are chemical-based approaches, such as medications and vitamin and herb supplements. The forms in this section can help you do so effectively. Complete these forms weekly.

REMEMBER You can also find treatment tracking forms online at www.dummies.com\ADHD.

When you fill in the information on these forms, keep these things in mind:

>> **Write down all the specifics about the treatment.** That includes the time and the amount that you used, took, or gave.

>> **Record your observations of the symptoms for the day.** Include any changes you see throughout the day. Doing so is especially important in the case of medication because the drug's effects change over time.

The first step to take is to complete the treatment effectiveness checklists in Tables A-1 and A-2. For each day of the week, both morning and evening, rate the positive and negative effects of your treatments on a scale of 1 to 10 (with 1 meaning poor results, 5 meaning acceptable, and 10 meaning excellent). Total your score for each time of day.

Next, complete the ADHD Treatment Tracking Form in Table A-3. In each section, note your total scores from the checklists for that treatment's positive and negative effects.

Performing Periodic Effectiveness Assessments

The treatment effectiveness forms in Tables A-1 and A-2 are things you want to complete every day. But you also want to take some time to assess your progress by doing the following:

>> **Do a quick review of your status once a week on the same day.** Use the forms in this appendix to quickly assess your plan. Make sure that you're following the proper protocol for each treatment and that you don't have any serious side effects that are making your life more difficult than it was.

>> **Get an outsider's perspective.** Ask someone close to you complete the forms in Tables A-1 and A-2 on your behalf once a week, if possible.

>> **Once a month, perform more careful analysis of your progress.** Compare where you are to where you were a month ago (or two or three months ago) and to where you thought you'd be given the treatment plan you drafted for yourself. Be honest with yourself about the results of what you're doing to treat your symptoms, and make adjustments to your plan based on what you see.

You may find it difficult to accurately assess your progress (or lack thereof). Getting input from someone else (such as a loved one or a professional) may be helpful to help you see how you're doing. Meet with this touchstone every month.

>> **Adjust your plan as needed.** After you do your weekly review or monthly assessment, don't be afraid to adjust your plan if you see things you don't like. If a medication isn't working, meet with your doctor and discuss changing it. If the diet you're trying makes you feel worse, change it. Rarely is the first treatment strategy you use the strategy you continue to use indefinitely.

Don't just drop a treatment from your plan if things aren't happening as fast as you want. Change takes time. So before you stop — unless the side effects are too hard to live with — consult the professional you hired to help you with a treatment. If you decided on the treatment on your own based on a recommendation or some research, talk to people or do more research into this treatment to see whether you're doing something wrong, and look for ways to adjust the treatment.

TABLE A-1 Positive Effects of Daily Treatments

Positive Effects	Mon am	Mon pm	Tues am	Tues pm	Wed am	Wed pm	Thurs am	Thurs pm	Fri am	Fri pm	Sat am	Sat pm	Sun am	Sun pm
Able to sit still, not feeling restless														
Able to focus and maintain attention on a task														
Accepted responsibility for actions														
Considered the needs and feelings of others														
Controlled impulses/considered consequences to actions before acting														
Able to handle frustrations														
Got along with others														
Followed through on an assignment or plan														
Remembered appointments/didn't lose personal items														
Emotions stable/moods under control														
Cooperative/respectful of authority														
TOTAL														

TABLE A-2 Negative Effects of Daily Treatments

Negative Effects	Mon am	Mon pm	Tues am	Tues pm	Wed am	Wed pm	Thurs am	Thurs pm	Fri am	Fri pm	Sat am	Sat pm	Sun am	Sun pm
Insomnia														
Agitation/irritability														
Nervousness/feeling "wired"														
Poor appetite/nausea														
Headache														
Grogginess														
TOTAL														

TABLE A-3 ADHD Treatment Tracking Form

Date: _____   Day of week: _____
Name: _____
Person completing form: _____

Medications taken:

Time of day: _____   Drug: _____
Dosage: _____ Positive effects score: _____
Negative effects score: _____

Time of day: _____   Drug: _____
Dosage: _____ Positive effects score: _____
Negative effects score: _____

Vitamin and herbal supplements taken:

Remember that the results of vitamin and herbal supplements are often subtle and can take a month or more to appear.

Time of day: _____   Supplement: _____
Dosage: _____ Positive effects score: _____
Negative effects score: _____

Time of day: _____   Supplement: _____
Dosage: _____ Positive effects score: _____
Negative effects score: _____

Other treatments used:

Name of treatment: _____
Time of day performed: _____ Positive effects score: _____
Negative effects score: _____

Name of treatment: _____
Time of day performed: _____ Positive effects score: _____
Negative effects score: _____

Index

chaos, 196, 254, 278

charter schools, 258

charts and boards, 112–113, 134, 218–219, 250, 259, 263, 275, 289–290

chemical activity, 10, 24–25

chemical sensitivities, 159–160. *See also* allergies and substance sensitivities

childhood disintegrative disorder, 77

children. *See* parenting children with ADHD; school

Children and Adults with ADHD (CHADD), 41, 99, 306–307

chiropractic, 89, 182–184

choline, 152–153

cleaning, 157–158

cleaning products, 159

clinical social workers, 47, 49–50

clonidine (Catapres), 108

coaching, 11, 47, 50, 90, 115, 124–125, 127–128, 241. *See also* ADHD coaches

cocaine, 37

coercion, 134

cognitive skills testing, 67

cognitive-behavioral therapy (CBT), 90–91, 120–121, 136–138

  aspects of, 136

  components of, 120

  example of, 137–138

  function of, 136–137

  metacognitions, 120

  motivations and circumstances, 136–137

colleges and universities, 241, 308. *See also* school

colognes, 160

color-coding, 229, 263, 275, 294

combined type ADHD, 8

comorbidity, 9

compassion, 135, 199, 205, 209, 301

complex carbohydrates, 146

compliments, difficulty accepting, 36

Concerta (methylphenidate HCl ER), 106

conduct disorder, 77–78

conferences, 99

conflict, 206–208, 223, 238, 256

continuous performance tests (CPTs), 68

convergence insufficiency, 187

co-occurring conditions

  anxiety disorders, 34

  depression, 35, 39, 76

  sleep disorders, 36

  substance abuse, 37

  treatment and therapy for, 49, 119, 176, 178, 185

co-parenting, 227

corpus collosum, 23

Cotempla XR (methylphenidate hydrochloride), 106

counseling and therapy, 90, 115–124

  behavior modification, 121

  cognitive-behavioral therapy, 120–121

  considerations before beginning treatment, 116–117

  differences between, 116

  family therapy, 122

  finding counselors and therapists, 127–128

  group therapy, 123

  insight-oriented therapy, 117–119

  lack of results before diagnosis, 118–119

  play therapy, 121

  psychoeducational counseling, 122

  support groups, 123–124

  supportive therapy, 119

couples therapy, 90

CPTs (continuous performance tests), 68

cranial rhythms, 182

craniosacral system, 182

CranioSacral Therapy (CST), 89, 182–183

creativity, 194–196

Crichton, Alexander, 16

criticism, 206–207, 210, 298, 300

CST (CranioSacral Therapy), 89, 182–183

D

Daytrana (methylphenidate hydrochloride), 106

deep breathing techniques, 138, 210, 272

default mode network (DMN), 23

defiance

  defiance/willfulness theory, 16

  discipline, 223–224

  oppositional defiant disorder, 77–78, 135, 224

delegating, 278

Delta waves, 162

denial, 117

depression, 35, 39–40, 75–76, 108, 155, 173, 176, 211

Desyrel (trazodone), 108

developmental vision evaluations, 188

Dexedrine (dextroamphetamine sulfate), 107

dexmethylphenidate (Azstarys), 106

dexmethylphenidate hydrochloride (Focalin), 106

dextroamphetamine (Xelstrym), 107

dextroamphetamine sulfate (Dexedrine; Procentra; Zenzedi), 107

diagnosing ADHD, 10–11

  acclimating to diagnosis, 70

  choosing a healthcare professional, 10–11, 46–52

  common emotions after diagnosis, 69–70

  considerations after diagnosis, 69–70

  diagnoses for legal purposes, 59

  differential diagnoses, 10, 71–84

  evaluating healthcare professionals, 54–56

  evaluation process, 61–70

    adequate evaluations, 62

    behavioral assessments, 67

    cognitive skills testing, 67

    discussing results and examining options, 69

    educational testing, 65–66

    medical testing, 65

    mental health evaluations, 63–64

    motor skills testing, 67

    performance testing, 68

    physiological testing, 68–69

    preparing for, 11, 62–63

    simple versus elaborate, 53, 61

    social skills testing, 67

  level of professional's involvement in, 55

  official diagnoses, 46, 53

  personal active role in, 55

  second opinions, 11, 57

Diagnostic and Statistical Manual of Mental Disorders (DSM-V), 8–9, 35, 37, 50, 63, 73, 309

diet and nutrition, 88, 141–150

  allergies and sensitivities, 144–146

  essential fatty acids, 143–144

  food textures, 147

  junk food, 144, 146–148

  making notes about before evaluation, 62

  poor diet theory, 16

  protein, 147

  simple carbohydrates, 146

  sugars, 148

  water and hydration, 143

  yeast, 148–150

differential diagnoses, 10, 34, 71–84

  defined, 72

  environmental influences, 83–84

  medical conditions, 79–81

  mental disorders, 73–79

  pseudo-ADHD, 83–84

  sensory processing disorders, 82–83

  steps for, 72

discipline, 220–224

  basic principles, 220–221

  consequences, 221–223

  defiance, 223–224

  self-discipline, 220

  steps for, 221

  suggestions for, 222

distractibility. *See* inattention/distractibility

DMN (default mode network), 23

dopamine, 10, 24–25, 104–105, 212

dorsolateral prefrontal cortex (DLPFC), 172

Dove, Heinrich William, 171

drugs. *See* substance abuse

DSM-V (*Diagnostic and Statistical Manual of Mental Disorders*), 8–9, 35, 37, 50, 63, 73, 309

dust, 156–157

dust mites, 157–158

dysbiosis, 149

E

ECT (electroconvulsive therapy), 175

educational diagnosticians, 47, 51, 60, 66–67

educational testing, 65–66

EEG (electroencephalography), 68–69

EEG-biofeedback. *See* neurofeedback

exercise, 231
homework, 260
sleep, 233
work, 267, 278

N

narcolepsy, 78
National Association of Professional Organizers (NAPO), 275
National Human Genome Research Institute, 22
National Institutes of Health (NIH), 22, 84
National Institutes of Mental Health (NIMH), 100
negative reinforcement, 134, 261
negative thought management, 210–211
neurofeedback (EEG-biofeedback; neurotherapy), 89, 96, 162–165
  brain wave levels, 162–163
  effects of, 164–165
  finding providers, 164–165
  goal of, 163
  process of, 163–164
neurological activity, 10
  brain damage, 17
  executive brain functions, 19–21
  research into ADHD, 23–24
  traumatic brain injury, 17
neurologists, 11, 47, 51, 81
neuromodulation therapies, 89, 161–176
  auditory brain stimulation, 165–172
    binaural beats, 171–172
    brainwave entrainment, 166
    neurostimulation, 166
    Rhythmic Entrainment Intervention, 166–168
    Tomatis-based approaches, 168–170
  electrical brain stimulation, 172–175
    finding providers, 174–175
    origin of, 173
    process of, 173
    results and effects, 174
    varieties of, 172–173
  magnetic brain stimulation, 175–176
    finding providers, 176

origin of, 175
process of, 176
results and effects, 176
varieties of, 175
  neurofeedback, 162–165
    brain wave levels, 162–163
    finding providers, 164–165
    goal of, 163
    process of, 163–164
    results and effects, 164–165
neurons, 24, 104–105
neuroplasticity, 26
neuropsychiatrists, 47, 51
neuroqueer individuals, 41
neuroscientists, 18–19
neurostimulation, 166
neurotherapy. See neurofeedback
neurotransmitters, 24, 104–105, 147
NIH (National Institutes of Health), 22, 84
NIMH (National Institutes of Mental Health), 100
Noah, Trevor, 194
nonverbal working memory, 20
norepinephrine (noradrenalin), 10, 24–25, 104–105, 212
norepinephrine reuptake inhibitors (NRIs), 107–108
nutraceuticals, 155–156
nutrition. See diet and nutrition
nutritionists, 57, 150, 155
Nuvigil (armodafinil), 107

O

obsessive-compulsive disorder (OCD), 74, 175–176
obstructive sleep apnea, 78
occipital lobe, 21
occupational therapists (OTs), 47, 52, 186
ODD (oppositional defiant disorder), 77–78, 135, 224
official diagnoses, 46, 53. See also diagnosing ADHD
omega-3 fatty acids, 143–144, 151–152
omega-6 fatty acids, 143–144, 151–152
OMT (osteopathic manipulative treatment), 182

PDD (pervasive developmental disorders), 77
pediatricians, 47–49
performance testing, 68
perfumes, 160
personal health journals, 97
personal space and boundaries, 237, 239, 255–256
Personalized repetitive Transcranial Magnetic Stimulation (PrTMS), 89
pervasive developmental disorders (PDD), 77
petit mal seizures, 80
Phelps, Michael, 194
phobias, 73–74
physical therapists, 67
physiological testing, 68–69
physiologists, 18
planning, 20, 289–291
  school, 250
  struggling with, 216
  work, 266
plastics, 160
play therapy, 90, 121
pollens, 159
polystyrene (PS), 160
polyvinyl chloride (PVC), 160
positives. *See* strengths and positives
posttraumatic stress disorder (PTSD), 74–75
power struggles, 134
prefrontal cortex, 21
premotor cortex, 21
primary auditory cortex, 21
primary hypersomnia, 78
primary motor cortex, 176
primary visual cortex, 21
private schools, 258
private tutors, 261–262
probiotics, 149
Procentra (dextroamphetamine sulfate), 107
prodrugs, 107
professional journal articles, 100–101
progress tracking
  educational plans, 247–248

medication, 109–114, 311–313, 316
  treatment plan development, 97–98
protein, 147, 232
protein powders, 147
Provigil (modafinil), 107
PrTMS (Personalized repetitive Transcranial Magnetic Stimulation), 89
PS (polystyrene), 160
pseudo-ADHD, 83–84
psychiatrists, 10, 47, 50, 64
psychoeducational counseling, 90, 122
psychologists, 11, 47, 49, 66–67
PTSD (posttraumatic stress disorder), 74–75
PubMed, 100
PVC (polyvinyl chloride), 160
pycnogenol (maritime pine), 153

Q

qi (life energy), 89, 178
Quelbree (viloxazine), 108
Quillichew (methylphenidate hydrochloride), 106

R

rapid-cycling bipolar disorder, 75
realism, 209, 301
rebalancing therapies, 89, 177–189
  acupuncture, 178–180
  homeopathy, 180–181
  manipulation therapies, 182–184
  sensory integration therapies, 184–186
  vision therapies, 186–189
rebound effects, medication and, 111
Red Dye No. 3, 16
Reddit forums, 100
REI. *See* Rhythmic Entrainment Intervention
reinforcement
  concrete, 134
  negative, 134, 261
  positive, 132–133
  of positive behaviors, 121, 132–133, 219–220
rejection sensitive dysphoria, 108

effects of, 169–170

finding providers, 170

Tomatis Method, 168–169

Tourette's syndrome, 79

toxic exposure, 17

TPN (task positive network), 23

traditional Chinese medicine (TCM), 178.
See also acupuncture

training, 90–91, 115, 125–128

awareness training, 91, 125–126, 138–140

finding trainers, 127–128

parent training, 91, 126

skills training, 90, 126–127

transcranial alternating current stimulation (tACS),
172–174

transcranial direct current stimulation (tDCS),
89, 172–174

transcranial magnetic stimulation (TMS), 89, 175

transcranial random noise stimulation (tRNS),
173–174

transdermal patches, 106

transgender population, 40

traumatic brain injury, 17, 81

trazodone (Desyrel), 108

treating ADHD, 87–101

behavior management, 91, 129–140

biopsychosocial model, 88–93

categories of treatment, 12

coaching, 115, 124–125

combining treatments, 93, 96–97

considerations after diagnosis, 69–70

counseling and therapy, 90, 115–124

diet and nutrition, 88, 141–150

disclosing all treatments to providers, 70

effectiveness assessments, 312–315

eligibility for services, 58–60

diagnosis for legal purposes, 59

insurance coverage, 59–60

school services, 60

examining options following diagnosis, 69

failure of treatment, 55

finding and nurturing strengths, 201

herbal remedies, 141–142, 150–156

homeopathy, 89, 180–181

learning about new therapies, 98–101

conferences, 99

Internet and social media, 99–100

professional journal articles, 100–101

support group meetings, 101

managing treatment, 57–58

medication, 88, 103–114

neuromodulation therapies, 89, 161–176

not feeling rushed into a plan, 69

not taking on too many treatments at once, 70

personal values and, 11, 53–54

rebalancing therapies, 89, 177–189

skills training, 90, 126–127

toolbox of strategies

tracking progress, 311–313, 316

training, 115, 125–128

treatment plan development, 93–98

trusting instincts about, 69–70

vitamin supplements, 141–142, 150–156

treatment plan development, 93–98

challenges, 94–95

combining treatments, 96–97

goals, 95

options, 95

prioritizing treatments, 96

steps for, 93–94

tracking progress, 97–98

tRNS (transcranial random noise stimulation),
173–174

truth, flexibility with, 216, 269

twins, 22

U

universities and colleges, 241, 308. *See also* school

University of California San Diego School of
Medicine, 187

unschooling, 258

Upledger, John E., 182

Upledger Institute, 182

U.S. National Library of Medicine, 100

USPhoneBook, 293

About the Authors

Jeff Strong is the creator of Rhythmic Entrainment Intervention (REI) and the director and CEO of the Strong Institute, a research center and provider of evidence-based custom auditory brain stimulation programs for individuals with neurological disorders. He is also the cofounder and chief creative officer of BrainStimAudio.com, a streaming music site containing personalized and custom-made music to enhance brain function.

A graduate of the Musicians Institute, Jeff is a percussionist, composer, recording engineer, researcher, clinician, and sought-after expert on the therapeutic use of musical rhythm. He is also an adult living with ADHD. He is the best-selling author of eight books, including *Drums For Dummies* (Wiley) and *Different Drummer: One Man's Music and Its Impact on ADD, Anxiety, and Autism* (Strong Institute).

Carol MacHendrie MSW, LCSW, has practiced family and individual therapy for over four decades. She has a BA from Hofstra University, an MSW from Syracuse University, and extensive postgraduate training in family therapy. She taught undergraduate and graduate classes on a variety of social science topics as adjunct faculty at Syracuse University School of Social Work and the College of Santa Fe. As a facilitator of ADHD workshops and groups for the past 25 years, she has specialized to focus on couples where one or both partners have ADHD. Carol has presented at national and international conferences on a variety of topics. She remains passionate about creating change through meaningful relationships and bringing forth each individual's gifts. She practices and lives in Santa Fe, New Mexico, which has proved a wonderful environment for being a different drummer.

Dedication

Jeff Strong: For Beth who has put up with my shenanigans, especially my incessant tapping, for the past three decades.

Carol MacHendrie: To my husband, Dr. Will MacHendrie. He was the first to recognize that he'd indeed married a different drummer and encouraged me to delve deeply into all the many aspects of ADHD. His love, acceptance, and celebration of my success and spirit are beyond measure.

Authors' Acknowledgments

Jeff Strong: I'd like to thank Elizabeth Stilwell who took the initiative to get the second edition of this book started. I'm also grateful to project editor Alissa Schwipps, copy editor Megan Knoll, and technical editor Dr. Jefferson Davis. Special thanks go to my coauthor, Carol MacHendrie, for helping make the second edition of this book better than the first. Most importantly, I'd like to thank my wife, Beth, and daughter, Tovah, for their love and support during this arduous process.

Carol MacHendrie: I'd like to thank my coauthor, Jeff Strong, for his respect, trust, and good humor as we created the easiest collaboration possible. I'd also like to thank Dr. Jefferson Davis, our technical editor, for his clinical expertise and our years of collaboration. Thanks to the many editors at Wiley for their efforts to bring this revision into being. To my clients throughout my career who have been a source of inspiration, learning, and joy, my humble gratitude for your trust and for the privilege of accompanying you on your journey of healing.

This project never would have come to fruition without my daughter Alexandra Ecklund being the conduit for it. Her support, inspiration, keen intellect, innovative lens, and love are central to this book. I am grateful to my trusted colleagues and dear friends Kate Cook, Karen Klinefelter, Martha Davis, Lynn Hillas, Naomi Fiske, Deanne Newman, Abby Braun, Jim Fickey, Gary Grimm, and Dr. Jonathan Beamer for their collaboration, support, and clinical acumen over many decades together. Marti Spiegelman for sharing her wisdom and knowledge. My sisterhood of caring women throughout the world have encouraged the feminine voice to come forward and be heard, especially my Santa Tierra sisterhood. Special thanks to my mentor Jose Luis Herrera who has shared his enormous heart and the priceless teachings from the wisdom keepers of the Andes.

My grandson Jens and my son from another mother Jonathan Ecklund have been a beacon of joy and love.

Publisher's Acknowledgments

Acquisitions Editor: Elizabeth Stilwell

Project Manager: Alissa D. Schwipps

Copy Editor: Megan Knoll

Technical Editor: Jefferson Davis, MD

Managing Editor: Murari Mukundan

Production Editor: Saikarthick Kumarasamy

Illustrator: Kathryn Born

Cover Image: © Maskot/Getty Images